For

Simon Thornley

and fellow contrarians

*Mark Blackham, Michael Jackson, Grant Morris, Grant Schofield
and Gerhard Sundborn*

T0325962

Le sens commun n'est pas si commun.
(Common sense is not so common.)

François-Marie Arouet (Voltaire),
writer, historian and philosopher
21 November 1694–30 May 1778

1. Prologue

In December 2019, a new coronavirus (SARS-CoV-2) emerged in Wuhan, China. The virus caused an acute respiratory disease, Covid-19. Within a few months, the disease had spread around the world. On 11 March 2020, the World Health Organization (WHO) declared Covid-19 to be a pandemic. With cases and deaths rising, public health systems under pressure and no effective anti-viral treatment, most countries in the world resorted to non-pharmaceutical interventions in an attempt to suppress/mitigate the disease.

Almost all of these measures across the world took the form of extreme physical (or social) distancing; often referred to as "lockdowns". These lockdowns included some or all of the following measures: border closures and cancellation of international flights; restrictions on large gatherings (typically more than ten, 50 or 100 people), leading to cancellation of games, concerts, weddings, funerals, conferences and closure of schools, movies, theaters, bars, restaurants, churches, gyms and other places that see large congregations of people at one time; workplace closures with people asked to work from home as far as practicable; and often even restrictions on internal mobility, including suspension of domestic travel. By April 2020, some countries, such as my home country of New Zealand, adopted harsher lockdowns in the form of shutting down everything other than those which were deemed essential services, for example, supermarkets and hospitals. Even industries where physical distancing came naturally and did not pose a serious constraint, such as construction, were shut down. India and Israel also adopted similar draconian mitigation policies.[1]

In most instances, people were in effect shut in; they were discouraged from venturing out of their homes except for essential work or to get exercise. If and when they did venture out, people were encouraged to behave as if they had Covid-19, wear protective equipment such as masks and gloves, and always stay within their "bubble" that included only people who were resident in the same household at the time the lockdown was announced. This also implied that often members of the same household were caught out if they were in different places at the time and had to shelter in place until such time as the lockdowns were lifted. Not surprisingly, allusions to the famous Albert Camus novel *The Plague* (*La Peste*) about a plague sweeping through the city of Oran were invoked repeatedly.

The strong support for lockdowns was surprising, since prior to this, the consensus in the epidemiological community seemed to be that large-scale lockdowns or quarantine were neither effective nor desirable in combating infectious diseases. Thomas Inglesby is Professor and Director of the Center for Health Security at Johns Hopkins University's Bloomberg School of Public Health. In the aftermath of the H5N1 (Avian flu) pandemic, Inglesby and his co-authors wrote in a 2006 journal article:

> There are no historical observations or scientific studies that support the confinement by quarantine of groups of possibly infected people for extended periods in order to slow the spread of influenza. A World Health Organization (WHO) Writing Group, after reviewing the literature and considering contemporary international experience, concluded that "forced isolation and quarantine are ineffective and impractical". Despite this recommendation by experts, mandatory large-scale quarantine continues to be considered as an option by some authorities and government officials.
>
> The interest in quarantine reflects the views and conditions prevalent more than 50 years ago, when much less was known about the epidemiology of infectious diseases and when there was far less international and domestic travel in a less densely populated world. It is difficult to identify circumstances in the past half-century when large-scale quarantine has been effectively used in the control of any disease. The negative consequences of large-scale quarantine are so extreme (forced confinement of sick people with the well; complete restriction of movement of large populations; difficulty in getting critical supplies, medicines and food to people inside the quarantine zone) that this mitigation measure should be eliminated from serious consideration.[2]

While reasonable people may disagree on whether large-scale lockdowns may or may not be the panacea, there was something about the uniformity of responses across different countries that was striking. Early on in 2020, it became evident that the lockdowns had little impact on Covid-19 mortality. This was true if we compared across countries at a point in time,[3] across counties in the United States[4] and within the same country over a span of time.[5] It was also evident early on that the main drivers of Covid-19 mortality had little to do with non-pharmaceutical interventions in the form of lockdowns. The main factors included: (1) population and population density (countries with higher populations and/or higher population densities reported more deaths, and countries whose citizens were on average older reported more deaths), (2) number of hospital beds per thousand of population (more hospital beds meant fewer deaths) and (3) whether a country had a land border or not (islands such as Australia, Iceland, Japan, New Zealand and Taiwan fared much better in experiencing fewer deaths per million).[6]

This meant that short-term policy responses, such as lockdowns, were not going to have a huge impact and we needed to look for alternatives. Most importantly, it seemed to make sense to adopt an empirical approach by looking around the world and taking lessons from various countries as to what was working and what was not. A skeptical reader may well interject at this point that time was of the essence. However, while this may have justified the early lockdowns in March and April 2020, it is hard to understand how the support for lockdowns remained unwavering even in November and December 2020, when the UK enacted strict lockdowns yet again.

* * *

I was in Cambridge, USA, in early 2020 teaching at Harvard Kennedy School, but when Harvard shut down its campus and all teaching moved online, I returned home to New Zealand and finished teaching remotely. Two things happened at this time that eventually led me to contemplate writing this book. First, one of my Harvard students asked me to talk about decision making in pandemics through the lens of some of the things we were studying. This led to the first of many articles I wrote at the time in the popular media.[7] Second, this first article and the associated discussion led to my becoming a member of a loose group of academics called Covid Plan B, which started asking questions about the sagacity of the lockdowns that were being implemented by countries around the world in an attempt to combat Covid-19. The reaction on social media to the questions being posed by Covid Plan B was swift and unpleasant; the calumny widespread.

However, as I engaged more deeply in this debate, I began to understand that while there were big gaps in my understanding of epidemiology and public health issues, there were equally yawning gaps on the other side regarding basic economic and psychological concepts. Worldwide, there was tremendous emphasis on calling upon epidemiological expertise without an adequate appreciation that Covid-19 was not merely an epidemiological crisis; it was an economic, social and moral crisis that required multidisciplinary expertise to assess and address different facets of the pandemic.

Covid Plan B was not the only group of people asking questions, though we were clearly in a minority, which gained us some degree of fame or notoriety; mostly the latter. Our arguments were not all that novel since many other scientists around the world were asking similar questions as well. In late 2020, some of these same people (including Jay Bhattacharya of Stanford, Sunetra Gupta of Oxford and Martin Kulldorff of Harvard) went on to publish the Great Barrington Declaration[8] opposing lockdowns, which in turn found strong opposition from the signatories of the John Snow Memorandum,[9] that strongly advocated the continued use of lockdowns as a means of combating this disease.

We, at Covid Plan B (and a few members of the group were original signatories of the Great Barrington declaration) thought that the point we were making was intuitive: the lockdowns may be necessary or not, but regardless, the lockdowns came with an *opportunity cost*; as we diverted scarce resources from other uses toward fighting Covid-19, there will be losses elsewhere in the economy, in the form of lower gross domestic product (GDP), job losses, lowered life expectancy, loneliness owing to reduced social interactions, inadequate treatment and screening of other diseases, delayed or abandoned vaccinations for children, mental health problems and self-harm, and adverse academic and social impacts on children shut in their homes and unable to go to school. To an economist such as myself, who is trained to look for these trade-offs, this seemed evident. Unfortunately, this was not obvious to everyone, and the vilification people asking these questions experienced was unexpected. We argued that in formulating policy, it was essential to consider the costs and benefits. What do we sacrifice by locking down? What do we sacrifice if we don't?

For instance, if tomorrow we all stopped driving (or shut down all heavy industries, which are the largest source of greenhouse gases), then this would lead to a massive reduction in pollution and pollution-related respiratory diseases. However, no one seriously suggests this as an option. So, what we do is utilize tools, such as carbon taxes or emissions trading permits, to equate the social costs of pollution to the social benefits of driving or heavy industries. Factories or businesses that emit larger amounts of pollutants typically have to pay more than those who emit less. Those who pollute more end up subsidizing those who pollute less. This provides an incentive for everyone to reduce as much of their pollution as possible until they equate the costs of pollution with the benefit from the pollution-generating activities.

Our argument was based on the simple idea that, as humans, we tend to focus excessively on the losses we can see in front of us, but tend to ignore losses that are more diffuse and occur in a more dispersed manner in the background, even if those latter losses are far larger. In attempting to combat the immediate losses in front of us, we often divert resources to preventing those losses, implying taking resources away from other areas, leading to losses in the latter.

Lockdown proponents have often justified their support by making arguments about excess mortality; that is, that there were many more deaths in 2020 than in other years (thereby defying historical trends) and this excess is owing to the deaths resulting from Covid-19. This debate will continue for a while since it will take time before we have reliable data to accurately assess this. However, evidence suggests that in numerous Western countries, excess mortality spiked *immediately after* the imposition of lockdowns. This could be explained via the standard epidemiological models, given a time lag between the onset of infection and death. I have more to say on this shortly. Alternatively, it could be argued that some of these additional deaths were those denied proper treatment for other ailments. It does seem strangely coincidental that in most countries, the spike is occurring virtually immediately after the imposition of lockdowns, which would require a very high degree of prescience on the parts of those respective governments.[10]

For instance, on 22 May 2020, the WHO announced that around the world, at least 80 million children under the age of one were at risk of diseases such as diphtheria, measles and polio as Covid-19 restrictions disrupted vaccination efforts,[11] and on the same day, the

New York Times wrote that the result of this disruption was going to lead to a surge in polio and measles.[12] In September 2020, the *Telegraph* of London reported that data from the UK's Office for National Statistics (ONS) shows:

> more than 6,700 extra deaths in homes across the UK in the past two months – of which just 203 involved coronavirus. The statistics show deaths from other causes are soaring, amid concern that millions of patients went untreated for killer diseases during lockdown. Among those under 65, the number of deaths caused by high blood pressure is up by one third, with the same rise seen in deaths caused by cardiac arrhythmias. Deaths from diabetes in this group have risen by one quarter. In older groups, deaths linked to high blood pressure rose by 15 per cent, while diabetes deaths were up by 14 per cent, the figures from May 8 to July 10 show.[13]

In late 2020, the International Monetary Fund predicted that the lockdowns and consequent job losses, coupled with the massive expansion of government spending in New Zealand, would imply that New Zealand's per capita GDP in 2025 will be lower than that in 2019.[14] This was not unique to New Zealand. During the second quarter of 2020 (April–June), India's GDP shrank by 25 percent and the UK's by 20 percent. In that same quarter, New Zealand's GDP shrunk by 12 percent, about the same as extremely hard-hit Italy. Both the drops for New Zealand and Italy were higher than the average for OECD countries.[15]

This is not to suggest that the lockdowns could not be of some value early on. At times, the lockdowns definitely helped in recovery rates by "flattening the curve" and thereby reducing pressure on over-extended public health systems. However, it is important to understand that even if the curve is flattened, the area under that curve remains unchanged, that is, the total number of infections (or cases) will remain unchanged. All that flattening the curve achieves is that it pushes the timing of those infections to a date in the future. Furthermore, given the presence of the disease within the community and given the widely acknowledged asymptomatic transmission potential of Covid-19, it was inevitable that when the lockdowns were lifted, disease transmission would resume.

Nevertheless, we could conceivably make a case along the following lines: yes, lockdowns do impose costs elsewhere but unchecked community transmission of the disease would also lead to social and economic harm. So, it makes sense to lock down temporarily and upgrade and bolster health facilities, particularly the ability to undertake contact tracing. If and when these upgrades to existing systems occur, there should be no need to continue to employ any further lockdowns in the future. What was not necessarily acknowledged was that this course of action may mean one of two things: either a lockdown of significant duration[16] or shorter lockdowns with periods of freedom but reinstatement of lockdowns when community transmission resumes. It seemed to me that there was an insufficient recognition that if and when governments tried to implement these repeated lockdowns, they were going to face massive protests and unrest among citizens.[17] Also, the lockdown proponents were necessarily relying on the invention of a vaccine. However, they seemed to be severely overestimating the probability of getting a vaccine in short order *and* the vaccine providing effective immunity not only from the current strain of SARS-CoV-2 but also from any future mutated form of the virus, which is common with coronaviruses. I discuss this issue of overestimating small probabilities in greater detail in Chapter 3.

HOW UNIQUE IS SARS-COV-2?

SARS-CoV-2 is the name of the virus that causes the respiratory disease Covid-19. Could it be that SARS-CoV-2 (or Covid-19) was, in the words of Nassim Nicholas Taleb, a "black swan" event – a highly unlikely event that still came to pass and if left unchecked, community transmission will ravage communities? This possibility is worth considering. As Tyler Cowen of George Mason pointed out, at the end of the probabilistic computations and mathematical modeling, the question came down to: whether we were "base-raters" or "exponential growthers"; whether we took the view that the trajectory of Covid-19 will follow that of other coronavirus-caused diseases, such as severe acute respiratory syndrome (SARS) or Middle Eastern respiratory syndrome (MERS). This would be the "base-rate" view, which says that we can be reasonably certain how Covid-19 will play out since we can rely on the evidence from the prior coronavirus outbreaks. I explain in more detail in the following pages about the idea of base rates. The "exponential growth" view argues that, on the contrary, this is indeed a black swan event and the old rule-book does not apply.[18]

In her article "Why did the world shut down for COVID-19 but not Ebola, SARS or swine flu?", Kaleigh Rogers of *FiveThirtyEight* expanded on this black swan view of Covid-19.[19] The argument is that while those other diseases may be far more deadly, they are not as contagious as Covid-19. Covid-19 spreads more quickly, particularly given its potential for asymptomatic transmission, and can be deadly for a large number of people who contract the disease and has the potential to quickly overwhelm public health facilities. This is what makes social (physical) distancing essential. (In what follows I often use the terms "social distancing" and "physical distancing" synonymously.) At the expense of reiterating my points, remember that social distancing does not eradicate the disease. It simply keeps it suppressed for it to reappear in the future. The necessity of social distancing is also predicated on other assumptions that I address at various places in this book. A key incorrect assumption is that, even when faced with a deadly pathogen, human beings will go about their business as usual and not adopt any preventive measures unless compelled by the authorities to do so. As I hope to convince you in the following pages, this view is misguided. I will also show you that the support for social distancing was based on mistaken assumptions of how long the lockdowns needed to be, and the probability of quickly finding an effective vaccine and distributing it around the world. I address the comparative contagiousness issue in the final chapter of this book.

I felt reasonably confident that the base-rate view or something close to it was true. This was because the early estimates by the WHO suggested that Covid-19 had a *case fatality ratio* (CFR) of 3.4 percent. (This compares with a CFR of about 50 percent for MERS and about 35 percent for SARS.) This means that out of every 100 people who contracted the disease, around 3.5 would die, or 7 out of every 200 people who caught Covid-19 would die. This is a reasonably high probability. However, the difficulty with this measure is that the denominator is the number of known cases. Let us say that we know of 200 cases, and of those, seven died. Suppose there are another 500 people who also contracted the disease and did not die, but we were not aware of those other 500 since they did not show any symptoms or were never tested. Now, we have 700 people who have or have had

Covid-19; we know about 200 of these but do not know about the other 500. Of these, seven people died. In this instance, the actual ratio (or to use jargon, the *infection fatality ratio*, IFR) becomes 7 out of 700, or 1 in 100, which is about a third of the CFR of 3.5 out of every 100. So, what we really care about is not the CFR, but the IFR; how many people contracted Covid-19 and how many of those died?

To answer this latter question, we needed to carry out serological tests for Covid-19 antibodies to see what proportion of a particular population may have been infected (without having been tested) and what proportion died. By September 2020, the US Centers for Disease Control and Prevention (CDC) had downgraded this ratio, the IFR, to 0.65 percent with a range of 0.2 percent (2 out of 1000) to 0.8 percent (8 out of 1000).[20] This means that out of every 100 people who contracted Covid-19, less than 1 person will die. Since 0.65 of a person does not make sense, a better way to think of this is that 1 out of 153 (or 6.5, say 7, out of 1000) people will die. To put this differently, and I will show you soon that the way an issue is framed makes a huge difference, this means that out of 153 people who contract Covid-19, 152 will survive. Out of 1000 people who contract Covid-19, 993 will be alright.[21] People may well disagree as to whether this is a large or small number, but this is much less than 7 in 200, and a risk of 1 in 153 is not dramatically different from many of the risks we take in our day-to-day lives. For instance, as John Ioannidis of Stanford and his collaborators have noted (and I have more to say on this in a later chapter), this risk is comparable to driving between 13 and 101 miles per day across a number of countries or across many states in the US. I doubt I need to mention that a vast majority of people routinely drive long distances to and from work every day.

Nevertheless, I was still quite willing to concede that those who were calling for lockdowns may have a point. However, to an economist like me, it seemed that the actual policy choice must depend on a consideration of the trade-offs. What are the potential number of deaths from Covid-19? What are the potential number of deaths that may result from locking down? Or, how many lives will we lose to Covid-19? Alternatively, how many lives will we lose elsewhere in trying to prevent the loss of lives from Covid-19? There is no denying that once the Covid-19 virus started spreading, it was going to cause output and employment around the world to drop. However, it was evident that for the countries that enacted stringent lockdowns, the drop would be much larger. So, these countries would suffer additional damage owing to the severe restrictions on economic activity over and above any damage they may have suffered from the virus. It is well known that declining output and employment lead to not only a loss of livelihoods but to a loss of lives as well. For example, it is well known that unemployment leads to decreased life expectancy. According to a 2018 report by the *Associated Press*, "An increase of 10 percentage points in the unemployment rate in a neighborhood translated to a loss of roughly a year and a half of life expectancy".[22]

The response to questions about the potential costs and benefits was along the following lines: How can you be so crass as to put a dollar value on human lives? Indeed, New Zealand's Minister for Health and Education at the time said the same thing: "Generally it's not something we would do. We don't put a dollar value on people's lives."[23] But we do! All the time! This is what every tort lawyer who sues for wrongful death does: ask for financial reparation for the lives lost. If a man in his forties, a non-smoker, in good health, with a high income and two young kids died in a car crash tomorrow and it could be ascertained beyond doubt that this was due to an equipment malfunction (the airbag did not inflate), it is highly likely that this man's family will be awarded much greater damages than the family of a 60-year-old with no children and a long history of smoking and health complications, such as obesity and diabetes. This is what actuaries and insurance companies do: set a price on how much a life is worth. Even the Ministry of Health in New Zealand has detailed guidelines on the value of a life, which guides policy making on, say, which drugs should be funded by the country's public health system and which should not.

My former colleague Martin Berka wrote at the time:

> We rightfully feel repulsed by the notion of putting a price tag on life. But every government uses estimates of a "value of statistical life" in designing its healthcare policies and decisions about which life-saving drugs to fund. There are hundreds of such estimates in the academic and policy literature. For example, the US Environmental Protection Agency uses a value estimate of around US$10 million per life, the Australian government indicates A$3.5 million and the European Commission estimates €1–2 million. If we assume value of statistical life of NZ$5 million (similar to the estimates in this report for the New Zealand Fire Service Commission), a back-of-the-envelope calculation suggests the policies

in the tougher Treasury scenario outlined above – of staying at level 4 lockdown for six months – would need to save at least 16,800 lives, statistically speaking, to have been worth it. These unpalatable "trade-offs" are nevertheless what government officials consider when deciding when to open up the economy, aware that moving to level 3 will likely cost lives.[24]

By November 2020, New Zealand had experienced only 25 deaths or five deaths per million. According to *Our World in Data*'s Covid-19 pandemic page,[25] Japan, without much of a lockdown, had reported 15 deaths per million while suffering far less economically. It is difficult to compare directly across countries, but I felt that it was reasonable to ask that policy decisions be made on the basis of weighing up the alternatives. For instance, suppose we did what Japan did. Given a population of 5 million, 15 deaths per million would mean approximately 75 deaths in New Zealand from Covid-19 but far fewer deaths from non-Covid related causes. What if the total non-Covid related deaths from locking down far exceeded the Covid-19 deaths prevented? Would this still be a worthwhile trade-off? It turned out I was completely mistaken that people will pay attention to such questions. The approach was, *we will minimize the loss of lives from Covid-19 regardless of the cost.* In most instances, no cost–benefit analyses were undertaken,[26] and when they were, it appeared that the cost of the lockdowns far exceeded any potential benefits,[27] at times by large magnitudes.[28]

I hasten to reiterate that while many of my citations come from New Zealand, this lack of cost–benefit calculations was not confined just to my country. This was true of most other countries as well, where epidemiological experts kept insisting on locking down regardless of the potential cost, with this insistence on disregarding the opportunity cost becoming embarrassing at times.[29] The use of New Zealand as a case study is also justified since the country was lauded around the world for its success.[30]

What was also striking was the uniformity of the response across the world in terms of the measures implemented. With the exception of Sweden, Japan, Iceland and Taiwan, which imposed fairly minimal restrictions, the vast majority of countries moved to impose strict lockdowns. These included rich countries and poor, advanced countries and backward ones, landlocked countries and islands. What was distinctive was the degree of "mimicry" in the extent to which countries followed one another in imposing such lockdowns. According to a group of Swedish researchers, four out of five countries in the Organization for Economic Cooperation and Development (OECD) adopted very similar measures within a period of two weeks in March 2020. Needless to mention, developing countries that rely on the developed ones for guidance in terms of science and policy soon followed suit. According to this group of researchers: "Given the heterogeneity among these countries in terms of the preparedness of their healthcare systems, their population demography, and the degree to which the pandemic had taken hold in each country at this time, the homogeneity in timing of adoption is striking."[31]

As the process played out across the world, it reached a point where even questioning the efficacy and rationale of lockdowns were tantamount to heresy and people who did so were dismissed as being "contrarian"[32] or offering "fringe" viewpoints.[33] There was scant recognition that those opposing lockdowns were not saying that the Covid-19 threat should be minimized or that we should do nothing to fight it. Instead, they were simply pointing out that locking down whole countries in order to fight a virus that had a more than 99 percent recovery rate[34] was overkill. If we consider an IFR of 0.2 percent (the lower limit of CDC estimates), then the recovery rate is 99.8 percent, while if we take the upper limit of 0.8 percent, then the recovery rate is 99.2 percent.[35]

In the meantime, what was not reported as widely is that a New Zealand High Court ruled that the first nine days of the country's lockdown was "unlawful" but "justified". Exactly how something that is "unlawful" can be "justified" was not clarified, and anyway, the public was happy and no one asked too many questions.[36] Two legal experts wrote at the time that the lockdown "imposes the most extensive restrictions on New Zealanders' lives seen for at least 70 years; perhaps ever. No matter how 'necessary' these may be, we should expect such restrictions to have a clear, certain basis in law and be imposed through a transparent and accountable process."[37]

New Zealand's left-of-center government brushed off the questions, including requests under the Official Information Act, ostensibly on the grounds that the government enjoyed public support and therefore there was no need to engage with anyone offering contrarian views. The New Zealand Ombudsman Peter Boshier commented that he was "horrified" to learn that in the aftermath of the pandemic, the government had considered suspending the Official Information Act, before backing down.[38]

Soon after, the government passed "under urgency" the Covid-19 Public Health Response Bill. According to one report: "the bill went through Parliament in less than two days and with no select committee hearings (and) grants police warrantless entry to premises if they reasonably believe virus-related orders are being breached." In doing this, the government had broad support across the political spectrum, including the main right-of-center opposition.[39]

THE LIMITATIONS OF EPIDEMIOLOGICAL MODELS

As Covid-19 spread through the world, we were repeatedly told to trust the science and the experts. The experts in this case were epidemiologists whose job is to model how infectious diseases propagate through the population. The problem with this view is twofold. First, some of the questions asked are not those that epidemiologists could feasibly answer. This issue was raised recently by the *New York Times* columnist Ross Douthat.[40] For instance, suppose an epidemiologist says that the infection fatality ratio is 7 out of 1000. It is now a job for our elected representatives to figure out what to do with this number. Is this high or low? How does it compare with other risks that we face in our day-to-day lives?[41] What and how much are we willing to sacrifice to reduce this number further, knowing fully well that it is impossible to get this number down to zero; that the number does not need to be driven down to zero; that it is costly to try to drive this risk down and that those costs rise exponentially as we try?[42]

Second, the epidemiological models that were being used to predict rates of infection or mortality rates were seriously incomplete. People undertaking mathematical models of disease propagation, such as Neil Ferguson of Imperial College, are primarily relying on the SIR model proposed by William Kermack and Anderson McKendrick in 1927, in which SIR stands for "susceptible", "infected" and "recovered" (where in the earliest formulation, "recovered" could mean "recovered live or dead"). In some instances, people refer to a

SIRD model where the "R" is for recovered and "D" is for dead. One assumption here is that "recovered" is an "absorptive" state; that is, when someone has recovered, he or she is immune.[43]

At the risk of gross simplification, here is how these models operate. On day one, you have a population of people who are all susceptible to a disease. These people then go about their lives. On day two, a proportion of these people become infected, while others do not. Some of the infected recover, while others die, but those who are infected go on to infect others and so the disease propagates within the community. Over time, the proportion of those who are susceptible decreases, and the proportion of those who are infected (and either recovered or died) increases. The process continues until a large enough proportion of the population is infected and the disease cannot find any new hosts. When this happens, we say that the population has acquired "herd immunity". However, models like these depend crucially on assumptions. What is the reproduction rate; that is, how quickly does the infection spread? How frequently are people meeting each other and what is the probability that any meeting between an infected person and a non-infected person will result in the latter being infected? And so on.

So far so good. The problem is that the SIR model considers these probabilities to be fixed. So the rate at which people get infected or the rate at which they recover is unchanging over time. This is not quite accurate. As people get to hear about the disease and change their behavior to some extent, as some wear masks, some self-isolate, some wash their hands more frequently, some work from home and some stay away from visiting elderly relatives, the probabilities change continually.

Now, even if you make appropriate adjustments to the probabilities, most SIR models were essentially comparing two binary benchmarks: locking down or letting it rip. In reality, we have a continuum of choices available. In order to accommodate those choices, we need more elaborate models, which incorporate theories of human decision making into the standard SIR models. When we do that, the limitations of the simplistic lockdown approach become obvious. A number of people have undertaken these comparisons to show that when we account for a variety of intermediate interventions, the outcomes are far better than either complete lockdown or complete lack of intervention.

A group led by Martin Eichenbaum at Northwestern University were one of the earliest to undertake this type of work. By its very nature, this work tends to be mathematical and therefore complex. Therefore, I am going to provide a sketch of the underlying ideas. This is where models incorporating human decision making start to deviate from standard SIR models. Even though people understand the health risks associated with market activity, behavior in pandemics generates a collective action problem similar to pollution. Collectively, we are all better off if we all stay home, but if everyone else stays home, then it does not make a big difference if one person goes out and about in order to engage in social and/or commercial activities. However, this person's activities increase the risk of infection for everyone else, but, if it is individually rational for one person to do this, then it must be individually rational for everyone else to do so as well. Consequently, we get unabated infection transmission.

Therefore, the primary focus of policy needs to be on reducing this negative externality of individual behavior. Most governments have proceeded as if the only way to do this is to implement lockdowns. The problem is that these lockdowns may need to be long lasting and will cause significant economic damage.

Eichenbaum and colleagues suggest that one natural intermediate step is testing people for their health status and then quarantining the infected. At any point in time, the population consists of people who are either infected or not. The problem is that neither the government nor the people themselves know for sure who is infected and who is not. Those who are already infected have less of an incentive to remove themselves from the population compared with those who are not infected and therefore susceptible.

Suppose that test results are used to implement the following simple-quarantine policy: infected people are not allowed to work and receive temporary benefits from government but they are allowed to engage in non-economic social interactions. Eichenbaum and colleagues refer to these policies as "smart containment". We could go a step farther and have "strict containment" which restricts infected people from non-economic social interactions too.

These are mere examples and there may be other options. The point is that Eichenbaum and his colleagues show that these selective containment techniques do much better on the aggregate compared with either indiscriminate lockdowns or no intervention at all. Countries such as Taiwan and South Korea followed policies along these lines based on rapid testing and contact tracing. As with all models, the Eichenbaum et al. approach has drawbacks. Their results also depend crucially on assumptions underlying different values. However, the big advantage to their model is that they are a step ahead of the more simplistic SIR models, since they embed models of human behavior within the SIR framework.

One main conclusion from Eichenbaum et al.'s work is that the returns to improving testing and contact-tracing abilities are massive. Also, work such as this or that carried out recently by V. V. Chari and colleagues, of Minnesota, are providing nuanced and sophisticated alternatives to lockdowns that go a long way towards total harm minimization without having to resort to indiscriminate lockdowns.[44]

This type of analysis is based on the recognition of trade-offs and opportunity cost; yes Covid-19 is a threat that needs to be dealt with, but focusing on this exclusively and diverting all our physical, human and cognitive resources to tackling Covid-19 means that we would necessarily have to take those resources away from alternative uses. Surprisingly, or maybe not surprisingly, while making this argument was often tantamount to heresy in many places, this was not so in and around economists. Economists as a clan may have their flaws, but trade-offs, scarcity and opportunity costs are their livelihoods. Economists realize that resources are finite and devoting them to one area means taking them away from another; so, even when economists disagreed on policy prescriptions or in their risk assessments of how deadly Covid-19 was (some were base-raters while others were exponential growthers), generally they all conceded the opportunity–cost argument; they all appreciated the distinction between loss of lives right in front of our eyes as opposed to more diffuse losses elsewhere and in the background.

* * *

Finally, a discerning reader will be well within his or her rights to say: it is easy for you to pontificate at length. If you are so opposed to lockdowns, then what would you have done, while making decisions in the midst of the whirlwind? My response is twofold. First, as noted above, my position is based on minimizing total costs. It might take time and resources to put effective contact-tracing systems in place; though I note that Taiwan and South Korea seem to have achieved this expeditiously. My reading of the evidence suggested that most countries around the world could have responded with restrictions on large gatherings, together with good hygiene and mask-wearing. This strategy seems to have succeeded quite well for Japan, which, of course, like Taiwan, has the benefit of being an island. This would have almost certainly meant more lives lost to Covid-19 in some countries, but the total cost in lives lost to Covid-19 plus lives and livelihoods lost to other causes would have been the smallest. I wrote this in April 2020 and so this is not based on hindsight.[45]

My second response is that I was more open to lockdowns than it might appear. All I wanted was for someone to crunch the numbers and show me when the net benefit of these policies exceeded the cost; under what assumptions? Why was there such insistence on two binary options: lockdown or let it rip? Why was there so little willingness to concede that there is a continuum of responses and that it makes sense to examine which response is better in a particular context? Is the optimal response for islands, such as Japan and New Zealand, the same as that for land-locked countries, such as Switzerland or other European countries with open land borders and a high degree of mobility among residents? Is the optimal policy the same for high-income and low-income countries? Should developing countries, such as India, Pakistan or Bangladesh, with a younger population on average and no effective social safety net, implement lockdowns similar to the more developed countries? Why did lockdowns receive so much support from across the political spectrum, from liberals to conservatives, from policy makers to members of the public? This is what I explore in this book. Along the way, I need to tell some stories and build a scaffolding in order to show how decision-making biases influenced our response to Covid-19.

No one expects governments to get this exactly right, but we do expect moderation. When the potential costs of a particular policy grossly exceed the potential benefits, we expect course correction, not the continued single-minded pursuit of the same misguided policy. This cost–benefit analysis is an integral part of all policy making. When doctors decide who on the waiting list gets the next available kidney, they are much more likely to give it to a 35-year-old mother of two than a 55-year-old person with grown children and a long-term history of smoking. We do this when we decide which of many potential life-saving drugs to fund and which ones not, based on expected costs and expected benefits. This is not a difficult calculation and the few undertaken suggest that the costs of the lockdowns exceed the benefits. The problem was, anyone who dared ask the question needed his or her own security detail.

However, these questions need to be asked. Are lockdowns the panacea they have been made out to be? Why the uniformity in response across countries with very different circumstances and demographics? If the benefits do outweigh the costs, then why the reluctance to undertake a cost–benefit analysis? Why not crunch the numbers? Why not convince the sceptics? Why shut down all these questions as being heretical and the questioners as being delusional fanatics? That does not seem appropriate to me. Does it to you? If it does, then this book is not for you. You would do well to bail now before the pillars underpinning your beliefs start to shake and rattle. For the rest of you intrepid souls who may be willing to engage in debate or are up for having some predispositions questioned and probed, why don't we get started?

NOTES

1. The Coronavirus Government Response Tracker at the Blavatnik School of Government of the University of Oxford (n.d.) provides measures of lockdown stringency depending on the exact form of the restrictions. According to the tracker, the countries that adopted the most stringent measures in early 2020 included India, Israel and New Zealand. https://www.bsg.ox.ac.uk/research/research-projects/coronavirus-government-response-tracker. There were countries that never implemented much in the way of lockdowns. This smaller list of countries includes Sweden, Iceland, Japan and Taiwan. Sweden's response was the subject of much heated debate. For Japan, it is likely that a long culture of limited physical contact (such as bowing rather than handshaking) and being comfortable with mask-wearing as a matter of practice made a big difference. Iceland and Taiwan set up extensive testing and contact-tracing mechanisms reasonably quickly. As always, sceptics may well ask, why did something work in one place and not in another? I am sure there will be a lot of research forthcoming on the epidemiological and public health aspects of Covid-19. I am going to sidestep much of this debate as being beyond the scope of this volume since I am less concerned about the response per se and more concerned about the thought processes that lay behind those policy responses and the near unanimity around the world about the need for lockdowns.

2. Inglesby, T. V., Nuzzo, J. B., O'Toole, T., and Henderson, D. A. (2006). Disease mitigation measures in the control of pandemic influenza. *Biosecurity and Bioterrorism: Biodefense Strategy, Practice, and Science*, 4(4), 366–375. doi:10.1089/bsp.2006.4.366. PubMed PMID: 17238820.

3. Chaudhry, R., Dranitsaris, G., Mubashir, T., Bartoszko, J., and Riazia, S. (2020). A country level analysis measuring the impact of government actions, country preparedness and socioeconomic factors on COVID-19 mortality and related health outcomes. *EClinicalMedicine*, 25, 100464. https://doi.org/10.1016/j.eclinm.2020.100464.

4. Gibson, J. (2020a). Government mandated lockdowns do not reduce Covid-19 deaths: Implications for evaluating the stringent New Zealand response. *New Zealand Economic Papers*. doi:10.1080/00779954.2020.1844786.

5. Meunier, T. A. (2020). Full lockdown policies in Western Europe countries have no evident impacts on the COVID-19 epidemic. *MedRxiv*. https://doi.org/10.1101/2020.04.24.20078717. (Not peer reviewed at the time of writing.)

6. Gibson, J. (2020b). Hard, not early: Putting the New Zealand Covid-19 response in context. Forthcoming, *New Zealand Economic Papers*. doi:10.1080/00779954.2020.1842796.

7. Chaudhuri, A. (2020a). A different perspective on Covid-19. *Newsroom*, 8 April. https://www.newsroom.co.nz/ideasroom/2020/04/08/1119994/a-different-perspective-on-covid-19.

8. The declaration is so named since some of the original signatories gathered in Great Barrington, Massachusetts, USA. https://gbdeclaration.org/.

9. In case you are wondering, this is not named after the character in *Game of Thrones*. John Snow (1813–1858) was an English physician and is considered one of the founders of modern epidemiology. He is credited with the adoption of anesthesia in surgeries as well as fundamental changes in the water and waste systems of London, which led to similar changes in other cities and a significant improvement in general public health around the world. https://www.johnsnowmemo.com/.

10. This is true of most Western countries, such as the UK, Spain, Belgium, the Netherlands and others. In each of these, the spike in deaths occurred shortly after the imposition of lockdowns. Pospichal, J. (2020). Questions for lockdown apologists. *The Medium*, 24 May. https://medium.com/@JohnPospichal/questions-for-lockdown-apologists-32a9bbf2e247.

11. "At least 80 million children under one at risk of diseases such as diphtheria, measles and polio as COVID-19 disrupts routine vaccination efforts, warn Gavi, WHO and UNICEF." World Health Organization Press Release, 22 May 2020. https://www.who.int/news/item/22-05-2020-at-least-80-million-children-under-one-at-risk-of-diseases-such-as-diphtheria-measles-and-polio-as-covid-19-disrupts-routine-vaccination-efforts-warn-gavi-who-and-unicef.

12. Hoffman, J. (2020). Polio and measles could surge after disruption of vaccine programs. *New York Times*, 22 May. https://www.nytimes.com/2020/05/22/health/coronavirus-polio-measles-immunizations.html.

13. Donnelly, L., and Gilbert, D. (2020). Non-virus deaths at home behind surge in excess fatalities, figures show. *Telegraph*, 2 September. https://www.telegraph.co.uk/news/2020/09/02/patients-dying-home-causes-covid-19-fuelling-excess-uk-deaths/.

14. Wilkinson, B. (2020). IMF's fiscal forecasts make for grim reading for New Zealand. *New Zealand Herald*, 21 October. https://www.nzherald.co.nz/business/bryce-wilkinson-imfs-fiscal-forecasts-make-grim-reading-for-nz/JVUUSP2JUIJBGBTJGVTJTSHTRQ/.

15. OECD stands for Organisation for Economic Co-operation and Development. Loosely, this is the group of rich countries of the world that include most of the industrialized nations of Western Europe together with others such as Australia, Japan, New Zealand, South Korea and the US.

16. Indeed, Neil Ferguson of Imperial College, London and his collaborators who undertook early mathematical modeling of Covid-19 transmission and deaths suggested that countries may need to implement some form of lockdown for extended periods of up to 18 months or two years in order to reduce the spread of the disease and to allow time for a vaccine to be produced. See Landler, M., and Castle, S. (2020). Behind the virus report that jarred the U.S. and the U.K. to action. *New York Times*, 2 April. https://www.nytimes.com/2020/03/17/world/europe/coronavirus-imperial-college-johnson.html.

17. Henley, J. (2020). Latest coronavirus lockdowns spark protest around Europe. *Guardian*, 2 November. https://www.theguardian.com/world/2020/nov/02/latest-coronavirus-lockdowns-spark-protests-across-europe.

18. Cowen, T. (2020). Bill Gates is really worried about the coronavirus: Here's why. *Bloomberg*, 4 March. https://www.bloomberg.com/opinion/articles/2020-03-03/how-fast-will-the-new-coronavirus-spread-two-sides-of-the-debate.

19. Rogers, K. (2020). Why did the world shut down for COVID-19 but not Ebola, SARS or swine flu? *FiveThirtyEight*, 14 April. https://fivethirtyeight.com/features/why-did-the-world-shut-down-for-covid-19-but-not-ebola-sars-or-swine-flu/.

20. Readers should bear in mind that, as with any other average, this number masks variances among different age groups. The mortality risk of people over 70 or 80 years old is much higher, say 1 in 100; and the mortality risk of those in that age group with other underlying health conditions is even higher, say 1 in 20. Conversely, the mortality risk of the younger age group is much lower. For those below 40 years old, it may be as low as 1 in 1000. These are approximate numbers but generally representative of what we know about Covid-19 mortality. This data was available from a number of sources, including the US CDC website, by August–September 2020 if not earlier.

21. At the time of writing, there is controversy about the long-term neurological effects of Covid-19. There is no conclusive evidence regarding this since other either virus- or bacteria-borne respiratory diseases, such as pneumonia, can also cause similar damage. It is possible that in future the infection consequences of Covid-19 may need to be reassessed. I revisit this debate in the final chapter of this book.

22. Forster, N. (2018). Unemployment, income affect life expectancy. *Associated Press*, 15 December. https://apnews.com/article/ea3be7fb82bf4bec90a00d759 57f833b.

23. MacNamara, K. (2020b). Can we put a cost on a human life? *New Zealand Herald*, 14 September. https://www.nzherald.co.nz/business/kate-macnamara-can-we-put-a-cost-on-a-human-life/AP7GDUZRSHVNXFG723OTA2ECQ4/.

24. Berka, M. (2020). Protecting lives and livelihoods: The data on why New Zealand should relax its coronavirus lockdown from Thursday. *The Conversation*, 17 April. https://theconversation.com/protecting-lives-and-livelihoods-the-dat a-on-why-new-zealand-should-relax-its-coronavirus-lockdown-from-thursday-136242. In New Zealand, level 4 implied the most stringent form of lockdown with everything other than essential services shut. Level 3 allowed for greater economic activity; for instance, industries that could safely distance workers, such as construction, were allowed. Restaurants could open for take-out service. There was also greater freedom of movement in relation to people being allowed to socialize outside of their bubble.

25. Ritchie, H., Ortiz-Ospina, E., Beltekian, D., Mathieu, E., Hasell, J., Macdonald, B., et al. (2020a). Coronavirus pandemic (COVID-19). *Our World in Data*. https://ourworldindata.org/coronavirus. Founder and Director: Max Roser.

26. MacNamara, K. (2020a). Why productivity at the Productivity Commission seems to be a low ebb. *New Zealand Herald*, 11 September. https://www.nzher ald.co.nz/business/kate-macnamara-why-productivity-at-the-productivity-com mission-seems-to-be-at-a-low-ebb/XR7PNKKLTZ5N4FV7YMUOHKO3R4/.

27. Miles, D., Stedman, M., and Heald, A. (2020). Living with Covid-19: Balancing costs against benefits in the face of the virus. *National Institute Economic Review*, *253*, R60–R76. https://doi.org/10.1017/nie.2020.30. Published online by Cambridge University Press, 28 July.

28. Heatley, D. (2020). *A Cost Benefit Analysis of 5 Extra Days at COVID-19 Alert Level 4* (Research Note 2020/02). New Zealand Productivity Commission. https://www.productivity.govt.nz/research/cost-benefit-analysis-covid-alert-4/.

29. For example, see interview of Professor Gabriel Scally of Independent SAGE (a strong proponent of a nationwide lockdown in England in November 2020) with Maajid Nawaz. Hickey, S. (2020). Maajid Nawaz corners epidemiologist over cost of second lockdown. *LBC*, 31 October. https://www.lbc.co.uk/radio/presenters/maajid-nawaz/epidemiologist-on-cost-of-second-lockdown-coronavi rus/. Maajid Nawaz hosts a radio show on LBC (formerly London Broadcasting Corporation), a London-based national phone-in and talk radio station.

30. NZ Herald. (2020). In awe of NZ: How world media reacted to New Zealand eliminating Covid-19. *New Zealand Herald*, 9 June. (No byline.) https://www.nz herald.co.nz/nz/in-awe-of-nz-how-world-media-reacted-to-new-zealand-elimin ating-covid-19/MMOWHK3HHQCYU3TWV7G3TSJJK4/.

31. Sebhatu, A., Wennberg, K., Arora-Jonsson, S., and Lindberg, S. (2020). Explaining the homogeneous diffusion of Covid-19 nonpharmaceutical interventions across heterogenous countries. *Proceedings of the National Academy of Sciences*, *117*(35), 21201–21208.

32. Daaldar, M. (2020). "Contrarian" academics oppose lockdown. *Newsroom*, 14 April. https://www.newsroom.co.nz/contrarian-academics-oppose-nz-lockdown.

33. Sample, S. (2020). Why herd immunity strategy is regarded as fringe viewpoint. *Guardian*, 7 October. https://www.theguardian.com/world/2020/oct/07/why-herd-immunity-strategy-is-regarded-as-fringe-viewpoint.

34. WebMD. (n.d.). Coronavirus recovery. https://www.webmd.com/lung/covid-recovery-overview#1. The website states:

> Scientists and researchers are constantly tracking infections and recoveries. But they have data only on confirmed cases, so they can't count people who don't get COVID-19 tests. Experts also don't have information about the outcome of every infection. However, early estimates predict that the overall COVID-19 recovery rate is between 97% and 99.75%.
>
> WebMD has been accused of being funded by big pharma and, therefore, may or may not be a credible source of information. In this case though, we would expect WebMD to suggest lower recovery rates, thereby creating greater urgency for vaccines and other medicines. In any event, the main point here is that the recovery rates for Coronavirus are high. WebMD. (n.d.). Coronavirus recovery. *WebMD*. https://www.webmd.com/lung/covid-recovery-overview#1.

35. Katz, D. L. (2020). Is our fight against coronavirus worse than the disease? *New York Times*, 20 March. https://www.nytimes.com/2020/03/20/opinion/coronavirus-pandemic-social-distancing.html.

36. Nightingale, M. (2020). Coronavirus lockdown unlawful for first nine days high court finds but says action was justified. *New Zealand Herald*, 19 August. https://www.nzherald.co.nz/nz/covid-19-coronavirus-lockdown-unlawful-for-first-nine-days-high-court-finds-but-says-action-was-justified/AI2WQ3PZ5QYEWUYGSTS3MNKE6Q/.

37. Geddis, A., and Geiringer, C. (2020). The legal basis for the lockdown may not be as solid as we've been led to believe. *The Spinoff*. 28 April. https://thespinoff.co.nz/covid-19/28-04-2020/the-legal-basis-for-the-lockdown-may-not-be-as-solid-as-weve-been-led-to-believe/.

38. Sachdeva, S. (2020a). Coronavirus: Officials pitched OIA suspension during Covid-19 lockdown. *Newsroom*, 24 April. https://www.stuff.co.nz/national/politics/121237698/coronavirus-officials-pitched-oia-suspension-during-covid19-lockdown.

39. Sachdeva, S. (2020b). Covid-19 powers approved under urgency. *Newsroom*, 13 May. https://www.newsroom.co.nz/2020/05/13/1171049/covid-19-powers-approved-under-urgency.

40. Douthat, R. (2020). When you can't just "trust the science". *New York Times*, 19 December. https://www.nytimes.com/2020/12/19/opinion/sunday/coronavirus-science.html.

41. I recently had an extended debate with a colleague who is an internationally renowned scientist. He is very much in favor of lockdowns since he believes that the cost of community infection is very high and he obviously assigns a large probability to the risk of Covid-19 getting out into the community. So, when it comes to Covid-19, he appears to be extremely risk averse; yet, his passion is rock climbing, an inherently risky sport! Evidently there is some cognitive dissonance

here, where he is risk averse in one sphere and risk loving in another. These are no longer epidemiological questions but, instead, relate to intrinsic individual and social preferences that lie beyond the expertise of epidemiologists.

42. According to an October 2020 report from the Imperial College London, there is a striking difference in the mortality rates between high-income countries with generally older populations and low-income countries where the population tends to skew younger. The underlying risk may be as high as 1 percent (1 in 100) in richer countries with older populations but as low as 0.2 percent or 2 in 1000 among low-income countries where the median age is much lower. Van Elsland, S. L. (2020). COVID-19 deaths: Infection fatality ratio is about 1% says new report. Imperial College London, 29 October. https://www.imperial.ac.uk/news/207273/covid-19-deaths-infection-fatality-ratio-about/. So, even if it makes sense to enact stringent lockdowns in high-income countries, does it make sense to do so in low-income ones? In low-income countries, there are myriad other easily preventable diseases that claim more lives than Covid-19. Many of these such as malaria, dengue or cholera claim the lives of many children and young people. Should these countries be devoting scarce resources to fight Covid-19 when these resources could be used to fight other diseases? These are no longer questions for epidemiologists but pose significant moral and ethical debates.

43. This assumption is currently up for debate. A recent (non-peer reviewed) study from New Zealand suggests that certain antibodies against Covid-19 stay in the blood for up to eight months following mild to moderate infection. Whitcombe, A. L., McGregor, R., Craigie, A., James, A., Charlewood, R., Lorenz, N., et al. (2020). Comprehensive analysis of SARS-CoV-2 antibody dynamics in New Zealand. *MedRxiv*, 11 December. https://doi.org/10.1101/2020.12.10.20246751.

44. In New Zealand, early in 2020, Sam Morgan, the founder of Trade Me (New Zealand's version of eBay) suggested something along these lines when he recommended that the government invest resources in rapidly developing Bluetooth enabled Covid cards that would make it a lot easier to undertake contact tracing. However, this did not happen. In September 2020, Morgan stepped down from the government's Covid-19 response team and expressed frustration at the lack of action in this area. The Minister in charge at that point commented that mandatory Covid cards of this type would be "the last resort". It was not quite clear why indiscriminate lockdowns were considered acceptable but universal Covid cards a bridge too far by the government. See Pullar-Strecker, T. (2020). Sam Morgan gives up on CovidCard in frustration with Ministry of Health. *Stuff*, 1 September. https://www.stuff.co.nz/business/122626522/sam-morgan-gives-up-on-covidcard-in-frustration-with-ministry-of-health.

45. Chaudhuri, A. (2020a). A different perspective on Covid-19. *Newsroom*, 8 April. https://www.newsroom.co.nz/ideasroom/2020/04/08/1119994/a-different-perspective-on-covid-19.

2. Gut feelings: biases, heuristics and Covid-19

This chapter looks at why there was such near unanimous support around the world for lockdowns in dealing with Covid-19 given that much evidence suggests that the unidentified losses from lockdowns are larger than the potential benefits. In doing so, I write about:

- the distinction between "identified lives" and "statistical lives";
- system-1 or intuitive thinking and system-2 or deliberative thinking;
- how it is important to realize when we can rely on system 1 and when we need to engage system 2;
- the role of priming, framing, anchoring and the availability heuristic;
- how we routinely put dollar values on human lives;
- the role of cognitive biases in responding to the pandemic.

* * *

In his book *Risk Savvy*, Gerd Gigerenzer notes that, in the immediate aftermath of 11 September 2001 (9/11), many Americans decided that flying was too risky. Instead, they chose to drive. In the 12 months following the attacks, an additional 1500 people lost their lives on the road while trying to avoid the risk of flying. This is more than the total number of passengers on the planes used in the 9/11 attacks. In deciding to drive instead of fly, people were essentially focusing on *identified* lives, the loss of lives that happened right in front of us on 9/11. In doing so, people were ignoring the additional loss of lives from road accidents, since these occurred in a scattered manner and therefore did not garner as much attention. This secondary loss of lives, which results from diverting many of our resources to save the lives right in front of us, is referred to as loss of *statistical* lives.

Gigerenzer calls this "dread risk", the fear of losing many lives in a short span of time.

A similar phenomenon afflicted our thinking about Covid-19. From the very beginning, epidemiologists, policy makers and members of the public became keenly focused on saving identified lives. Every day, newspapers reported how many people died of Covid-19 around the world. This is not surprising, since this is exactly what our instincts tell us to do: take all possible safety measures to avoid the pathogen and prevent the deaths right in front of our eyes. However, this came with significant trade-offs. The question is not only: how many lives will we lose to Covid-19? Equally: how many lives and livelihoods will we lose to other causes as we divert scarce resources (such as hospital beds and other medical services, including emergency ones) to a single-minded fight against Covid-19?

Given that resources such as time, money, energy and attention are finite, whenever we decide to use one or more resources in one area, we must decide not to use it for another. For instance, your decision to buy this book or even read this book required a number of trade-offs; another book you could have read or another activity you could have pursued; taking a leisurely stroll or even a nap. This is the *opportunity cost* of doing what you are doing; the value of the best alternative activity forgone. The opportunity cost of holding a large amount of cash in your wallet is the interest income you are forgoing by not putting your money in the bank. The cost of our recent fantastic family trip to Europe (which, alas, may have been the last for a while under the current circumstances) was the part of the mortgage that I could have paid back had we not taken the trip. In some cases, such as the cost of our Europe trip or forgone interest earnings, assigning a dollar cost to the forgone alternative activity is easier. If you think hard about it, you could also possibly assign a dollar value to other things; activities that you gave up in order to pursue this current activity. Economists call this the *imputed value*; the idea that you could and should assign a value to activities. When you decide to undertake a particular activity, you have implicitly decided not to undertake another activity.

For instance, I often forgo searching for bargains, especially on items that are not hugely expensive. I figure that I might have to spend an extra hour in order to save $50, but this is not really a saving, since to me that extra hour is valuable. I could have spent that hour reading, writing or listening to music. If someone asked me how much I was willing to forgo in order not to spend extra time looking for a bargain, I might say that I am willing to pay as much as $50. So, even if in the end I save $50, effectively it is equal since the imputed value of my extra time is also $50. Hunting for the bargain only makes sense if I can save more than the opportunity cost of my time. My wife and daughters accuse me of putting too high a value on my time, and some people do derive pleasure out of the act of shopping itself. *De gustibus non est disputandum* (In matters of taste, there can be no disputes). However, trade-offs such as this are often neither obvious nor intuitive. Let us take a closer look why.

GUT FEELINGS

We are often confronted with choices where decision-making is not easy. Should I get the ultra-high definition television or organic light-emitting diode (OLED) television? How big; 55 or 75 inches? Which is the right house to buy? Will it still be "right" when the kids are older? What neighborhood? Which school zone? Close to the ocean? Better lifestyle but a longer commute. Or close to the highway, reducing commuting time but in a less nice area. As Theodore Geisel (Dr Seuss) noted in his book *Oh, The Places You'll Go!* we often find that it is not a simple matter "for a mind-maker-upper to make up his mind". When it comes to such decision-making, it is not unusual for us to go with our gut feeling. Or someone we ask may well say: "Go with your gut" or "What does your gut tell you?" Often this seems like common sense; to rely on our instincts.

Former US President George W. Bush held that he was the type of guy who preferred to make his decisions with his gut.[1] In 2006, Stephen Colbert, who was the featured speaker at the White House Correspondents' dinner,[2] made a joke out of Bush's reliance on gut feelings. Here is part of Colbert's famous riff:

> We are not that different, he and I. We both get it. Guys like us, we are not some brainiac on nerd patrol. We are not members of the "fact"-onista. We go straight from the gut. That is where the truth lies. Right down here in the gut. Do you know that there are more nerve endings in your gut than in your head? You can look it up. Now, I know some of you will say that "I did look it up and that is not true." That's because you looked it up

in a book. Next time, look it up in your gut. I did. My gut tells me that's how our nervous system works.

Colbert's comments notwithstanding, there is significant evidence that we often rely on our gut feelings to make decisions, and both academic research and popular writing suggests that this is often useful. According to Gerd Gigerenzer, a behavioral scientist at the Max Planck Institute of Human Development in Berlin, going with your gut is fine in many situations since millions of years of evolution have endowed us with this ability to make quick judgments. In the African savannah, this may have meant the difference between life and death. If there is a slithering noise in the bush behind you, you might be better off jumping, assuming a snake, rather than investigating the source of the sound. According to Gigerenzer, evolution has molded our minds in such a way that we can, often, rely on these instincts to good effect.

The idea of relying on our gut received extensive support in the book *Blink* by Malcolm Gladwell. Gladwell starts his book by discussing an example where a number of art experts were invited by the J. Paul Getty Museum in Los Angeles to judge the authenticity of a Greek sculpture (a "kouros").[3] A geologist had already certified that the statue was made of dolomite marble from the Greek island of Thasos and that the statue was old; it was not a contemporary fake. However, when the museum called in the art experts, even before the experts had had a chance to examine the statue's provenance or undertake other detailed analysis, all of them knew in their gut that the statue was a fake. Many of these experts could not articulate why they felt that way; they variably attributed this to a hunch; an instinctive sense that something was amiss.

* * *

Take a look at Table 2.1. This shows the opponents from the round of 16 of the 2019 US Open men's tennis tournament and is taken from my book *Behavioural Economics and Experiments*. I am using 2019 since 2020 was a strange year with many unexpected outcomes including the ousting of Novak Djokovic early in the tournament for hitting a lineswoman with a ball. Can you figure out who won each game? Go ahead and give it a shot before you read on.

Table 2.1   List of matches: round of 16 of the 2019 US Open Tennis Championship men's tournament

Djokovic vs Kudla	Majcharzak vs Dimitrov
Wawrinka vs Lorenzi	De Minaur vs Nishikori
Koepfer vs Basilashvili	Rublev vs Kyrgios
Medvedev vs Lopez	Berrettini vs Popyrin
Federer vs Evans	Shopalov vs Monfils
Goffin vs Carreno Busta	Bublik vs Andujar
Schwarzman vs Sandgren	Bedene vs Zverev
Nadal vs Chung	Isner vs Cilic

Source: Reproduced from Chaudhuri (2021a).

Here is the answer. The winner was the first-named player in the first column and the second-named player in the second column. How did you do? Chances are you did well even if you are not a regular follower of tennis. How? Most likely because you adopted a simple rule of thumb: in each pair, you picked the player who was better known or at least the player you had heard of before. If you did this, you would have done well. I did, even though I did not know the outcomes of these games. Except for a few cases, I did well on the others, simply by relying on what Gigerenzer terms the *recognition heuristic*. A *heuristic* is a fancy name for a rule of thumb. If it was a name I had heard before, this probably meant that he was the better player, so I picked that player.

So far so good; relying on gut feelings or instincts sounds like a good bet. Now let me ask you another question. Rank the following rugby union players by the total number of test tries (analogous to touchdowns in American football) they have scored: David Campese (Australia); Christian Cullen (New Zealand); Bryan Habana (South Africa); Doug Howlett (New Zealand); Brian O'Driscoll (Ireland); Daisuke Ohata (Japan); Hirotoki Onozawa (Japan); Joe Rokocoko (New Zealand); Julian Savea (New Zealand); Rory Underwood (England); and Shane Williams (Wales). No idea?

Let me make it simpler. Pick the top five try scorers. Still nothing? Would it surprise you to know that two of the top five are from Japan? Here is the correct ranking: (1) Daisuke Ohata; (2) Bryan Habana; (3) David Campese; (4) Shane Williams;

(5) Hirotoki Onozawa; (6) Rory Underwood; (7) Doug Howlett; (8) Brian O'Driscoll; (9) Christian Cullen; (10 tied) Joe Rokocoko and Julian Savea. How did you do? I am betting that you chose five people from among the Australians, New Zealanders, South Africans and British since your instinct told you that these are the countries that have strong rugby teams. I am also absolutely certain that none of you picked Ohata or Onozawa in your top five. Assuming that you did not cheat by looking at Wikipedia, which is where I got this information from, I bet you are surprised since you probably were not even aware that Japan played rugby. Baseball yes, Sumo, yes, but the Japanese do not seem cut out for rugby. Out of these players, Ohata is the only one with an average of greater than 1, meaning that he scores at least one try (touchdown) per game he plays.

One more puzzle before I get to my point. Among the following cricket players, rank the top five batsmen by their lifetime batting averages in test cricket (number of runs scored per innings played) and the top five bowlers by the number of wickets they have taken in their lifetime in test matches. Don Bradman (Australia); Sachin Tendulkar (India); Virat Kohli (India); Steven Smith (Australia); M.S. Dhoni (India); Herbert Sutcliffe (England); Ken Barrington (England); Everton Weekes (West Indies); Kapil Dev (India); Imran Khan (Pakistan); Glenn McGrath (Australia), Anil Kumble (India); Muttiah Muralitharan (Sri Lanka); Shane Warne (Australia); James Anderson (England); Courtney Walsh (West Indies); and Stuart Broad (England).

Lost? Chances are you know that cricket is big in India, Australia and England, and so you picked names from those countries. You may even have heard the names Tendulkar, Dhoni and Kohli in passing from Indian friends and/or acquaintances since the three of them are huge superstars. Let me give you the answers. Of those players who have played at least 40 tests or more, the top five batsmen in batting average, in sequence, are Bradman, Smith, Sutcliffe, Barrington and Weekes. Highest wicket takers in order? Muralitharan, Warne, Kumble, Anderson, McGrath, Walsh and Broad. How did you do? Did your list of batsmen feature some bowlers or vice versa?

There is no reason for you to feel bad. I follow both rugby and cricket. I had no idea about the rugby try-scorers and even in cricket I would have struggled to pick the top batsmen. I have a feeling that many cricket aficionados will struggle too. Bradman is a shoo-in since he is the Babe Ruth of cricket but I would never have thought of Sutcliffe, Barrington or Weekes. They are certainly not household names.

What is my point? The reason that you probably did not fare well in the rugby or cricket questions is because you have no experience with those games and therefore there was no recognition heuristic to rely upon. The word "experience" comes from the Latin "experiential". The verb *experior* comes from Latin *perior*, which is related to the Greek verb *peirao*, meaning to try, attempt, test or get experience. The following words all come from that same root: expert, expertise, experiment and experienced. For the recognition heuristic to work, you need to have a minimal amount of experience in the task at hand. When people read the kouros story from Gladwell, they often ignore the role of expertise. The experts had the instincts; they knew intuitively that something was off.

Tom Brady, the long-time quarterback for the New England Patriots (before he left for Tampa Bay in 2020), is legendary for his ability to make fast decisions in the pocket. He may well be the best quarterback of all time. Brady has won seven Super Bowls and was elected to be the most valuable player (MVP) in five of them. He has been the National Football League MVP three times. What makes Brady so good? It turns out that Brady is particularly good at split-second decision making on where to throw the ball in the face of on-rushing tacklers. For someone in Brady's position, there is really no time to pause and ponder the alternatives; he needs to decide very quickly and the only way to do that is to rely on his instincts.

On 15 January 2009, Chesley Sullenberger was the captain of US Airways Flight 1549. This was an inter-continental flight departing from LaGuardia Airport in New York City and headed for Seattle. Shortly after take-off, a flock of Canadian geese flew into the plane, resulting in the plane losing power in both engines. Sullenberger quickly realized that there was no way the plane could get back to LaGuardia or any other airport in the locality. Using deft instincts, he guided the plane to a water landing on the Hudson River. All 155 people on board survived.[4] Talking about the experience later, Sullenberger said that on that fateful day, his 42 years of experience paid off.

Most of us are not Tom Brady or Chesley Sullenberger. An important caveat to bear in mind is that in order to reap the greatest benefits from our gut feelings, we may need to have substantial expertise in the task at hand. Otherwise, gut feelings or common sense can drive you astray, especially when it comes to problems that are complex, decisions that we encounter infrequently and situations in which we have little experience. So, ultimately, whether you rely on your gut feelings or not may come down to how much familiarity you have with the task in question. If this is a task or decision that you encounter infrequently, then you are better off doing some research rather than going with your gut.

LIMITATIONS TO INTUITIVE THINKING

Consider the following problems posed by Shane Frederick of Yale University. Try answering them before you read on. You will get more out of them if you do.

Problem 1: A bat and a ball together cost $110. The bat costs $100 more than the ball. How much does the ball cost?

Problem 2: In a lake, there is a patch of lily pads. Every day, the patch doubles in size. If it takes 48 days to cover the entire lake, how long does it take for the patch to cover half of the lake?

Problem 3: Suppose you are running a race and you have just passed the person running in second place, what place are you in?

For problem 1, most people intuitively say that the ball costs $10. This is clearly incorrect, because if that were so, the bat must cost $110 since the bat costs $100 more than the ball. However, if that were true, then the two together cost $120, not $110. The correct answer is that the ball costs $5 and the bat costs $105. Our intuition does not come up with this answer as $105 is not intuitive. For the second problem, the answer is not 24 days as intuition suggests. The correct answer is 47 days. Since the lily pads double every day, if the pond is half-full after 47 days, then it doubles and gets filled the very next day, the forty-eighth. For problem 3, an intuitive response is to say that you are in first place, but this is not right; if you overtook the second place person then you are now in second place. In all these problems, the answers seem obvious but the correct answer is not the most obvious one. This led Daniel Kahneman, who won the 2002 Nobel Prize in

Economics,[5] to coin the acronym WYSIATI: what you see is all there is! However, often there is much more than meets the eye.

Gut feelings are sometimes termed *system 1* thinking. They involve automatic or intuitive thinking and operate quickly, with little or no effort and no sense of voluntary control. System 2, however, is deliberative and effortful. It allocates attention to effortful mental activities that demand it, including complex computations, but it takes conscious effort to engage system 2. System 1 quickly gets into action as soon as we receive a signal or a threat or a stimulus. A good analogy is to think of system 1 as an elephant that lurches into action quickly, while system 2 is the rider trying to guide the elephant; this can be done but is not easy and requires practice.[6]

Take a look at Figure 2.1. This is known as the Müller-Lyer illusion. Looking between the arrows, which line segment do you think is longer? You will appreciate the point more if you first try the test yourself. Seems intuitive, does it not? Line A is clearly longer than line B? Now look at Figure 2.2. Still convinced A is longer? The lines are of equal length. Now go back and look at Figure 2.1 again. Line A does seem longer again. Once you have seen Line A as being longer, it seems difficult to "unsee" it. This is system 1 at work. It is hard to overcome your instincts even after the correct answer has been revealed.

This implies that once our system 1 became fixated on the number of deaths from Covid-19 in banner headlines on our newspapers and television screens, we found it increasingly difficult to take a step back and engage our system 2. We tended to forget that many of those people would have died in the normal course of events, from a variety of reasons, such as heart attacks or flu. The median age of those who died from Covid-19 is around 82. Approximately 50 million people die every year from a variety of causes, including old age. The vast majority of deaths across the world were of those in their eighties, and in most cases, there were other co-morbidities (that is, other diseases). For instance, in October 2020, the BBC reported the following about Covid-19 deaths in Scotland:

Figure 2.1   The Müller-Lyer illusion

Figure 2.2 The Müller-Lyer illusion explained

The average age at death for those who died with Covid-19 in Scotland was 79 for men and 84 for women. Elsewhere in the NRS report it showed that life expectancy in Scotland is 77.1 for males and 81.1 for females. The report says the age profile of those dying with Covid was significantly older than that for deaths in general. More than three quarters (77%) of all those who died were aged 75 or over and 43% were aged 85 or over. This compared with overall deaths in 2019 where 63% were aged 75 or over and 33% were aged 85 or over.[7]

The issue is not so much how many people died from Covid-19, but how many more? In focusing on identified lives, we ignore the loss of statistical lives. It is almost certain that the total impact of the loss in statistical lives and livelihoods will be greater than any loss of lives owing to Covid-19. However, those deaths will register less on our collective psyche, since they will be diffuse, scattered all over the world and will not be reported on in the same breathless manner.

Beyond a particular point, it is just not worth keeping the economy shut down in order to save more people. As economic activity came to a standstill, businesses went bankrupt. By late March 2020, more than 6 million people had filed for bankruptcy in the United States. The corresponding number at the start of the Global Financial Crisis in 2008–09 was less than 1 million. In New Zealand, as international flights all but stopped, the national carrier's (Air NZ's) revenue fell from roughly NZ$6 billion per year to only about NZ$500 million.[8]

Globally, and especially in less developed countries, this massive economic shock resulted in poverty, hunger and death. In India, migrant workers from other states lost their jobs and were also unable to travel back home. In the absence of any type of social safety net, these workers were literally starving. Estimates suggest that a ten percentage point increase in unemployment results in a decrease in life expectancy of approximately one to one-and-a-half years. The diversion of resources, including health facilities, around the world to reduce deaths from Covid-19 meant that other tests, screenings and surgeries were postponed, leading to a sharp spike in deaths from other causes. The lockdowns around the world meant that roughly 80 million children were not vaccinated, leading to a sharp increase in measles, diphtheria and polio. A similar argument would be true of countries that use the BCG vaccine against tuberculosis.

Writing for the *New York Times* in April 2020, columnist Ruchir Sharma summed it up by saying that some countries faced an awful question: death by coronavirus or by hunger? As Sharma noted, while millions filed for unemployment benefits in the US, in developing countries, more than 2 billion people were facing unemployment without any social safety net. At the time Sharma was writing, nearly 80 countries had approached the International Monetary Fund (IMF) for bail-out packages. What happens when the healthcare infrastructures of these countries collapse? People will die. They will die of easily preventable diseases, such as cholera. Children will die owing to lack of adequate care or lack of vaccination. Diseases that we thought had been eradicated, such as measles, will come roaring back. Confinement in close quarters, even in countries such as New Zealand, is going to lead to a resurgence of tuberculosis; especially among the socio-economically deprived. Sharma quoted Imran Khan, the legendary ex-cricketer and current Prime Minister of Pakistan, who said that South Asia is "faced with the stark choice" between "a lockdown" to control the virus and "ensuring that people don't die of hunger and our economy doesn't collapse".

COGNITIVE BIASES AND COVID-19 DECISION MAKING

A bigger and older fish swims by two much younger fish and asks: "Hey boys, how's the water?" One of the younger fish looks at the other and asks: "What's water?" We are social creatures and are intimately affected by people and events around us, even without realizing that what we take as routine and commonplace in our social environment is, nevertheless, socially constructed. It is the consequence of prior policy and design choices. The tendency to go with our gut often means that we take the status quo as being right and questioning this as being problematic. This, in turn, makes us susceptible to a series of cognitive biases that can lead to systematic judgment errors. Three that played a significant role in the early days of the pandemic were priming, framing and anchoring. Collectively, they can be thought of as an availability heuristic; a tendency to focus excessively on information that is right in front of us without thinking too much about where that information came from or whether it is necessarily correct.

PRIMING AND COVID-19

In his books *The Better Angels of Our Nature* and *Enlightenment Now*, Steven Pinker makes the point that over the past century or so, human conditions have improved massively. There have been fewer wars and therefore fewer deaths from wars. Life expectancy and standards of living have increased. Deaths from easily preventable diseases have dropped. Hans Rösling, Ola Rösling and Anna Rosling Rönnlund make a similar point in their eminently readable and highly recommended book *Factfulness*. The vast majority of the world's population now live, not in low-income countries, but in middle-income countries. Sixty percent of girls finish high school. The population living in abject poverty has halved within the last two to three decades. Average life expectancy around the world is now 70 years. Eighty percent of the world's children have been vaccinated against one or more diseases, implying that 80 percent of the world's children have access to some type of healthcare. Yet, the majority of the world, including educated citizens, remain unaware of the progress we have made. In *Enlightenment Now*, Pinker writes that pessimism is "equated with moral seriousness. Journalists believe that by accentuating the negative they are discharging their duty as watchdogs, muckrakers, whistle-blowers, and afflicters of the comfortable. And intellectuals know they can attain instant gravitas by pointing to an unsolved problem and theorizing that it is a symptom of a sick society."

This makes us receptive to doom-and-gloom messages and so, when Covid-19 hit, it was not surprising that the collective hysteria soon took hold via a process of priming to expect the worst. In New Zealand, for instance, the Prime Minister, Jacinda Ardern, set the tone by calling upon the "team of 5 million" to "unite against Covid-19" and to always "be kind". Giant signs saying the latter appeared all over the place. Ardern also claimed that while New Zealand did adopt very stringent measures, this was essential, and by going "hard and early", we would be much better placed to tackle the problem. It soon became clear that we did not really go hard and early. New Zealand's restrictions were imposed after the "inflection point" of Covid-19 transmissions; that is, the restrictions were imposed when the growth rate of cases (number of cases in any given day divided by the number of cases in the previous day) had started to decline. This was true of many, if not most, other countries, where the lockdowns were brought in after the country had already crossed the inflection point. Later we would also find that while lockdowns imposed prior to this inflection point, when the growth rate of cases is rising, do make a difference in at least flattening the curve, restrictions imposed after the inflection point have no effect.[9]

* * *

All around the world, offices have a coffee corner. They work on an honor system. You can help yourself to a cup of coffee but in return you are expected to leave some money in the box. Not surprisingly, some people leave money; others do not. If you want more people to leave money, then you can resort to a simple trick. Put a pair of eyes on top of the donation box. Or even better, add a message underneath the pair of eyes: Put 50 cents in the box; we are watching you. No one is really watching. It is just a pair of eyes drawn on a piece of paper, but more people will put money in with the watching eyes.

I did not make up the watching eyes idea. Moe Fathi, Melissa Bateson and Daniel Nettle of the University of Newcastle in the UK did. They were also interested in designing a choice mechanism for charitable contributions. Participants in their study are confronted with a charity jar that is either filled with loose change (mostly small coins, 10p, 20p, and so on) or with large change (£1 and £2 coins). Except, in some cases these jars are placed under a poster which has nothing to do with the study in question. The poster contains a message forbidding people from eating or drinking in the laboratory, and at the top of the poster is a large pair of watching eyes.

What happens is striking. When the jar is filled with loose change, the median contribution is 20p. When that same jar filled with loose change is placed directly underneath the poster with a pair of watching eyes, the median contribution increases more than threefold to 73p. When the jar is filled with large coins, the median contribution is zero and 23 percent of contributions are large. Placing that same jar under the pair of watching eyes increases the median contribution to 50p and large contributions almost double to 43 percent.[10]

However, priming can, at times, be seriously detrimental. Priming can lead to unwanted peer effects and social pressure, leading to conformist behavior. One of the most well-known examples of the desire for such conformity in groups comes from the experiments carried out by Solomon Asch. Asch carried out his work in the 1950s as the world was trying to recover from the horrors of World War II. Asch was interested in exploring how so many ordinary Germans willingly conformed to Nazi propaganda. Asch asked participants to take a "vision test". Participants are shown two cards. The card on the left has the reference line and the card on the right has three comparison lines. Figure 2.3 shows the relevant information. The job of the participant is to identify which of the three comparison lines is of the same length as the reference line. It is clear or should be clear to everyone with reasonable vision that the reference line on the left-hand card is the same length as line C on the right-hand card. In reality, all but one of the participants in any group were research confederates of the experimenter. The participants – the real one and the confederates – were all seated in a classroom, and each in turn was asked which line on the right-hand card was longer than, shorter than or of equal length to the reference line on the left-hand card. The confederates had been instructed to provide incorrect answers.

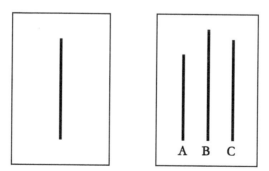

Figure 2.3   The three lines from Asch (1956) study of conformity

So, in one treatment, all the confederates would say that the reference line is the same length as line A on the right-hand card. While a number of the real participants answered correctly, a high proportion (32 percent) conformed to the majority view of the others, even when this view was evidently erroneous, in which the majority said that two lines were of the same length even though they differed by several inches.[11]

The problems do not end there. It is certainly a problem that a substantial number of people agree with an assessment that is clearly incorrect. But a great deal of evidence suggests that you actually do not need one participant and multiple confederates. When one participant is willing to ignore his or her own estimate and go with the group, successive participants are also willing to do so, primarily because there are so many people on one side and so few on the other. Once they have taken that position, people are often convinced of the correctness of that position. They are locked in and no longer willing to change their minds or scrutinize how they came to hold that position. This is because changing our minds makes us look like flip-floppers and it can be psychologically painful. Minds can be changed, but once set, this is no longer easy and we need to marshal substantial evidence before success can be achieved.

I should note that this phenomenon of conformism is quite different from what is often termed "the wisdom of crowds". James Surowiecki, formerly of the *New York Times*, has an excellent book of the same name. There are different ways to explain this. I will refer to what happens in the National Geographic's *Brain Games* episode hosted by Jason Silva.[12] A giant glass bowl is filled with gumballs. Silva invites a large number of people to guess how many gumballs the bowl contains. The answers differ massively ranging from tens to thousands. Then Silva asks a teenager armed with a calculator for his answer. He does some quick calculations and comes up with an answer that is very close to the actual number of gumballs. What is his secret? It turns out that he simply took all the answers and averaged them to come up with an answer that was nearly correct.

Why can we not take conventional wisdom at face value? What is the difference between Asch's study and the wisdom of crowds? The difference is that in the latter, in guessing the number of gumballs, each respondent is using his or her independent estimate. It turns out that given a large number of people, even if each individual is off by a lot, as long as they are erring both on the higher side as well as the lower side, averaging their answers will get you close to the correct answer. This principle can be used in a variety of settings and has even been used in solving crimes. Ask a large number of people to name a list of suspects and then pick the one or ones who appear in multiple lists. However, this is not true for Asch's or other similar studies of conformism. In these studies, the estimates of subsequent respondents are not independent. After one or more initial respondents have chosen to ignore their private estimates (or "private signals", to use a bit of jargon), this becomes a moral dilemma for the subsequent respondents. I can see that the reference line seems the same length as line C, but so many others seem convinced that line A is the correct answer. How could so many people ahead of me be so wrong? Should I then go with my private signal (which says that the correct answer is line C) or should I go with this public signal suggesting that line A is the correct answer? Do I dare to stand on my own or just go with the flow? Economists term this an "information cascade", where we start ignoring our independent estimate (signal) and rely on a public signal. We go to restaurants (watch movies/read books/vote/invest in shares) that everyone says are great, even though we are personally not as convinced. We think that our inability to find them great is a deficiency in ourselves. How could so many people be wrong? Unlike the gumball experiment, in the latter, these decisions are no longer independent; instead, they are correlated. Each person makes decisions that are no longer based on his or her own independent guess, but on what the majority (or those who came before) think.

* * *

Globally, the gloomy messages and the accompanying worries implied that not a lot of people were inclined to invest a lot of time and effort into thinking critically about the exact nature of the Covid-19 pandemic and the extent of the threat that it posed. In New Zealand, Ardern's choices set the tone for the policy debate that followed, or actually did not follow as, from this point on, asking questions about the government's policy became tantamount to heresy. If you did so, you were no longer welcome in the team of 5 million. Journalists were taken to task if they asked "tough" questions of the Director General of Health, Dr Ashley Bloomfield, who was in charge of overseeing New Zealand's efforts against Covid-19.[13] In one memorable stretch, the government refused to allow members of Parliament to ask questions of the Director General, even though as a public servant, this is part of his job description; to respond to questions from Parliament.[14] This is similar to the Attorney General or another government official refusing to attend a Congressional hearing. It also needs to be noted that subsequently in New Zealand and most other countries around the world, people questioning the sagacity of lockdowns were *personae non grata*. Yet, in Sweden, the exact opposite was true. Those who were calling for lockdowns were looked down upon.

Policy makers were trying to convince people that there were win–win options; that we could combat Covid-19 without making sacrifices elsewhere. The attitude was, deal with Covid-19 now and worry about the economic and social damage later. This was not a realistic option as it would be difficult to undo the economic damage that was being inflicted. Taking New Zealand as an example, government debt is forecast to peak at over NZ$200 billion by 2023, from around NZ$57 billion pre-Covid-19. That is NZ$143 billion of additional borrowing. This will become a significant burden for today's younger workers, who will also be the most adversely affected by the economic fallout of Covid-19. The IMF prediction is that New Zealand's per capita GDP in 2025 will be lower than that in 2019.

In September 2020, New Zealand's Finance Minister gave an interview to the *Financial Times*, where he claimed that the best economic response was a strong health response.[15] It was not clear how he knew this, given that no cost–benefit analysis had been carried out. Indeed, the only cost–benefit analysis carried out by the New Zealand Productivity Commission suggested that the cost of extending the country's April lockdown by an additional five days than previously proposed outweighed the benefits by more than 90 to 1.[16] Similar results were reported from the UK.[17] Evidently, neither the epidemiologists nor the policy makers had a firm grasp on the concept of opportunity cost. I was happy to accept the point that a strong health response was indeed the right approach but, as I wrote at the time, all I wanted was for the Minister to show some evidence to back this up.[18] Very few of these analyses have been undertaken, and the findings of those that have are the opposite of what the Minister claimed. The costs of lockdowns outweigh the benefits. This is true of all countries where similar cost–benefit analyses have been carried out. The problem is that these analyses were few and far between.

* * *

FRAMING THE MESSAGE

I noted previously that it makes a huge difference when someone says 1 in 153 will die as opposed to saying 152 out of 153 will live. It seems surprising, but the way information is presented to us can make dramatic differences. Saying 3 in 100 people will die sounds dramatically different from saying that 97 out of 100 will live.

Take a look at Figure 2.4, which shows the rates of deceased organ donations (post-mortem donations of organs such as heart, lungs, kidneys or liver) across different European countries. This is taken from work by Alberto Abadie and Sebastien Gay of Harvard. I have taken data from their paper and recreated this chart. It is clear that the rates are quite different across countries. These countries share a swath of cultural and economic norms. But even if you look at countries located literally next door to each other, such as the Netherlands and Belgium, you will see big differences. Belgium is doing better than the Netherlands and has access to many more organ donors.

As you look at Figure 2.4, your system 1 has already started formulating arguments and creating a narrative as to what could cause these differences. You may be tempted to frame these differences in relation to these countries' culture, history and demographics. However, it turns out that there is a very simple reason why these differences came about. Believe it or not, these differences are caused by a single question on driver license forms. Some countries in the world ask applicants: "Would you like to be an organ donor? If so, check the box below." Other countries state: "We will assume that, in the event of your death, you will be willing to donate your organs. If you are not willing to do so, then check the box below."

The first option is referred to as "opt-in"; that the driver has actively chosen to be an organ donor. The second option is known as "opt-out"; here, everyone is presumed to be an organ donor unless he or she explicitly chooses not to be. The countries that implement the opt-out option are referred to as countries with "presumed consent",

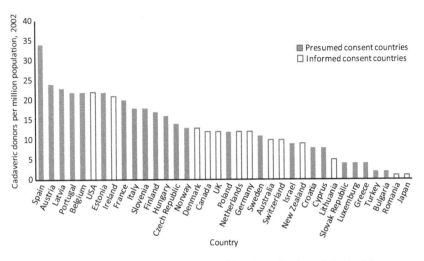

Source: Figure recreated by author on the basis of data from Abadie and Gay (2006).

Figure 2.4   Differences in deceased organ donations across 36 Western countries

that is, we assume that you have given consent to donating your organs unless you specifically tell us otherwise. On the other hand, the countries that rely on the opt-in option are "informed consent" countries; the assumption being that you have not consented to donating your organs unless you explicitly indicate this on your driver license.

It may be surprising but, in the opt-in case, people do not check the box, and therefore do not become organ donors. In the opt-out case, people also do not check the box, and therefore become organ donors by default. Now go back and look at Figure 2.4 again. Guess what is common to all the countries that have higher rates of organ donation? They all provide the opt-out option: Check the box if you do not want to donate your organs. The countries that do not do so well on the organ donation scale are those that provide the opt-in option: do you wish to donate? All of this over a simple decision (or the lack of a decision) to check a box. Behavioral scientists often refer to this as changing the default option.

Let us look at another example that is more immediately relevant to Covid-19. In one of their studies, Daniel Kahneman and Amos Tversky asked participants to express their preference between two treatments, A and B, which will affect 600 people. Half of the participants get one message while the other half get a different message. Half of the participants get the following "positively framed" information, which is put in terms of lives saved:

> Treatment A is predicted to save 200 lives.
> With Treatment B, there is a 1/3 chance of saving everyone but there is 2/3 chance of saving no one.

The other half of the participants see the information below, which is more "negatively framed" in relation to lives lost:

> Treatment A is predicted to result in 400 deaths.
> With Treatment B, there is a 1/3 chance that no one would die but there is 2/3 chance that everyone will die.

A large majority of respondents chose Treatment A when the message was framed positively in terms of lives saved, while a majority chose Treatment B when the message had a negative framing in terms of lives lost. This is surprising, since the informational content of the two messages is identical. Given that there are supposed to be 600 people, if Treatment A saves 200 lives, then it leads to the loss of 400 lives. If Treatment B has a 1/3 chance of saving everyone, then under Treatment B, there is a 2/3 chance that everyone will die. Simply presenting this information in the form of lives saved versus lives lost makes a huge difference. The policy implications of this are massive because this is not a mistake committed by uninformed lay people. It happens to experts, professionals and policy makers. Simply changing the default may result in differences as to which life-saving drugs we fund and which we do not.

This, in turn, implied that when the news media put the number of deaths from Covid-19 front and center of their messaging, we took those messages at face value. We were deathly scared by the fact that 7 out of 1000 people had died but ignored the fact that 993 of those same 1000 recovered. Neither did media outlets provide any comparable numbers for deaths caused by other diseases. No one asked: "Okay so, I realize that X number of people died from Covid-19 this week. How many died from other causes?" In 2018, more than 650 000 people in the US died from heart disease. In the same year, nearly 600 000 died from cancer and around 167 000 from accidents and unintentional injuries. More than 150 000 died from chronic lower respiratory diseases; 85 000 died from diabetes, 51 000 from kidney diseases and 48 000 from suicides.[19] By November 2020, 240 000 people had died from Covid-19 in the US. However, while the newspapers highlighted the number of people who died from Covid-19, they did not mention the numbers dying from these other diseases, to provide context. It is highly likely that the deaths owing to respiratory illnesses will be dramatically lower in 2020 compared with earlier years. This is because those who would have died from respiratory illnesses will have succumbed to Covid-19, which implies that what Covid-19 resulted in was displaced mortality but not necessarily additional (or excess) mortality. In order to figure this out, we had to consistently take a step back, engage our system 2, and try to evaluate the information we were receiving in the proper context. However, in times of stress and cognitive load, this is not easy, especially if everyone around us is convinced that we are in the grip of a mortal pandemic that threatens our very existence.

ANCHORING, AVAILABILITY AND COVID-19

The third prong of the availability heuristic is the idea of anchoring. In life we often do not evaluate events or outcomes *de novo*, but instead start from a reference point, which is usually some sort of status quo. This typically leads to anchoring effects. Some examples will make this easier to understand. Researchers and lecturers around the world carry out the following exercise with a group of people, usually their students. The students are asked to pick small identical slips of paper from a box. They are told that the slips of paper are numbered from 1 to 100, except in reality, there are only two numbers possible: 10 and 65. So half of the students get a slip of paper with "10" on it, while the other half gets a slip with "65". Then they are asked to answer the following question: "How many countries are there in the continent of Africa?" The correct answer is 54. On average, members of the group who picked "10" always chose a lower number than those who picked "65". It is a trivial thing that has no connection with the Africa question but the act of picking a smaller number establishes a lower anchor (reference point) for one group, while the act of picking a larger number establishes a higher anchor for the other group.

This matters in different ways and, as always, does not just apply to regular people. Professionals fall prey to this as much as the rest of us. In a study by Gregory Northcraft and Margaret Neale, a collection of seasoned real estate professionals were divided into two groups and shown a house and an asking price. One group saw a high asking price while the second group saw a low asking price. Then, the two groups were asked for their best guess. Not surprisingly, the guesses were far apart. For example, if the high anchor is $100 000 more than the low anchor, so that one group is shown a price of $500 000 and another group is shown a price of $400 000, then the average guess of the $500 000 (high-anchor) group was approximately $41 000 more than that of the $400 000 (low-anchor) group. Furthermore, the real estate agents were absolutely confident in their ability to come up with a reasonably accurate price for the house and were certain that the asking price shown to them at the beginning of the exercise had no influence in their price predictions.

Asking someone to guess the price of a house is different from asking whether this price is more than or less than $400 000. No matter how much we deny it, the availability of the additional information influences subsequent decision making. When asked, a majority of people around the world will say that in any given year, more lives are lost owing to war and/or terrorism than to respiratory diseases. The reality is the exact opposite. Many more people die of respiratory diseases than die from violence. However, the ubiquitous news coverage of violence makes us much more prone to focus on this and ignore the many more deaths caused by illnesses that do not make the headlines. Similarly, someone who is told that 1 out of every 153 people who contract Covid-19 will die, will have a very different reaction and perspective on the disease than another person who is told that 152 out of 153 people who get Covid-19 will live. These two people will differ radically in their policy response to the disease.

Just to be clear and to reiterate an earlier point, there are similarities between the three concepts of priming, framing and anchoring that I have collectively referred to as an availability heuristic. Framing (or changing the default) refers to the fact that different ways of presenting the same information can often lead to dramatically different responses. Priming consists of a large set of subtle or not so subtle nudges influencing people to act in particular ways. Anchoring can also be thought of as priming. An anchor (a piece of information), even if completely superfluous, is also a nudge in a particular direction, except anchoring involves the establishment of a well-defined reference point, which in turn influences subsequent judgment. So one way to think of anchoring is that it is priming plus a well-established, albeit arbitrary, reference point.[20]

An additional difficulty is that once people have arrived at a conclusion, they become invested in it. This is referred to as a "confirmation bias". So, even if I, a real estate agent, stated a higher price because I was prompted by a higher asking price, even though I may deny it, once I have arrived at this price, I am loath to change my mind. Once I have decided, I try to find all sorts of *post facto* reasons in support by looking at evidence that bolsters my position, while ignoring evidence that refutes it.

Charles Lord, Lee Ross and Mark Lepper of Stanford had 48 undergraduates, who either supported or opposed capital punishment, look at two purported studies, one seemingly confirming and one seemingly disconfirming their existing beliefs about the deterrent effects of the death penalty. As the authors conjectured, both proponents and opponents of capital punishment rated the study results that confirmed their own beliefs to be the more convincing, leading to corresponding shifts in their beliefs. The net effect was an increase in attitude polarization. Lord and his colleagues comment:

> People who hold strong opinions on complex social issues are likely to examine relevant empirical evidence in a biased manner. They are apt to accept "confirming" evidence at face value while subjecting "disconfirming" evidence to critical evaluation, and, as a result, draw undue support for their initial positions from mixed or random empirical findings. Thus, the result of exposing contending factions in a social dispute to an identical body of relevant empirical evidence may be not a narrowing of disagreement but rather an increase in polarization.

FROM "FLATTENING THE CURVE" TO "ELIMINATION"

Following a lockdown of five weeks in April, New Zealand had a period of 128 days of no community transmission. This allowed the government to claim that we had eliminated the virus. It was also played up in the news and all over social media, both in New Zealand

and overseas. All of a sudden, we were the team of 5 million that had shown up the rest of the world. Then something strange happened. All this time, the mantra had been "flatten the curve" to relieve pressure on public health systems, but now "flatten the curve" quickly morphed into "eliminate Covid-19". It was once again left unexplained how you eliminate a disease in the absence of an effective vaccine. We were told that "elimination" is not the same as "eradication" since the latter does require a vaccine. Except, according to the WHO, "local elimination of a virus means interruption of transmission for at least 12 months, high quality surveillance, and supporting genotyping evidence".[21]

Not surprisingly, New Zealand could not eliminate the virus. Eventually, community transmission started again and, in August 2020, the Auckland region, which houses approximately one-third of the country's population and accounts for nearly 40 percent of the country's GDP, was placed under lockdown again, with a slightly less stringent lockdown for the rest of the country. It was not explained why, given New Zealand's low population density, it was necessary to lock down the South Island, which is an entirely different island from the North Island, where Auckland is located. (Auckland, the commercial capital, and Wellington, the national capital, are located in the North Island. Two other big cities, Christchurch and Dunedin, are located in the South Island.)

In the meantime, for reasons I explain later, the team of 5 million had started to develop cracks. New Zealand's GDP in the second quarter of 2020 had dropped 12 percent, the largest drop in recorded history. The economy was officially in recession and governments around the world and in New Zealand were beginning to wake up to the collateral damage being caused by the single-minded focus on Covid-19. However, course correction was still not easy, as now what is known as "the sunk cost fallacy" kicked in. The thinking was: we have worked so hard and made so many sacrifices; we need to stay the course; we cannot give up now. This is the wrong way of thinking about the situation. The sunk cost is sunk and not recoverable. The reasonable basis for policy making needed to be: what is the additional cost of pursuing this goal and what is the benefit? Pursue the policy only if the benefit exceeds the cost. However, as before, no attempts were made to weigh the costs and benefits, and we continued down the lockdown path just because we had come so far and sacrificed so much. Put this down to ego, hubris or the psychological pain of admitting mistakes, support for lockdowns remained unwavering.

In late 2020, parts of Europe, including the UK, were also placed under a four-week lockdown again.[22] On 16 March 2020 Neil Ferguson and his collaborators at Imperial College London predicted that, in the absence of stringent interventions, Great Britain would experience more than 500 000 deaths.[23] Using the same Imperial College model of Ferguson and colleagues, it was predicted that in Sweden, "at least 96,000 deaths would occur by 1 July (of 2020) without mitigation".[24] The real figure for Sweden by that date was around 6000. Based on these differential estimates, Rickard Nyman and Paul Ormerod of University College London suggest that earlier lockdowns in Britain saved at most 20 000 lives and possibly fewer.[25]

David Miles is a Professor of Economics at Imperial College Business School and a former member of the Bank of England's monetary policy committee. In July 2020, Miles wrote:

> What is the lowest plausible estimate of the cost of the lockdown? Suppose we only count lost GDP. The Office for Budget Responsibility and the Bank of England put this at 13–14% of GDP if restrictions are eased now and the economy bounces back. If we ascribe only two thirds of this lost GDP to the lockdown (since behaviour would clearly have changed with no government restrictions), this generates a cost of around £200 billion. This cost ignores all future lost GDP beyond 2020, it excludes all medical side effects (not treating cancer patients, stopping screening for serious conditions, etc.), and it ignores the future damage of huge disruption to education.

Miles then goes on to provide a breakdown of prospective costs and benefits. In Table 2.2, I present part of his results. Instead of showing the projected costs and benefits, for the ease of exposition, I present only the numbers for net benefits (numbers that have positive signs in front of them) or for net losses (numbers that have negative signs in front of them). It may or may not come as a big surprise to you at this time that there are no numbers with positive signs in front of them. All of the numbers come with negative signs, implying that the projected costs always outweigh any projected benefits.[26]

The numbers in Table 2.2 speak for themselves. There are no situations where the benefits outweigh the costs. If the UK experienced a

Table 2.2   Net benefits (+) or net losses (−) of a March to June lockdown in the UK (£ billions)

Lives not lost (i.e., lives saved)	Loss in GDP			
	9%	15%	20%	25%
440 000	−68	−198	−308	−418
250 000	−140	−270	−380	−490
100 000	−170	−300	−410	−520
50 000	−185	−315	−425	−535
20 000	−194	−324	−435	−544

Source: Reproduced from Miles (2020).

9 percent drop in GDP and managed to save 440 000 lives, the total loss would have been £68 billion (in italic). If Nyman and Ormerod are correct, and the lockdowns saved only 20 000 lives and led to a 9 percent drop in GDP, then this came at the cost of £194 billion to the economy. However, if the lockdowns saved 20 000 lives but led to a loss of 15 percent or 20 percent of GDP, then the cost to the economy is either £324 billion or £435 billion respectively. This is a lot of lives and livelihoods. I cannot help but paraphrase Churchill. Never have so many been asked to sacrifice so much for the so few.

* * *

In this chapter, I have shown how excessive reliance on gut feelings can introduce systematic biases in our decision making, including priming, framing, anchoring, confirmation bias, and ignorance of trade-offs and opportunity costs. I have also shown how these biases impacted the global response to Covid-19 and how the sunk cost fallacy prevents a course correction even when it starts to become obvious that the costs outweigh the benefits. In *A Theory of Justice*, John Rawls notes that we are often forced to choose between utilitarianism (the principle of the greatest good for the greatest number) and intuitionism. Rawls adds: "Most likely we finally settle upon a variant of the utility principle circumscribed and restricted in certain ad hoc ways by intuitionist constraints. Such a view is not irrational; and there is no assurance that we can do better. But this is no reason not to try."

In the next chapter, I turn to two other crucial pieces of the puzzle; first, a general lack of ability to understand probabilities, particularly small probabilities, and, second, our risk perceptions, before discussing how these applied to thinking about Covid-19.

NOTES

1. For instance, on 29 August 2004, *NBC News* reported that the "43rd president is 'gut player' who eschews personal change". Associated Press. (2004). 43rd president is "gut player" who eschews personal change. *NBC News*, 29 August. https://www.nbcnews.com/id/wbna5762240.

2. For those who do not know, this is an annual event organized by the journalists who cover the White House. It brings together the movers and shakers of Washington, DC: politicians, including the President of the United States, journalists and a liberal sprinkling of Hollywood glitterati. The main event features a roast of the assembled dignitaries (including the President of the United States) by a comedian, with the President getting his (and there is no point in saying "his or her" for obvious reasons, though hopefully this will change soon) turn to retaliate afterward. This was the convention until, in 2017, Donald Trump decided to skip the event, which featured Hasan Minhaj. Minhaj did his best, but without the President, the butt of his jokes, it was not the same. Trump never attended this event (and sometimes asked other members of the administration to stay away too), thereby considerably diminishing the event's luster. Some have blamed Seth Myers for Donald Trump's decision to run for President. At the 2011 dinner, Myers said of Trump, who was one of the attendees, and I am paraphrasing: "I (meaning Myers) hear that Donald Trump is thinking of running for President as a Republican. I am surprised since I thought he was running as a joke." As the camera zoomed in on Trump, it was clear that he was not laughing. It is arguable that matters were not helped when Barack Obama, who followed Myers, also ripped into Trump. After making fun of the whole "birther" controversy regarding whether Obama was born in the US or not, Obama pointed out that the controversy had been settled with the release of Obama's long-form birth certificate by the state of Hawaii. Obama went on to quip that now that this was settled, Trump could go back to devoting his attention to other weighty topics such as whether the moon landing was faked, what happened at Roswell, and where Biggie and Tupac are.

3. A kouros (plural kouroi) is a free-standing Greek sculpture of nude male youths. It is believed that these sculptures date from the archaic period, approximately eighth century BCE until fifth century BCE.

4. Sullenberger was the last to leave the plane after making sure that everyone else was safely out. Among other accolades, the newly elected President, Barack Obama, invited Sullenberger and his crew to join the Presidential Inauguration

ceremony on 20 January. In 2016, Clint Eastwood directed the movie *Sully*, with Tom Hanks playing the role of Chesley Sullenberger.

5. The cognoscenti among you may be aware that the Economics Nobel Prize was not part of the original set of prizes endowed by the funds left by Alfred Nobel. The Economics Nobel Prize was started in 1969 and is actually named the Sveriges Riksbank Prize in Economic Sciences in Memory of Alfred Nobel. "Real" scientists like the ones who win the prize for physics, chemistry or medicine often do not consider the Economics Nobel Prize as a "real" Nobel Prize. As far as I know though, they all come with the same prize money; so I guess the economists are not too bothered. The 2002 Nobel Prize was awarded to Daniel Kahneman together with Vernon Smith. The latter is a pioneer in using decision-making experiments to understand behavior in economic transactions. Much of Kahneman's work is co-authored with Amos Tversky of Stanford and it is likely that Tversky would have shared the Nobel Prize too, but unfortunately Tversky passed away in 1996 and the Nobel Prize is not given posthumously.

6. I believe I may have taken this elephant analogy from Jon Haidt's book, *The Righteous Mind*.

7. The average age of those who died with Covid-19. Report by the BBC, 6 October 2020. https://www.bbc.com/news/uk-scotland-54433305.

8. At the time, the New Zealand dollar was worth around 60 US cents.

9. Gibson, J. (2020b). Hard, not early: Putting the New Zealand Covid-19 response in context. *New Zealand Economic Papers*. doi:10.1080/00779954. 2020.1842796.

10. In the interests of full disclosure, I should note that this type of priming research has come under scrutiny in recent times, for its failure to replicate. A good article to read on this topic is Shimmack, U., Heene, M., and Kesavan, K. (2017). Reconstruction of a train wreck: How priming research went off the rails. 2 February. https://replicationindex.com/2017/02/02/reconstruction-of-a-train-wreck-how-priming-research-went-of-the-rails/. However, while individual studies may have faced questions, I believe the broader point that priming does make a difference in many circumstances still stands. In any event, both organizational and state actors still rely on priming techniques extensively.

11. The National Geographic Channel has an excellent show *Brain Games* hosted by Jason Silva. The show has an episode on the Asch study using real participants. I highly recommend the show. If you watch this episode, you will see how many people are willing to ignore their own assessments and go with the judgments of others. You can see this particular episode at: https://www.youtube.com/watch?v=BOBhKR4MK3w.

12. For those interested in this episode, here is the link to a YouTube clip: https://www.youtube.com/watch?v=Qfh-k9P8ZPI. Or simply, open your browser, type in "Brain Games Wisdom of the Crowd" and enjoy.

13. Donnell, H. (2020). A backlash over tough questions for Dr Ashley Bloomfield. *Radio New Zealand*, 23 August. https://www.rnz.co.nz/national/programmes/mediawatch/audio/2018760556/a-backlash-over-tough-questions-for-dr-ashley-bloomfield.

14. Coughlan, T. (2020). Coalition MPs say no to grilling Bloomfield over outbreak. *Stuff*, 20 August. https://www.stuff.co.nz/national/politics/300087522/coronavi rus-coalition-mps-say-no-to-grilling-bloomfield-over-outbreak. Stuff.co.nz is an umbrella website owned by its parent company Nine Entertainment. It publishes news content on its own website and provides content to newspapers that it owns, such as the *Wellington Dominion Post* in the capital city of Wellington.

15. Smyth, J. (2020). New Zealand backs lockdown despite record contraction. *Financial Times*, 17 September.

16. Heatley, D. (2020). *A Cost Benefit Analysis of 5 Extra Days at COVID-19 Alert Level 4* (Research Note 2020/02). New Zealand Productivity Commission. https://www.productivity.govt.nz/research/cost-benefit-analysis-covid-alert-4/.

17. Miles, D., Stedman, M., and Heald, A. (2020). Living with Covid-19: Balancing costs against benefits in the face of the virus. *National Institute Economic Review*, 253, R60–R76. Published online by Cambridge University Press, 28 July.

18. Chaudhuri, A. (2020c). Time to walk the talk, Minister. *New Zealand Herald*, 22 September.

19. Meszaros, L. (2020). Top 10 causes of death in the US in 2020. *MDLinx*. 28 February. https://www.mdlinx.com/article/top-10-causes-of-death-in-the-us-in-2020/MNpEowpA8DXKBUNcbmkpY. This is an internet-based service for physicians and healthcare professionals provided by M3 USA Corporation. It offers physicians and other healthcare professionals a means of staying current with academic literature.

20. Here are two examples. The speed limit on roads within Auckland City is 50 kilometers per hour. Priming can take the form of billboards with eyes saying: "Drive to the speed limit; we are watching you!" This does not specify how careful you should be. Police will typically leave you alone driving at a higher speed, as long as this is not more than 10 kilometers per hour over the speed limit. So, even if you are driving carefully at 55 kilometers per hour, it might be okay. However, we could be more specific and include a specific anchor. Something along the lines of: "Drive to the speed limit; we are watching you! Are you below 50 km/hour?" It is most likely that average speeds will be lower with the second message than with the first message.

21. World Health Organization. (2013). Framework for verifying elimination of measles and rubella. *Weekly Epidemiological Record*, 88(9), 89. https://www.who.int/wer/2013/wer8809.pdf.

22. BBC. (2020). Covid-19: PM announces four-week England lockdown. *BBC News*, 31 October. https://www.bbc.com/news/uk-54763956.

23. Ferguson, N., Laydon, D., Nedjati Gilani, G., Imai, N., Ainslie, K., Baguelin, M., et al. (2020). Report 9: Impact of non-pharmaceutical interventions (NPIs) to reduce COVID-19 mortality and healthcare demand. *Imperial College Covid-19 Response Team Research Report*. Imperial College, London.

24. Gardiner, J. M., Willem, L., Van Der Wijngaart, W., Kamerlin, S. C. L., Brusselaers, N., and Kasson, P. (2020). Intervention strategies against

COVID-19 and their estimated impact on Swedish healthcare capacity. *MedRxiv*, 15 April. https://doi.org/10.1101/2020.04.11.20062133.

25. Nyman, R., and Ormerod, P. (2020). How many lives has lockdown saved in the UK? *MedRxiv*, 21 August. https://doi.org/10.1101/2020.06.24.20139196.

26. Miles, D. (2020). The UK lockdown: Balancing costs against benefits. *VoxEU*, 13 July. This is an extended version of an article that was published in *The Times* of London on 25 June 2020.

3. Pathogens and probabilities

In this chapter, I explore the role of probabilities in understanding pandemic responses. I write about:

- the concept of risk aversion;
- the overweighting of small probabilities and underweighting of large ones;
- prospect theory, loss aversion and their implication for Covid-19 risk perceptions.

* * *

Pandemics, or any crisis for that matter, create an acute sense of uncertainty. We worry about ourselves, our families and our friends. We worry about our jobs and finances. The uncertainty imbues us with a sense of losing control, that we are no longer in charge of our destinies. We feel stressed and anxious. In the previous chapter, I discussed how gut feelings and cognitive biases make us prone to errors of judgment; how we often tend to ignore trade-offs between statistical lives and identified lives. These problems are especially exacerbated in times of crisis, owing to the uncertainty. Crises require us to think about probabilities and risks, but this is exactly where cognitive biases can lead us even further astray as we are not intuitive statisticians. Often, we seriously overestimate small probabilities while underestimating large ones. In times of stress, risks that are relatively minor, and often comparable to other risks we routinely accept in our day-to-day lives, loom large in the individual and collective psyche.

In a previous chapter, I mentioned this cognitive dissonance on the part of a colleague who is extremely afraid of Covid-19, yet goes rock climbing. A healthy young adult is more likely at greater danger of death or significant injury from rock climbing than from Covid-19. In New Zealand, with its strong adventurist and do-it-yourself culture, most healthy adults are at far greater risk of injury from many of these

54

activities than from Covid-19. Yet collective group-think and hysteria makes us far more fearful of Covid-19 than bungee jumping, rock climbing, hang-gliding, para-sailing, playing rugby, cleaning gutters or undertaking extensive home renovations on our own.[1] In this chapter, I first introduce a few concepts in order to illustrate some simple fallacies that often plague our decision making. I then address how our Covid-19 decision making was plagued by many of the same fallacies.

BASE RATES AND DIAGNOSTIC TESTS

I love the movie *12 Angry Men*.[2] I have watched it many times and often use one of my early lectures in decision-making courses to show it to my students, because invariably, very few of them have seen it. I show the 1957 black and white version starring Henry Fonda, Martin Balsam, George C. Scott and Ed Begley Sr, not the later remake with Jack Lemmon, James Gandolfini and Tony Danza. The movie provides a succinct distillation of the tussle between system-1 and system-2 thinking; between automatic and deliberative decision making; between relying on our gut and taking a careful evidence-based view of the world.

A juvenile boy stands accused of killing his father. The movie starts with the judge handing the case over to the jury. The jury members then proceed to the jury room to deliberate. After some preliminary chit-chat, the jury decides that it would be a good idea to take a vote at the very beginning to figure out who stands where. At the first vote, 11 out of 12 jurors are convinced that the boy is guilty; the sole person holding out is Henry Fonda, Juror No. 8. He does not say that he is certain the boy is not guilty; he just wants to talk a little about the evidence, while the others try to convince him of the boy's guilt. Most of the jurors just know in their guts that the boy is guilty and find it astounding that Juror No. 8 feels otherwise. At the beginning at least, Juror No. 8 is the only person who seems willing to be the rider rather than the elephant; to take a step back and ask questions about what the evidence really shows rather than relying on his gut feelings about what is right.

The other aspect of the movie that stands out is the role of probabilities and how the jurors perceive them. Many of the jurors are not willing to invest the time and/or energy to ask if something is, on balance, likely or unlikely. If likely, how likely is it? Over and over again, when a juror claims that he is certain something did or did not happen, Juror No. 8 asks whether something is possible or how likely a particular event is.

At one point in the movie, Henry Fonda (Juror No. 8) says that he would like to find out "if an old man who drags one foot when he walks, 'cause he had a stroke last year, could get from his bedroom to his front door in 15 seconds". At this, Juror No. 3 comments: "You're talking about a matter of seconds! Nobody can be that accurate." Fonda responds: "I think testimony that could put a boy into the electric chair should be that accurate." Could the old man who limps badly get to the front door in time to see the boy running down the stairs and out of the building? Could he really hear the boy yell "I will kill you" when an L-train was roaring past his window? Could a woman, who was not wearing her glasses, clearly see the boy stab his father through the windows of that L-train even if the train was completely empty?

Most things in life come with an element of uncertainty. It turns out that we are not naturally good at thinking in terms of chances. When it comes to probabilities, our gut feelings often misguide us. To use Kahneman's WYSIATI (what you see is all there is) paradigm, when it comes to probabilities, the need to look carefully and dig deeper is all the more important because there is often much more to what you see.

* * *

In most developed countries, we are now marrying later in life and having children later in life. Looking at New Zealand, in 1961, the median age at first marriage was 25 for men and 22 for women. By 2016, the median age for men was 32 and for women 30, and this trend has remained steady since then. A similar pattern would be true for most other developed nations. Given that, even now, most people have children when married rather than out of wedlock, this has also come to imply that a lot of women are having children later in life.

One problem with having a first child later in life is that children born to older mothers are much more likely to have Down's Syndrome.[3] This does not mean that younger mothers cannot have babies with the syndrome; it simply means that as a woman gets older, her chances of having a baby with Down's Syndrome increases rapidly. For instance, the chances that a 25-year-old mother will have a baby with the syndrome is 1 in 1300. This probability increases to 1 in 1000 for a 30-year-old mother, 1 in 365 at 35, and 1 in 90 at 40. These are often referred to as *base rates* or *prior probabilities*. This does not mean that a 25-year-old mother can never have a baby with Down's Syndrome or that a 40-year-old mother certainly will. It means that, on average, the chances of a 25-year-old mother having a baby with Down's Syndrome is very small and nothing to be excessively worried about. For a 40-year-old mother, the probability is much higher; something that needs to be considered seriously, together with other medical factors.

Typically, the first step in screening for Down's Syndrome is to undertake a nuchal translucency. This is an ultrasound technique usually carried out at around ten weeks of pregnancy. It is designed to measure the thickness of fluid build-up at the back of the baby's neck. Higher than normal thickness can be an early indication of Down's Syndrome. A more reliable screening test is the maternal blood serum test, which can be carried out at around the same time (approximately 11–13 weeks into pregnancy). The mother can also undergo an amniocentesis, which can tell for certain whether chromosomal abnormalities are present or not. However, amniocentesis is an invasive procedure that requires inserting a needle into the uterus to pull out amniotic fluid for testing, and there is a small chance of miscarriage when undertaking an amniocentesis. Consequently, many mothers tend to stop after the maternal blood serum test. They look at what the probabilities are and then decide whether to continue with the pregnancy or to consider termination at that point.

Let us assume that you are in a situation where you have chosen to have a baby later in life. You are 35 and having a baby for the first time. You have just received a telephone call from your obstetrician telling you that you have tested positive on the maternal blood serum test. This means that your unborn child may have Down's Syndrome. Naturally, you will be worried at this point. You ask the doctor how accurate the test is, and the doctor tells you that the test is accurate 90 percent of the time. This means that if 100 mothers, whose baby has Down's Syndrome, took this test, then the test will correctly predict that the baby has Down's Syndrome in 90 cases (which is usually referred to as a *true positive*), and in the remaining ten cases, the test will fail to predict the existence of the disease (a *false negative*; the baby has the disease but the test fails to pick that up). This can be a problem too, but usually the probability of false negatives tends to be low. For those with a medical background, the terms used most frequently are the "sensitivity" (which is the true positive rate) and "specificity" (the true negative rate) of a particular test. These are different ways of arriving at the same thing: how accurate a particular test is.

If you are reasonably well informed, then you will know that these tests are not infallible. There is a chance of a false positive. This means that the test will say that the baby has Down's Syndrome even though the baby does not. Suppose you find that this particular test has a 5 percent chance of a false positive. This means that 5 out of every 100 mothers will be told that her baby has Down's Syndrome even though the baby does not. So, how worried should you be? Remember that, as with most things in life, there is seldom certainty about events; all we can rely on are probabilities. How high is the fatality ratio for a certain disease? Is it 3.4 percent or 0.65 percent? These numbers look small and the difference negligible, but they have radically different implications for formulating policy.

Let me put this information into a table in order to facilitate decision making. The real *base rate (prior probability)* that a 35-year-old mother will have a baby with Down's Syndrome is 1 in 365, or 0.00274, or about 0.3 percent. Since this is not an easy number to deal with, I am going to pretend that the prior probability is 1 in 100, or 0.01 (1 percent). This will make the calculation easier. By assuming a base rate of 1 in 100 rather than 1 in 365, I am estimating that the chance of Down's Syndrome is about three times higher than it actually is. This means that I will overestimate the correct probability by a factor of three. Therefore, any answer I come up with will need to be scaled down by one-third.

The maternal blood serum test is accurate in 90 percent of cases. This means that the test correctly predicts the existence of the disease in 90 out of 100 cases (true positive) but fails to indicate the existence of the disease in 10 out of 100 cases (false negative). The test also results in a false positive in 5 percent of cases. This means that out of 100 mothers who take the test, for 5 mothers, the test suggests the presence of Down Syndrome incorrectly (a false positive). This means that in 95 out of 100 cases, the test accurately predicts the absence of the disease when the baby does not have Down's Syndrome (true negative).

Now suppose we take a thousand 35-year-old mothers who take the maternal blood serum test. One percent (1 in 100) of them will have babies with Down's Syndrome. This amounts to 10 mothers out of 1000. This, in turn, also implies that 990 mothers will not have Down's Syndrome babies. Of the 10 mothers who have babies with Down's Syndrome, 9 will be identified correctly. There is one mother who will receive a false negative; she will receive a negative test even though her baby most likely has Down's Syndrome. This is a problem too. But, given a 5 percent false positive rate, out of the 990 mothers whose babies do not have Down's Syndrome, 5 percent of them, or approximately 50 (the actual number is 49.5), will receive a positive test result. The other 940 will receive a true negative. Table 3.1 illustrates this breakdown.

What we need is the probability that the baby has Down's Syndrome when the test turns out to be positive. Again, bear in mind that the test can be positive in two ways: (1) *correctly*, when the baby actually has Down's Syndrome and the test turns out to be positive, and (2) *incorrectly*, when the test turns out to be positive even when the baby does not have Down's Syndrome. The latter occurs since the test gets things wrong in 5 percent of cases where the test suggests that the baby has Down's Syndrome even though this is incorrect.

What can we conclude? We know that 59 mothers will receive positive tests. But out of them, only nine have babies with Down's Syndrome (true positive), while the remaining 50 are false positives. So, the chances that your baby has Down's Syndrome are 9/59 = 0.15, or about 15 percent. This is termed the "posterior probability". This rate is certainly much higher than the prior probability, which was

Table 3.1 Breakdown of maternal blood serum test results to check for Down's Syndrome

	Baby has Down's Syndrome	Baby does not have Down's Syndrome	Total
Positive test	9 *True positive*	50 *False positive*	59
Negative test	1 *False negative*	940 *True negative*	941
Total	10	990	1000

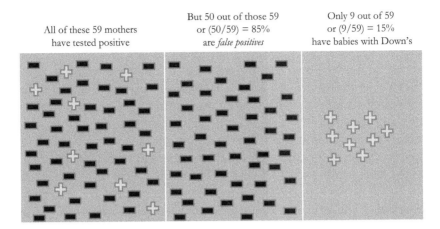

Figure 3.1   The chances of a mother having a baby with Down's Syndrome when she tests positive on the maternal blood serum test

1 in 100, or 1 percent. So, the chances of having a baby with Down's Syndrome has gone up dramatically by 15 times, but it is certainly not 90 percent. In Figure 3.1, I depict this outcome pictorially.

Remember, however, that I worked out this simple numerical example with a prior probability of 1 in 100, which is about three times the true prior probability of 1 in 365. This will make a big difference in the calculations. If we use the actual prior probability of 1 in 365, which is about one-third of our make-believe prior probability of 1 in 100, then we need to lower the posterior probability by about a third, or from 15 percent down to 5 percent (or 5 in 100).

If and when a mother receives the positive blood serum test, her actual probability of having a baby with Down's Syndrome has increased manifold from the base rate of 1 in 365 to 5 in 100, or from around 0.3 percent to around 5 percent, but the posterior probability is still nowhere near 90 percent. She still may need to make some decisions as to how to proceed but it is important to bear in mind that we are talking about an event that has a 5 in 100 chance of occurring, not 90 in 100. I am sure we would agree that whether in personal life or in the public arena this can and should make a huge difference.[4]

I realize that this above example may seem to be a needlessly complicated exercise, but there is method behind the apparent madness. It is not important if you did not follow all the steps, as long as you take away two key points. First, what seems obvious on the face of it may not be so. Even if you test positive for a syndrome, that does not automatically mean you have it; the base rate or the prior probability matters. Second, when it comes to diagnostic tests, both false positives and false negatives are a source of concern.

FALSE POSITIVES AND COVID-19

Previously, I explained why we need to worry about the infection fatality ratio (IFR), rather than the case fatality ratio (CFR). This is because looking at the latter and looking only at people who have been tested and, in turn, have tested positive for the disease, will probably give us an inflated estimate of the likelihood of death. However, an equivalent concern relates to the appropriate use of the CFR itself. Remember that the CFR is the number of people who have died divided by the number of people who have tested positive. In looking at those who have tested positive it is important to bear in mind that this can be either a true positive or a false positive. (This was especially true once the focus shifted from "deaths" to "cases".) This in turn means that if and when we read media reports on either death rates or number of cases, we need to approach this with a modicum of skepticism since it is not WYSIATI; there is more to the story than meets the eye.

As regards Covid-19, the primary concern was the dreaded false negative, wherein a test mistakenly deems an infected person to be virus free. This means that someone who has Covid-19 but receives a negative test result then goes about their life and ends up spreading the disease to unsuspecting others. However, false negatives are not the only concern regarding coronavirus diagnostics, especially given the stress and hysteria around the disease. False positives, where someone tests positive even in the absence of the disease, are a concern too.

As Katherine Wu noted in the *New York Times*,[5] while false positives may seem relatively harmless in comparison with their false-negative cousins, nevertheless, false positives also set off a cascading and often catastrophic chain of events. In places where the virus is relatively scarce, false positives may even outnumber true positives, eroding trust in tests and, under some circumstances, leading to unnecessary isolation of healthy people for as long as two weeks, which is time spent away from friends and family, and may even mean time away from home if, as in the case of New Zealand, people could not self-isolate but had to stay in a mandatory quarantine facility during that time. The time lost also meant missing school or work. This was particularly difficult for caregivers, as it could force them to separate from children, older family members or other vulnerable contacts. Also there is the undue stress caused.

EXPECTED VALUES

You have all seen the signs specifying penalties for littering along highways. Have you ever wondered why the fines are so large? For instance, one sign might say that the fine for littering is US$2000. Why is the fine for flicking a candy wrapper out of your car window so high? The answer is that, while the magnitude of the fine is very large, the *expected* fine is small. What is the expected fine? It is the magnitude of the fine multiplied by the probability of getting caught. You see, if everyone who littered got caught, then we could impose a $50 fine on everyone and this fine would likely be enough to deter litterbugs. But on a highway, what are the chances of actually getting caught? Is it 1 in 100? If so, then the expected fine for littering is $(1/100) \times \$2000 = \$20$. This is much smaller than $2000 but still a substantial amount. Given the low probability of getting caught, in order to deter littering, the amount of the fine needs to be large.

Suppose you are asked to place a bet that a random card drawn from a deck of 52 cards is an ace. If the card turns out to be an ace then you win $5; otherwise, you get nothing. What are the chances that a random card will turn out to be an ace? Four out of 52, or 1/13. So, there is only a 1 in 13 chance of you winning this bet. This means that if the winning prize is worth $5, then your expected winnings are $(1/13) \times \$5$, or just 38 cents; you should *expect* to win only $0.38 on average. So, if you paid $1 to buy a ticket for this lottery with a winning prize of $5, then you would expect to lose about $0.62 on average. Even if the winning prize was $10 and you paid $1 for a ticket, you should expect to lose around $0.23. This is because with a prize of $10, your expected winnings are $(1/13) \times \$10$, which is around $0.77.

The same is true for most lotteries or casino games on a much larger scale. Even if the jackpot is very large, the probability of winning is vanishingly small. For example, suppose the jackpot for a particular lottery is $40 million and the ticket costs $25. Should you buy a ticket? It depends. Suppose 5 million people buy tickets. Then, your expected probability of winning is 1/5 000 000. This means that even if the jackpot is $40 million, the amount you expect to win is: (1/5 000 000) × (40 000 000) or $8. Someone or more than one will win, but on average, most people will lose and their expected loss is ($25 − $8) = $17. This implies that the expected value of any win is typically less than the price of the lottery ticket or the price of entering the casino game. This is why "the house usually wins"; because the total amount the house receives in ticket sales or entry fees from participants exceeds the amount the house has to pay out. People do routinely accept these bets and we will see shortly how this decision may be justified.

RISK AVERSION

So far, so good. We have a good way of thinking about probabilistic outcomes. Consider the payoffs and then multiply those with the corresponding probabilities and calculate the expected value in order to decide whether something is worth the price or not. If the expected prize is larger than the cost of entry, then undertake the project, but if the expected value falls short, then do not. People who behave like this, that is, make their decisions purely on the basis of expected costs and benefits, are termed "risk neutral".[6]

Now consider the following lottery, which has come to be known as the *St Petersburg paradox*. A fair coin is tossed and the game ends once tails comes up. If the first toss throws up tails, then the game ends and the player wins $1. If the first toss is heads and the second toss is tails, then the player wins $2. If the first two tosses are heads and the third is tails, then the player wins $4. If the first three tosses are heads and the fourth results in tails, then the player wins $8, and so on. How much should you be willing to pay for this gamble?

The first step is to calculate the expected value of this lottery. What is the expected value? This problem is simple since the probability of getting either heads or tails on a given toss is always fixed and equal to 1/2. The probability of getting tails on the very first toss is 1/2. The probability of getting tails for the first time on the second toss is 1/4. This is because if you get tails on the second toss, then you must have had a heads on the first toss. So, the probability of getting a head on the first toss and a tails in the second toss is $(1/2) \times (1/2) = 1/4$. Following the same logic, the probability of getting tails for the first time on the third toss is Probability(Heads) × Probability(Heads) × Probability(Tails) = 1/8 and so on. How much should you expect to win on average? With probability 1/2 you win \$1, with probability 1/4 you win \$2, with probability 1/8 you win \$4, and so on. Therefore, the expected value is (\$0.50 + \$0.50 + \$0.50 + ...). The expected value of the game is infinite. A risk-neutral person should be willing to pay a relatively large amount for this lottery with a high expected prize. Yet, few people would be willing to pay a lot of money to accept this gamble. This is because most people are not risk neutral; they are *risk averse*.

The resolution, proposed by Daniel Bernoulli in 1738, was that the "value" of this lottery is not the same as its monetary value.[7] Instead, people attach some subjective value, or what economists refer to as "utility", to monetary outcomes. You can think of utility as happiness, satisfaction or joy; something that you typically want more of rather than less. Thus, people do not seek to maximize expected values, but instead seek to maximize expected utility (happiness/satisfaction/joy). Furthermore, the utility we obtain from consuming various goods (including money, since money is a means of buying goods that in turn bring us utility) is not constant but shows *diminishing sensitivity*. This means that as we consume more of something, our utility may increase, but it does so by smaller and smaller increments.

Diminishing sensitivity seems complicated but most of us have an intuitive understanding of what this means. If you are hanging out at the beach on a lazy summer afternoon, the first ice-cream tastes great but the second one not as much. By the fifth ice-cream you might start to feel a little sick. This is what diminishing sensitivity means; as we consume more and more of the same good, the additional utility (happiness/satisfaction) we obtain from each additional unit becomes smaller and smaller. This does not have to be true for everyone. It is conceivable that you might be the type of person who loves to consume three ice-cream cones with double scoops each in one sitting. However, even for you, a point will come when diminishing returns set in. Beyond that point, you do not want to spend any more money on ice-cream since the extra happiness is just not worth the extra spending.

The vast majority of humans behave like this even when it comes to money; they are risk averse rather than risk neutral.[8] As we get larger and larger sums of money, our utility does not increase at a constant rate; instead, with more income (more consumption), the additional utility we obtain from each additional dollar of money (or each extra unit of a good) goes down. This has dramatic implications for our risk perceptions. Later in this chapter I will show you that, when it came to Covid-19, there was another twist to our risk aversion: it makes a big difference whether we are looking at a gain or a loss. Losing $100 causes a lot more unhappiness than the happiness caused by winning $100. We evaluate outcomes on the basis of the status quo. Gains make us happy; losses make us unhappy, but the impact of the latter is felt much more acutely than the former.

PROCESSING RISK: SHOULD ANA BUY THE SUPER-COVER WARRANTY?

Ana has just bought a fancy new 65-inch Sony OLED smart television (TV) for $5000. The salesperson tells Ana that since these TVs are so "thin" they tend to be delicate and could topple over easily. The salesperson suggests that Ana should take out the super-cover insurance that provides a longer warranty on top of the usual one-year warranty that comes with her purchase. This additional insurance costs $300. Should Ana take out this insurance? The answer depends on what risk Ana attributes to the TV toppling over and how risk averse Ana is.

Put yourself in Ana's shoes. The first question you need to ask yourself is, what is the chance that the TV will indeed topple over? For the sake of argument, let us assume that this chance is 10 percent (or 1 in 10). This means that there is a 90 percent chance that nothing bad will happen but there is a 10 percent chance that the TV will topple over, crash and become valueless. So, with 10 percent chance you will be left with nothing (no TV) and with 90 percent chance the $5000 TV works fine. In this instance, your expected payoffs are $0 with 10 percent chance, and $5000 with 90 percent chance. What is the expected value? The answer is $(0.9) \times (\$5000) + (0.1) \times (\$0) = \$4500$. So, factoring in the risk of a crash, your expected loss is $500; the actual $5000 cost of the TV minus the expected value of $4500 in the event of a catastrophe. In this instance, you should certainly buy the super-cover warranty since you will have to pay $300 for this extra cover but it insures you against an expected loss of $500. You are better off by $200 in expectation.

However, this depends on Ana's (or your) risk perception. Is the risk of the TV toppling over really 10 percent? This would mean that 1 out of every 10 such TVs will crash. What if the risk is only 5 percent? In this instance, the expected value with the risk of a crash is $(0.95) \times (\$5000) + (0.05) \times (\$0) = \$4750$. Now your expected loss is only $250 ($5000 for the TV minus the expected value of $4750). So, if you buy the additional insurance for $300, then you are effectively losing $50. Is a 5 percent risk of breakage realistic? You can do a quick Google search and look at online bulletin boards to find out how often these TVs break. What if the actual risk is only 1 in 100? In this instance, the expected value is $4950 and you stand to lose only $50 in expectation. Here, if you buy the super-cover warranty by paying $300, you are paying this amount to insure yourself against an outcome whose expected loss is only $50. You can do this but it depends crucially on how risk averse you are. So, unless Ana or others like her have some astoundingly high degree of risk aversion, typically buying the super-cover warranty does not make sense unless you assume a fairly high probability (such as 1 in 10) for the TV to topple over and crash. We see further on in this chapter how an inability to correctly perceive small probabilities and an extreme amount of risk aversion came to dominate our Covid-19 responses.

REFERENCE POINTS, GAINS AND LOSSES

Previously, I mentioned that in addition to risk aversion, a second key feature of our decision making is that we evaluate gains and losses not in a vacuum, but starting from a reference point, which is usually the status quo. Much of what follows is taken from the extensive work done by Daniel Kahneman and Amos Tversky in this area, known as "prospect theory".

Kahneman and Tversky asked a group of respondents to choose between the following two lotteries:

Lottery 1 (Choose A or B):
Choice A: 80% chance of winning $4000.
Choice B: Win $3000 for sure.

Lottery 2 (Choose A or B):
Choice A: 80% chance of losing $4000.
Choice B: Lose $3000 for sure.

Notice that the first lottery poses a choice between an expected win of $3200 (80 percent chance of winning $4000) or a sure win of $3000. Lottery 2 poses a choice between an expected loss of $3200 versus a sure loss of $3000. When it came to the first lottery, 80 percent of respondents went for the sure win of $3000 over the expected win of $3200, but for the second lottery, 92 percent chose the larger expected loss of $3200 (80 percent chance of losing $4000) over the sure loss of $3000. It seems strange that people are choosing a larger expected loss over a certain smaller loss. Kahneman and Tversky provide other examples to show that this is not driven by an inability to understand expected values. This suggests that people apply very different calculations when it comes to gains as opposed to when it comes to losses. Kahneman and Tversky called this tendency to choose larger expected losses over smaller sure losses, "loss aversion". People are eager to avoid sure losses; losses that are right in front of them, even if this implies accepting larger probabilistic losses.

SMALL VERSUS LARGE PROBABILITIES

As part of this research program, Kahneman and Tversky also discovered another interesting fact: *All probabilities are not the same.* That is, Kahneman and Tversky found that humans have a pronounced tendency to "overweight" small probabilities and "underweight" large ones. I explain this in Figure 3.2.

The horizontal axis in Figure 3.2 shows the actual probabilities of an event, ranging from zero to one. The vertical axis measures what I have termed *perceived probabilities*. These are how we assign subjective or psychological values to the actual probabilities. These are not always equal. If these subjective or psychological values of the probabilities (perceived probabilities) were always the same as the actual probabilities, then the perceived probabilities will look like the solid straight line going from the bottom-left to the top-right of the figure.

When actual probability is 0.2, perceived probability is 0.2; when actual probability is 0.4, perceived probability is 0.4; when actual probability is 0.8, so is the perceived probability. This is what will happen if everyone was risk neutral; their perceived probabilities will coincide exactly with the actual probabilities. However, Kahneman and Tversky discovered that given most people are risk averse rather than risk neutral, their perceived probabilities do not look like the solid straight line going from bottom-left to top-right in Figure 3.2. Instead, they look like the sideways-tilted inverse "S" shaped dotted line. Let me explain.

For some cut-off probability value, the subjective (psychological) value we assign to that probability, that is, the perceived probability, is larger than the objective (actual) value of the probability; that is, the probability *appears* to be larger than it really is. For probability values higher than this cut-off, we assign a smaller subjective (psychological) value than is actually the case, implying that large probabilities

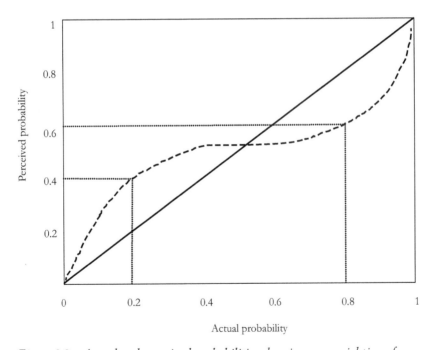

*Figure 3.2   Actual and perceived probabilities showing overweighting of
              small probabilities and underweighting of large probabilities*

are underweighted; the perceived probability appears to be smaller than the actual probability. The way I have drawn the dotted curve in Figure 3.2, it looks as though this cut-off occurs at an actual probability of 0.5. For all actual probabilities less than 0.5, perceived probabilities are higher than the actual probabilities. For all actual probabilities more than 0.5, perceived probabilities appear to be less than the actual probability. I hasten to add that this depends very much on the nature of the inverted and sideways-tilted "S" curve. This may intersect the solid straight line at a value less than or more than 0.5. This depends on the curvature of that inverted "S" curve and may well vary from one individual to the next.

Here is what this implies. This means that even if some events have a very low probability, in our minds, we overweight it and the subjective probability appears to be much larger than it actually (objectively) is. This is why we routinely buy lottery tickets, even though the probability of winning the jackpot is vanishingly small. Similarly, we often underweight large probabilities. So, if you look at Figure 3.2, you will see that this particular person is assigning a value of 0.4 (overweighting) to an event that has an actual probability of only 0.2, while he or she is assigning a value of 0.6 (underweighting) to an event with 0.8 probability. The former (probability of 0.2) is an unlikely event; it occurs in 20 percent or 1 out of 5 cases. The latter is a likely event; it occurs in 80 percent or 4 out of 5 cases. However, because this person is overweighting the smaller probability and underweighting the larger probability, he or she is treating both events as if they are reasonably close in terms of their probabilities. He or she is assigning a value of 0.4 (40 percent or 2 out 5) to the first event and a value of 0.6 (60 percent or 3 out of 5) to the second, making it appear that the probabilities of the two events are much closer (40 percent and 60 percent, respectively) than they actually are. This is not correct. The second event (probability 0.8 or 80 percent) is four times more likely than the first (0.2 or 20 percent probability).

LOSS AVERSION AND COVID-19

Here is how loss aversion played a role in the response to the pandemic. As I noted previously, most epidemiologists both in New Zealand and elsewhere were adamant about strict social distancing measures in an attempt to suppress the disease, no matter what the cost. However, in doing this, the epidemiologists are focusing on identified lives; the sure loss of lives we can see right in front of our eyes. Therein lies the connection with loss aversion. Faced with the prospect of a large-scale loss of lives, medical professionals are willing to accept much larger probabilistic losses later rather than accept smaller sure losses owing to people succumbing to Covid-19. Part of this also has to do with the underweighting of large probabilities. However, the probabilistic losses are less obvious, especially as, even if the probability of the event is high, our brains tend to underestimate that probability.

This meant that we were constantly overweighting the relatively small probability of deaths owing to Covid-19 and underweighting the very high probability of significant economic damage (and consequent loss of lives) from locking down to deal with Covid-19. This also played a role in how we evaluated the risks. First, if and when a particular risk has become small, the costs of reducing it even further start to become prohibitive. Getting a probability down from 1 in 10 to 1 in 100 may not be very costly but getting this down to 1 in 200 is more costly, 1 in 500 even more costly, 1 in 1000 costlier still. At some point, we need to stop and think: is it really worth incurring additional costs to try and push this probability even lower? That is, consumers such as Ana need to stop and think: how large is the probability of the TV toppling over? Does it really make sense to shell out a large amount in buying super-cover warranty if the probability is actually very small?

This applies both to R_0 (the contagion rate) and the IFR. The contagion rate is the rate at which each person infected with Covid-19 infects others. If this number is bigger than 1, then we have a serious problem and the makings of an epidemic. This is because now, one infected person infects two others, who in turn infect four others. A series such as this $(1 + 2 + 4 + 8 + ...)$ is termed a geometric progression which blows up into huge numbers very quickly. Alternatively, if the contagion rate is less than 1, say 4/5, then the story is quite different. Here, the first person infects only 4/5 others. Since this is not very intuitive, another way of thinking about this is, five people infect four, who in turn infect less than four, and so on. This is also a geometric series of the form $(1 + 4/5 + 16/25 + ...)$ but this one starts dwindling to smaller and smaller numbers.

A similar argument could be made about the IFR. Once the IFR is brought down to a relatively small number, the benefits of bringing this down even further may be limited or prohibitively costly. According to John Ioannidis of Stanford and his collaborators:

> The Covid-19 death risk in people <65 years old during the period of fatalities from the epidemic was equivalent to the death risk from driving between 13 and 101 miles per day for 11 countries and 6 states, and was higher (equivalent to the death risk from driving 143–668 miles per day) for 6 other states and the UK. People <65 years old without underlying predisposing conditions accounted for only 0.7–2.6% of all Covid-19 deaths (data available from France, Italy, Netherlands, Sweden, Georgia, and New York City).[9]

Many of us drive similar distances on a routine basis if not daily. A careful reader is justified in asking at this stage: but are you not ignoring that a small fraction of a very large population is still a large number? This is a valid point and one made by many. Even if the IFR is 0.65, meaning less than 1 in 100, this still translates to 6500 per million. For a country such as the United States, with 330 million people, this would imply more than 2 million dead. This is what some of the initial modelers of the pandemic were saying in arguing for stringent lockdowns.

Let us engage our system 2 a little differently. Let us assume that the 0.65 percent IFR is correct. It could be lower since the US Centers for Disease Control and Prevention (CDC) suggests a range of 0.2 percent to 0.8 percent. However, let us proceed and take the value of 0.65 percent. For this IFR to translate into more than 2 million deaths in the US, it must be that every single person is infected with the disease. How likely is that? Not very likely, because, as I argue in the next chapter, humans are not automatons. When confronted with a potentially lethal pathogen, they will voluntarily undertake precautionary measures. They will wash their hands, wear masks, stay away from elderly relatives, especially if they are feeling feverish, and they will do this voluntarily without having to be coerced by the authorities. This in itself will reduce significantly the spread of infection.

Further, this IFR value is heavily skewed towards the elderly and those with other underlying health conditions. For healthy adults, the IFR is much lower and indeed very small. Children seem virtually immune to the disease, with extremely few cases (close to zero) reported of any child dying from Covid-19. The number of adults under 65 years old who died from Covid-19 are small. None of this suggests that these lives, especially the elderly, are not worth saving; but at what cost? Remember, trying to save these lives is costing us lives elsewhere. This is a choice; a heartbreakingly difficult one certainly, but a choice nonetheless. Which lives should we be saving? An 82-year-old dying of Covid-19 or a 30-year-old who kills himself because his business went under?[10] Medical professionals are routinely called upon to decide on similar trade-offs. Previously, I wrote about the calculations that go into deciding who gets to receive a new heart, lung, liver or kidney. At the height of the Covid-19 pandemic, hospitals were routinely triaging to decide who gets treated and who is turned away. They were deciding this from among Covid-19 cases, those suffering more than others. They were doing this for other ailments too, or choosing to treat Covid-19 patients over others in distress. There is no win–win here. Hard choices often need to be made and there is nothing particularly callous or heartless in asking which lives will be saved and which not. No matter how much the lockdown proponents insist, we were constantly faced with these trade-offs. We were focusing on saving lives right in front of our eyes at the expense of discarding lives that were in the background.

In these situations, following the philosopher John Rawls, I have nothing better to offer than the Benthamite utilitarian principle of the greatest good for the greatest number, or to turn the maxim on its head, minimizing total harm. This is the more humane and rational position; not the position which says that we will prevent Covid-19 deaths no matter what the cost. It is the proponents of lockdowns who were prioritizing some lives over others while accusing the opponents of being guilty of the same thing. All evidence suggests that the costs are indeed much higher than the benefits. I am more than happy to concede that I may be wrong but, if I am wrong, then the lockdown proponents need to make a stronger case (or just make a case) to convince us skeptics as to how the benefits justify the massive social and economic costs that we are or were imposing on our citizens. The kids who did not attend school for one year, or those who could not because they did not have reliable Internet connection for online classes; the weddings that were postponed or canceled; the funerals that went unattended; those who died alone far away from their loved ones, or those who could not be at the bedside of elderly parents or relatives as they passed away, not to mention those who died from other diseases that were not detected at the right time; and the millions who lost their jobs and turned to unemployment benefits in countries that provide such benefits, or simply starved in countries where no social safety net was available.

Most readers will know that New Zealand has a flourishing agricultural industry, which relies to a large extent on migrant workers from the surrounding islands, such as Fiji, Samoa and Tonga. When the economy closed down, these migrants were left jobless with no sources of support. New Zealand's then Deputy Prime Minister declared that they should probably go home. How were they supposed to get home? We live on an island, which had closed its border and shut down all flights![11]

New Zealand is a founding member of the International Labour Organization (ILO). Referring to migrant workers, Article 8 of ILO Convention 143 (1975) states:

> (1) On condition that he has resided legally in the territory for the purpose of employment, the migrant worker shall not be regarded as being in an illegal or irregular situation by the mere fact of the loss of his employment, which shall not in itself imply the withdrawal of his authorisation of residence or, as the case may be, work permit. (2) Accordingly, he shall enjoy equality of treatment with nationals ... (with respect to) ... security of employment, the provision of alternative employment, relief work and retraining.

THE QUEST FOR RAPID VACCINE DEVELOPMENT

There was yet another way lack of facility with probabilities played into this zeal for locking down. This was the belief that given the huge amount of money being poured into the enterprise and the global effort to develop a vaccine, it would not be too long before a vaccine would come along, making future lockdowns redundant. This is an area where the overweighting of small probabilities played a major role.

People were ignoring that the typical timescale for an "effective" vaccine was eight to ten years and the fastest vaccine ever developed took four years; the vaccine for mumps. The varicella vaccine providing immunity against chicken pox took 28 years, as did FluMist (for types A and B influenza). Rotavirus and human papillomavirus (HPV) vaccines took 15 years each. The pediatric combination of diphtheria, polio, tetanus and pertussis vaccines took 11 years. For Covid-19, the aim was to find a vaccine within 18 months.[12] I have put the word "effective" within quote mark because most of the vaccines that are currently utilized such as those for HPV, diphtheria, polio, and so on, provide fairly long-term immunity. Some of these need to be followed by boosters. For instance, doctors believe that if we receive a tetanus vaccination once every decade, this provides adequate immunity.

This was not true for the early Covid-19 vaccines; at least, the vaccine trials were not set up to look for long-term immunity owing to the severely compressed timeframe. So, while the early vaccines were certainly going to produce a degree of immunity, it was not clear if they would be successful in reducing severe Covid-19 (hospital admission, intensive care unit treatment or death) or interrupting transmission (person-to-person spread).[13] Here is how the trials were designed. Suppose you recruit 200 people from the community. (The real numbers are much larger, in the thousands.) You put 100 of them in the treatment group and the other 100 in the placebo group. The first group receives the vaccine; the second group does not. Now, suppose you estimate that approximately 10 percent of the population should contract Covid-19 in the absence of any intervention. This means that you expect 10 out of every 100 people to catch the disease. But now suppose that 10 out of the 100 people in the placebo group do contract the disease, but in the vaccinated group, only 1 does. This means that 9 people in the treatment group who should have caught the disease did not. This in turn means that the vaccine is 90 percent effective. Given the pressure to develop a vaccine quickly, this was all that could be tested.

By early 2021, four vaccines had been approved in the Western world: those by Pfizer, Moderna, Johnson & Johnson, and AstraZeneca. The Russians produced their own vaccine, Sputnik V, and the Chinese produced Sinovac. Neither of the latter were being used extensively in developed industrialized nations and therefore garnered less interest and exposure than the others, although by mid-2021, more than 40 countries around the world including large South American nations, such as Brazil and Argentina, were vaccinating people with the Chinese-made Sinovac. Early reports suggest that Sinovac is less effective than the four Western vaccines mentioned previously. The Pfizer, Moderna, and Johnson & Johnson vaccines are a radically new type of mRNA (messenger ribonucleic acid) vaccine that have not been used beyond clinical studies before. Typical viral vaccines (such as that from AstraZeneca) work by injecting humans with a very small amount of live attenuated virus or a fragment of the virus. This at times generates some mild symptoms in the recipient, but confers immunity against the virulence of the actual disease. The mRNA vaccines work differently than traditional vaccines and are easier to develop, which partially explains why these types of vaccines (or their producers) reported success earlier than others working on traditional vaccines. Coronaviruses such as SARS-Cov-2 generally invade human cells via "spike proteins" that allow the virus to latch onto the cell. An mRNA vaccine works by introducing into the body an mRNA sequence (the molecule which tells cells what to build) which is coded for a disease-specific antigen, in this instance the spike protein. Once produced within the body, the antigen is recognized by the immune system, in turn telling our bodies which antibodies need to be produced to fight the disease off. So, if and when the Covid-19 virus tries to invade the cell, the spike protein it generates to do so is recognized by our immune system, which will disable the virus and kill any cells that have become infected.

OTHER VACCINE CHALLENGES

Since the mRNA vaccines are unique, obtaining raw material for them and scaling up production will be a challenge. The mRNA vaccines need to be frozen at negative 70 degrees Celsius. According to some news reports, negative 70 degrees Celsius (or approximately negative 94 degrees Fahrenheit) is a very cold day in the South Pole. This makes the risk of spoilage high and adds another hurdle in relation to storing these vaccines. Finally, and again probably not surprisingly, none of these calculations take into account that the virus could mutate, as it did in late 2020. This new mutated strain of the virus was first reported in the UK, but spread rapidly across the world, and by the early part of 2021 became the dominant strain of SARS-Cov-2. No one had any clear idea as to whether the existing vaccines provided immunity against the new strain. (It is generally well accepted that when we vaccinate against the seasonal flu, we are often vaccinating against the strain from the past year. This is why, without much change in the actual vaccination rates from one year to the next, we sometimes get "bad" flu seasons.)

We still need to produce and distribute enough vaccines to immunize 7 billion people around the world. Other than the vaccine being developed by Johnson & Johnson, every vaccine needs to be frozen or chilled – a serious challenge in less developed tropical countries with high temperatures and often unreliable power supplies. Then, enough doses need to be produced, transported and kept frozen/chilled. While this is certainly possible, it is highly unlikely to occur in a short span of time. When the early vaccination efforts in the US and the UK got off to a much slower than anticipated start, there arose a significant debate about whether people really required two doses as recommended by the drug companies, or was one dose enough? That is, should we go for stronger immunity among a smaller subsection of the population or weaker immunity among a wider cross-section?[14]

This discussion is not meant to minimize the effort of the scientists who came up with a vaccine in record time; neither does this suggest that the vaccines are useless. These vaccines will, at the least, slow the spread of infection, even if they are not successful in completely eradicating Covid-19. I am referring primarily to how we perceived the probabilities associated with these events, and that we were routinely overestimating how quickly we could get this done and significantly underestimating the scale of the task involved. This, in turn, meant that the opportunity costs being incurred in this pursuit of eliminating Covid-19 were inevitably going to be much larger than anticipated.

To take the example of New Zealand once more, the country has imposed tight restrictions on border entry, thereby hobbling its biggest export industry, tourism, and its fifth largest, higher education, with international students not allowed to enter the country. New Zealand and other countries with similar border restrictions in an attempt to eliminate the virus will have to keep those restrictive measures in place for a long time if they are really being serious about eliminating the virus.

Then there is the issue of cost and availability of the vaccine. The distribution of this vaccine is being organized by Gavi, the Vaccine

Alliance, a philanthropic enterprise, through its COVAX facility. According to a press release from Doctors Without Borders, Gavi does not have experience of negotiating with pharmaceutical companies on behalf of these countries.

> Meanwhile, the WHO Pandemic Influenza Preparedness (PIP) Framework is an example of WHO's global normative and operational role to develop public health instruments that help to prepare for and respond to global pandemics. The PIP Framework includes requirements from manufacturers that they set aside specific quantities of medicines or vaccines in the case of a global influenza pandemic, with WHO determining the equitable allocation of those medical tools.[15]

Gavi envisages a two-tiered system for vaccine distribution: "self-financing" countries (developed countries that can afford to pay) and "funded" countries (developing countries that need help). When a vaccine is available, the self-financing countries will be entitled to receive enough vaccines for at least 20 percent of their population. Countries will then decide who gets those vaccines. The funded countries that need help will only get the vaccine if and when all the self-financing countries have received their 20 percent quota. However, 20 percent is nowhere near the threshold required for herd immunity. Most estimates suggest that herd immunity requires a much larger proportion of the population to be vaccinated. How long will that take?

Questions remain: the US, China and Russia are not signatories to COVAX. If and when a vaccine is produced and demand far outstrips supply, it is not clear why and whether pharmaceutical companies will sell to Gavi at a cost-plus pricing model rather than to others. The relationship with Gavi does not rule out other bilateral relationships.

Even assuming that some vaccine makers do agree to provide vaccines to Gavi, there is currently no plan for generic production. Indeed, in late 2020, the developed countries of the world such as the US, the UK, Canada and Australia barred a proposal from India and South Africa to allow generic production of Covid-19 vaccines. Under the World Trade Organization (WTO) rules, such proposals, which fall under the WTO's guidelines for safeguarding intellectual property rights (TRIPS), must be adopted unanimously. Given the opposition of the developed countries, the proposal was doomed to fail. However, generic production is essential in order to make the vaccine available cheaply. Again, according to Doctors Without Borders, until recently, the only two producers of the pneumonia vaccine have been Pfizer and GlaxoSmithKline, who were selling it to Gavi for US$9 per child in the low-income countries and for US$80 in middle- and higher-income countries. The Serum Institute of India has offered to sell the same vaccine at US$6 per child in low-income countries and for no more than about US$11 per child in middle-income countries. These lower prices are only possible when we allow generic production.[16]

It seems likely that in the near future, we will be in a world of vaccine haves and vaccine have-nots. Citizens of countries in the former group will be able to travel freely among each other, but travel and trade relations with vaccine have-not countries will be severely curtailed. This, in turn, will have a seriously adverse impact on the lives and livelihoods of those countries' citizens. As Joseph Stiglitz, the 2001 Nobel Laureate in Economics, notes, it is likely that our policy responses will exacerbate inequalities both within and across countries.[17]

One issue that is not sufficiently highlighted is that extreme mitigation strategies are not equally well suited to everyone. It depends crucially on people's socio-economic status, and a great deal of this burden is falling and will fall on the socio-economically disadvantaged; those who are not able to engage in social (physical) distancing; those who do not have the luxury of working or studying from home; those who are forced to spend long periods cooped up in cramped spaces without access to unlimited broadband; those who live from pay check to pay check; those who need to show up at our supermarkets and hospitals as part of essential services; those who need to take public transit in order to do so; and those who are being exposed to the disease at a higher rate than their more fortunate counterparts. Stiglitz states: "One of the reasons the United States has been afflicted with the highest number of cases and deaths (at least as this goes to press) is because it has among the poorest average health standards of major developed economies, ... and the highest levels of health disparities."

Looking across international borders, mitigation strategies and the potential for incomplete and/or inadequate vaccine coverage implies that low-income countries and their citizens will face greater hurdles.

Some of these hurdles will arise from the limited contact between low-income countries and developed countries caused by the vaccine disparity. Covid-19 may not go away soon, and even when it does, the fear of future similar pandemics will linger. This has implications for global supply chains. The pandemic will accelerate the existing trend of moving away from low-skilled work toward automation but, in the absence of an adequate safety net for those workers, this will increase existing disparities both within and across countries. While I am a firm believer in market-based solutions, markets work well only while the playing field is level. As Stiglitz writes in that same article (and although he is talking primarily about the US, the lessons apply broadly):

> We have an economy rife with market power and exploitation. The rules of the game matter. Weakening constraints on corporate power; minimizing the bargaining power of workers; and eroding rules governing the exploitation of consumers, borrowers, students, and workers have all worked together to create a poorer-performing economy marked by greater rent seeking and greater inequality.

* * *

In this chapter, I have argued that one reason for the strong support behind lockdowns was a belief that a vaccine will be available shortly. However, this is predicated to a large extent on overweighting events with a small probability of happening. Let me be clear. It is a stupendous achievement that we managed to get an mRNA vaccine, something that has not been tried before and was probably developed primarily because of the time-pressure exerted by Covid-19. There is no doubt that either the vaccines already developed or that will be developed will make a substantial difference in combating Covid-19, but this is not going to happen any time soon; at least, not for large parts of the world. What is the game plan then? Keep borders closed? Keep schools closed? More lockdowns? At what cost? Or, while we try to get people vaccinated, could we also explore things like asking people to wear masks, wash their hands, stay home if they feel sick and exercise various other common-sense measures to ward off the disease? We do not need everyone to do everything, but as long as enough of us do enough things, enough of us wear masks, enough of us stay home as and when possible, enough of us avoid large gatherings, enough of us practice physical distancing, we will be okay.

As Aaron Carroll wrote in the *New York Times*,[18] think about safety as a pile on the floor. We want to make the pile as large as possible. So every time some of us put on masks or work from home where possible, we are throwing some safety onto that pile. Could this make enough of a difference? I think so; but this also requires governments to chart a consistent course, provide appropriate advice and, most importantly, *trust their citizens to do the right thing*. A great deal of evidence suggests that a large proportion of lockdown proponents start from the viewpoint that people cannot be trusted and hence need to be coerced into doing things under the threat of punishment for not following those orders. This view of humanity is mistaken, and is what I turn to in the next chapter.

NOTES

1. In New Zealand, compensation for all accidental injuries is administered by a government agency called the Accident Compensation Corporation (ACC) set up by the Accident Compensation Act 1972. According to the ACC website (https://www.acc.co.nz/newsroom/media-resources/injury-claim-statistics/), between 1 July 2018 and 30 June 2019, ACC accepted more than 2 million claims in a population of 5 million people. Some of these are minor and some may be the same person suffering multiple injuries. Also, 29 percent of these, or roughly 580 000, are the result of falls and 21 percent, or roughly 420 000, are the result of sports injuries.

2. *12 Angry Men* (1957); screenplay by Reginald Rose; directed by Sidney Lumet; producers: Henry Fonda and Reginal Rose; Orion-Nova Productions. It is not exactly clear why the movie is called *12 Angry Men* since not all 12 are angry; Henry Fonda's Juror No. 8 is always calm, methodical and precise. I guess "11 Angry Men and 1 Composed Man" or "11 Men Guided by System 1" would not have the same evocative appeal. If you have not seen the movie, I strongly recommend that you watch it.

3. Down's Syndrome is also known as Down Syndrome or Trisomy. This is a genetic disorder caused by the presence of all or part of a third copy of chromosome 21. Down's Syndrome is usually associated with physical growth delays, mild to moderate intellectual disability and characteristic facial features. Those with Down's Syndrome typically have a much lower IQ compared with their peers and usually have a lower life expectancy. There is no cure for this. Babies born to older mothers are particularly susceptible to having Down's Syndrome. This issue is particularly problematic for the first child of older

mothers. Older women having a second or later child do not seem to create similar problems.

4. This type of calculation, updating prior probabilities on the basis of available information to form new posterior probabilities, is known as Bayesian reasoning or simply Bayes' rule. The rule is named after Thomas Bayes (1701–1761), an English statistician, philosopher and Presbyterian minister. Bayes never published this rule or theorem, which was published in 1763, after his death, by Richard Price (1723–1791), a British moral philosopher and mathematician. Price spent most of his adult life as minister of Newington Green Unitarian Church and was a Fellow of the Royal Society.

5. Wu, K. (2020a). In coronavirus testing, false positives are more hazardous than they might seem. *New York Times*, 25 October. https://www.nytimes.com/2020/10/25/world/in-coronavirus-testing-false-positives-are-more-hazardous-than-they-might-seem.html; Wu, K. (2020b). Why false positives merit concern, too. *New York Times*, 15 December. https://www.nytimes.com/2020/10/25/health/coronavirus-testing-false-positive.html. I believe the second article is an updated version of the first article, but they have different titles and the content is not exactly the same. In the interests of completeness, I have provided both citations.

6. I need to point out an important caveat here. I will often use the terms risk and uncertainty synonymously much as they are used in day-to-day parlance. However, to economists, these are two different and distinct concepts. Both are probabilistic events, meaning that they are not certain and occur with some probability. Risk refers to circumstances where these probabilities are known. Uncertainty or ambiguity refers to situations where these probabilities are unknown. Most of the examples I discuss in this chapter are about risk, since I typically assume that the probabilities are known. This is not true in many cases, where the actual probabilities are unknown. As Donald Rumsfeld, who was George W. Bush's Defense Secretary, noted during the second Iraq War: there are often "known unknowns" and "unknown unknowns". Rumsfeld took a lot of ribbing, but these are legitimate concepts in logic, philosophy and statistics.

7. The paradox takes its name since Daniel Bernoulli was a resident of the city and published his arguments in the Commentaries of the Imperial Academy of Science of Saint Petersburg (Bernoulli 1738 [1954]).

8. There is a third category of risk lovers. An example would be a recent *Jeopardy!* winner, James Holtzhauer, who, every time he hit a "Daily Double", bet it all, and typically won big in all the games that he won. In his day job, James Holtzhauer is a sports bettor in Las Vegas, but this is typically a highly specialized group that constitute a small minority in any population.

9. Ioannidis, J. A., Axfors, C., and Contopoulos-Ioannidis, D. G. (2020). Population-level COVID-19 mortality risk for non-elderly individuals overall and for non-elderly individuals without underlying diseases in pandemic epicenters. *Environmental Research*, *188*, 109890. https://doi.org/10.1101/2020.04.05.20054361.

10. Biddle, D.-L. (2020a). South Auckland Mad Butcher owner dies suddenly after business goes into liquidation. *Stuff*, 12 May. https://www.stuff.co.nz/busi ness/121491315/south-auckland-mad-butcher-owner-dies-suddenly-after-busin ess-goes-into-liquidation. Another report from the same reporter quoted the victim's sister, who did not want to speculate on the reasons for her brother's death but said the Government-enforced lockdown rules did not help. "I wasn't part of his business or anything and can't comment too much, I just know that Covid-19, and the restrictions put on his small business did not help, and it just added to the burden." See Biddle, D.-L. (2020b). Family of Auckland butcher who died suddenly say Covid-19 restrictions "added to burden". *Stuff*, 13 May. https://www.stuff.co.nz/national/121497895/family-of-auckland-butcher-who-died-suddenly-say-covid19-restrictions-added-to-burden. "Died suddenly" is a New Zealand euphemism for suicide. It may come as a surprise to many, but the BBC reported in 2017 that:

> according to UNICEF, New Zealand has by far the highest youth suicide rate in the developed world. The UNICEF report found New Zealand's youth suicide rate – teenagers between 15 and 19 – to be the highest of a long list of 41 OECD and EU countries. The rate of 15.6 suicides per 100,000 people is twice as high as the US rate and almost five times that of Britain.

Hence the media reluctance to explicitly use the term "suicide", instead relying on the above-mentioned euphemism. See Illmer, A. (2017). What's behind New Zealand's shocking youth suicide rate? *BBC*, 15 June. https://www.bbc.com/news/world-asia-40284130.

11. Wade, A. (2020). Covid 19 coronavirus: Winston Peters tells struggling migrant workers "you should probably go home". *New Zealand Herald*, 13 May. https://www.nzherald.co.nz/nz/covid-19-coronavirus-winston-peters-tells-stru ggling-migrant-workers-you-should-probably-go-home/C47ZGBC3BELTLBIN D47N6J5JXM/.

12. Thomson, S. A. (2020). How long will a vaccine really take? *New York Times*, 30 April. https://www.nytimes.com/interactive/2020/04/30/opinion/coronavir us-covid-vaccine.html.

13. Doshi, P. (2020). Will covid-19 vaccines save lives? Current trials aren't designed to tell us. *BMJ*, *371*, m4037. https://www.bmj.com/content/371/bmj.m4037.

14. Wu, K. J., and Robbins, R. (2021). As rollout falters, scientists debate new vaccina-tion tactics. *New York Times*, 3 January. https://www.nytimes.com/2021/01/03/health/coronavirus-vaccine-doses.html.

15. Doctors Without Borders. (2020). COVID-19 Vaccine Global Access (COVAX) Facility: Key considerations for Gavi's new global financing mechanism. MSF Media Briefing, June. https://msfaccess.org/sites/default/files/2020-06/MSF-AC_COVID-19_Gavi-COVAXFacility_briefing-document.pdf.

16. Some readers may be thinking, but do the companies producing the vaccines not have a right to earn a profit? Yes, they do, but do not forget that these companies have already received billions of dollars in subsidies from various governments. Further, most of the companies are relying on work undertaken by scientists at public universities all around the world, work funded by the public via their

taxes. Even with generic production, these companies still stand to make large sums of money, albeit not as much as they will make in the absence of generics.

17. Stiglitz, J. (2020). The pandemic has laid bare deep divisions, but it's not too late to change course. *Conquering the Great Divide, International Monetary Fund Finance and Development* (Fall). https://www.imf.org/external/pubs/ft/fandd/2020/09/COVID19-and-global-inequality-joseph-stiglitz.htm.

18. Carroll, A. (2020). When it comes to Covid-19, most of us have risk exactly backward. *New York Times*, 28 August. https://www.nytimes.com/2020/08/28/opinion/coronavirus-schools-tradeoffs.html.

4. Should we trust people to do the right thing?

In this chapter, I discuss the role of trust in our everyday lives. I write about:

- whether we can trust people to wear masks or self-isolate on their own accord;
- whether people must be compelled to do the right thing on the basis of penalties for non-compliance;
- the distinction between extrinsic and intrinsic incentives;
- whether a model of humanity that starts from a large degree of mistrust is borne out by the evidence.

* * *

Following a five-week lockdown in April 2020, New Zealand had a period of 128 days without community transmission. At this point, New Zealand's government, flush from this success and basking in the adulation of the global media,[1] decided to make a fateful decision. New Zealand decided that "flattening the curve" was no longer enough: we were going to "eliminate" the virus. It was not quite clear what "elimination" really meant. The government was certainly not talking about "eradication" since this requires a vaccine and the only viral disease successfully eradicated is smallpox. As I noted in a previous chapter, the World Health Organization definition of "elimination" is also dramatically different, implying no community transmission for at least a year or more together with extensive surveillance, contact tracing and genotyping. These conditions were not met. What the government most probably meant was that we do not have Covid-19 among citizens anymore and we intend to keep it that way.

This led to the establishment of a huge bureaucracy in the form of managed isolation and quarantine or MIQ, as the system came to be known. From now on, anyone entering the country would be taken to a quarantine facility (hotels around New Zealand; some extremely nice, others less so). Once you got off the plane, you would be put on a bus to take you to your quarantine hotel. This was a radical change from the existing practice at the time, which was to ask people to self-isolate. When I returned home from the US in April 2020 immediately prior to our first lockdown, self-isolation for two weeks was the policy. However, the government deemed that this was no longer secure enough.

There were, at least, two big problems with this elimination approach. First, given the potential for asymptomatic transmission of Covid-19, there was no way to ascertain that there were no dormant carriers of the disease in the community. This is especially since New Zealand was not carrying out any systematic serological testing.[2] Second, this meant that the MIQ facility needed to stay in place for the foreseeable future; most likely until a vaccine was developed. If and when that happened, would it be enough if 20 percent of New Zealanders were vaccinated? What about visitors from the rest of the world?

Among other things, this had a devastating impact on tourism, New Zealand's largest export industry. It also made sure that New Zealand's fifth largest export industry, higher education, suffered a massive blow, since international students were now barred from entering the country for the foreseeable future. In addition, the government decided that anyone entering the country would need to pay for the cost of the two-week quarantine. Initially, the idea was that everyone would have to pay, but after significant opposition from various quarters, the policy underwent changes as I explain below.

The government was not only overweighting the small probability of getting their hands on a vaccine in short order but they were also severely underestimating the high probability of the virus finding a way through. Not surprisingly, this is exactly what happened. After 128 days, community transmission started again. By this time, even the government had started to become wary of extensive lock-downs. So this time, instead of locking down the whole country, the Auckland region was placed under Level 3 restrictions. This meant that essential services and others, such as construction or take-away restaurants, where physical distancing was not a huge concern could continue to operate. Everything else, including schools, universities and workplaces, was closed. The rest of the country was put under a milder lockdown. However, given that the Auckland region accounts for nearly one-third of the country's population and two-fifths of the country's gross domestic product, this increased the potential for a further adverse shock to the economy.

It is important to understand that for much of this, the left-of-center government had strong support from the right-of-center opposition party. Indeed, the opposition was calling out the government for not being draconian enough in administering the facilities. This is because, and again possibly not surprising to those who study human psychology, there were a number of cases of people who broke out of isolation. In one instance, this involved a 37-year-old woman who had flown in from Brisbane with her children to attend the funeral of her husband who had died suddenly. The woman and her 18-year-old were hauled up in court. Thankfully, the younger minor children were spared this further ordeal. Eventually, the 18-year-old was allowed to go without a conviction while the mother was sentenced to jail for 14 days.[3] However, another man who broke out of his quarantine hotel to buy alcohol was sentenced to only community service.[4]

The news of these "escapes" made front page news. What did not make the news was that the thousands of people who were arriving at our borders were all dutifully obeying the restrictions. The escapees were the anomaly, were few and far between, and accounted for a vanishingly small fraction of the total number of returnees. However, remember the availability heuristic. The escapes were featured prominently in the newspapers and so the popular perception became that people were constantly trying to break out of the isolation facilities.

In order to prevent such break-outs, the government decided to turn over the running of the facilities to the military, another move supported by a large proportion of the opposition. It also quickly became apparent that administering the elaborate MIQ system was going to be very costly. Faced with these mounting costs, the government decided that people being put into isolation facilities would have to pay for this. Once again, these decisions had strong support from across the political spectrum. These charges were initially going to be imposed on everyone, including overseas New Zealanders returning home. As Sunetra Gupta of Oxford noted, the virus was already resulting in heightened nationalism, particularly among the developed nations.[5] In New Zealand, this took on a fascinating and morbid form. All of a sudden, there emerged a clear division between those New Zealanders who lived in New Zealand and those who did not. To me this seemed like a violation of the social compact between a country and its citizens. It seems to me that a fundamental part of being a country's citizen and carrying its passport is that you should be able to return to that country without being forced to pay for that privilege.

As I made this argument in the media,[6] some told me that it made sense because the overseas New Zealanders do not pay taxes in New Zealand. Left unsaid was that this is a key part of our economic system; that New Zealanders living and working in (say) the US pay taxes in the US while Americans living and working in New Zealand pay taxes in New Zealand. Typically, we do not expect people to pay taxes to two separate jurisdictions.

By now, the "team of five million" and "be kind" slogans had started to lose their sheen. Partly because it was not only me that balked at forcing citizens to pay. The amounts being asked were also substantial. Someone wishing to return to New Zealand had to pay for not only the plane fare (not easy to find and expensive given the disruptions to international travel), but also another US$2000 or so for the quarantine cost for an adult couple; more for those with kids. Overseas citizens were not happy and neither were their resident relatives.

Eventually, the government backed down and decided to create a series of exemptions. The government also made it mandatory that travelers had to apply for and receive quarantine vouchers for a place at one of the approved quarantine facilities before they could get on a flight to New Zealand. This in turn also meant that many New Zealanders were now caught in a sort of purgatory, where they may have lost their jobs overseas but could not return, since they could not procure isolation vouchers as, typically, there were shortages of these.[7]

I have never been one of those who rave and rant about "big government"; about government being the problem and not the solution. I have always believed that the government has a role to play, particularly in situations where markets are not able to handle particular features of the problem; for instance, in dealing with negative externalities such as pollution that affect many others besides the one doing the polluting; or when it is necessary to rein in giant monopolies. However, even I was horrified at the gargantuan bureaucracy that we had implemented. We were now in a situation where a large bureaucracy had to decide who was to pay and who was exempt. Were you returning to New Zealand permanently or temporarily? If permanent, then you are exempt. If temporary, then was it for more or less than 90 days? If more than 90 days then you are exempt; if not then you are not. Did you leave prior to the announcement? If yes, then you are exempt; if not then you are out of luck. If you had to pay, how much did you have to pay? How many people in your traveling team? Did you need one room at the hotel or more? Also, if and when you were placed into isolation, you could request compassionate leave to attend funerals and such. Who should be granted such compassionate leave? On what grounds?

The 37-year-old woman mentioned previously had applied for compassionate leave to attend her husband's funeral and decided to "break out" of isolation only after she had been denied permission. In some instances, when people wished to see dying parents or relatives, exemptions were not made or were made too late to make a difference. The family of an 11-year-old girl who died suddenly wanted to have her funeral in Northland (the northern part of the North Island), but given that they were located in the southern part of the North Island, in order to do so, they had to drive north through the Auckland region. However, Auckland was under a lockdown and so permission was refused initially, until eventually the family was allowed to travel through under police escort.[8]

The only word that came to mind again and again at this vast expansion of the bureaucracy was "Kafkaesque". It is hard to imagine that there were government officials sitting in a building, probably somewhere in Wellington, trying to distinguish between quanta of grief. What exactly were the criteria? Exemption if a parent passed away but not a partner? Exemptions to visit dying parents but not for funerals? Exemptions for funerals but not for weddings? Who got to decide this and how exactly could anyone reasonably make these calls? How do you establish rules for these things? Also, a very large number of people who had working visas for New Zealand were not exempted. This had implications for their own jobs and the prospects of their employers. I have already discussed the plight of the migrant workers earlier and there is little value to reiterating this. I also noted how many New Zealanders were stuck overseas because they could not get the isolation vouchers they needed to get on the plane. Many of them had already booked their plane tickets a while back, before the requirement for isolation vouchers were instituted. Now, they were forced to cancel those tickets with no guarantee when they could travel next.

Again, I hasten to add that this was not the left-of-center government that was so gung-ho; the main opposition party was as well. Indeed, the main opposition party was constantly trying to out-do the government. Any break-outs or breaches of the isolation facilities were touted as evidence of massive government failure. It was not recognized that it was the very nature of the gigantic machinery put in place that breaches were going to occur. Also, a virus is not a terrorist; bottling up the former is vastly more challenging than restricting the latter. The government could have saved themselves an enormous amount of angst simply by saying that they were going to do their best to keep their citizens safe. However, the harsh glare of the global spotlight and the degree of public adulation made it imperative that the government keep doubling down on elimination, which meant every breach was a source of embarrassment and proof of ineptitude.

The main opposition party's primary selling point was that as strict as the government was trying to be, this was nowhere near enough. Even more strict measures were required; the military should have been called in earlier; the government should expand the scope of the isolation facilities and privatize them; everyone must provide evidence of a negative Covid-19 test besides having their quarantine vouchers prior to getting on a plane. Their argument was not that the government was being profligate with taxpayers' money, where it was not at all obvious that the potential benefits were worth the cost, but that the government was not being stringent enough in enforcing border restrictions. This proved to be a less than winning strategy. Faced with a hugely popular and charismatic leader in the form of Jacinda Ardern, who enjoyed high levels of trust and support from the population, the right-of-center opposition party went down to a humiliating defeat in the country's October 2020 general elections.[9]

Now, I know what you are thinking. You are thinking that after lecturing us all this time about the difference between identified lives and statistical lives, he is now pulling a sleight of hand and focusing on identified lives himself. After all, there certainly were lapses and cases that make you feel sad and angry, but was it not all for the greater good? No, it was not.

There was a far more efficacious option: ask people coming into New Zealand to self-isolate at the risk of prosecution if they were found in violation of the protocol; ask them to show up for a three-day and 12-day nasal swab. Engage in contact tracing and then, if and when needed, prosecute those who defied the rules. In the meantime, encourage everyone to wear masks in confined spaces. This would have achieved the same result at a fraction of the cost. However, this was out of the question. As the host of a radio talk-show I appeared on told me with great confidence: the high-trust model does not work. People cannot be expected to self-isolate; they cannot be expected to wear marks assiduously. How can you be so naive to think that people can be trusted? However, this makes perfect sense and there is an enormous amount of research to back it up. I will show you below, how and why.

Following the second lockdown in the Auckland region, the government asked people to wear masks on public transport and in many public spaces. Guess what? They complied. This is hardly surprising since, similar to many Scandinavian countries, New Zealand is also a high-trust society and so it was not surprising to me that New Zealanders complied with this request. Furthermore, back in April 2020, the government was asking everyone to self-isolate, and all evidence suggested that this worked relatively well given the lack of community transmission following our first lockdown. Then, all of a sudden, a few people decide to break out of isolation and people could no longer be trusted. I posit that they broke out specifically because they were being forced into isolation against their wishes. A great deal of this displays a lack of understanding of the human psyche, the role of trust and trustworthiness, and the distinction between extrinsic and intrinsic motivation.

This misunderstanding of human psyche underlay a lot of the mathematical modeling of disease transmission too. Most modelers assumed that unless strong mitigation measures such as lockdowns were put into place, people would go about their business just as before. This is not true. When faced with the prospect of a contagious disease, people will automatically make compensatory changes to their behavior: they will wash their hands more often; they will wear a mask; they will stay home when feeling sick; they will stay away from elderly relatives; they will adopt a whole host of steps and measures that will have a mitigating effect on the disease even if not explicitly instructed by their governments. This is exactly why a 0.65 percent IFR will not turn into more than 2 million dead in the US or similar numbers elsewhere. Government policy can and does make a difference, but not making appropriate allowances for intrinsic human motivation to avert a crisis when required to do so is not reasonable. This is what I turn to next.

* * *

In the mid-1990s, three researchers, Joyce Berg, John Dickhaut and Kevin McCabe at the University of Minnesota, were interested in understanding the role of trust in human interactions. So, they came up with an ingenious game that they named the *investment game* but which has subsequently become popular as the *trust game*. Participants in this game are divided into pairs. One person is the "sender" and the other person the "receiver". Senders and receivers are placed in different rooms, and no one knows who he or she is paired with. Both the sender and the receiver are given US$10. Each sender is then told that he or she can simply keep all of the money, say "Thank you very much" and leave. The game will end if he or she does so, and the sender will get $10 and the receiver will get $10 too. But, if the sender wishes, he or she can send part or all of the $10 to the paired receiver. If the sender sends any money at all, then the experimenter will *triple* that amount and give that tripled amount to the receiver. For instance, if the sender sends $5 to the receiver, then the experimenter will triple that and give $15 to the receiver. Then the receiver is told the following: he or she can keep the entire amount sent to him or her and leave. The game will end at that point. Or if he or she wants, he or she can send some of the tripled amount received back to the paired sender in the other room. The game ends with the receiver's decision – regardless of whether he or she decides to send back any money or not – and any money sent back by the receiver is *not* tripled.

What do you think happens? First, notice that these people are not engaging in "cheap talk". If you say that you trust someone, the experimenters are asking you to put your money where your mouth is. You think you are a trusting person? Okay, here is $10. Why don't you trust a stranger to send money back to you? If you insist that you are a trusting person, then how about you walk the talk?

Before I tell you what happens, think about this. Let us start with the second player's, the receiver's, decision. The receiver has been sent a sum of money (say $5, which has been tripled to $15 by the experimenter), by a sender whom he or she does not know and will most likely never meet again. The receiver knows that the game will end after his or her decision. A self-interested receiver has no incentive to send any money back. If the receiver is sent any amount, then the receiver should simply keep all of it and send nothing back. Now let us put ourselves in the place of the sender. If the sender correctly anticipates the receiver's reaction, that is, the receiver has no incentive to return any money, then it would be foolish to send any money in the first place. By doing so, the sender makes himself or herself vulnerable to being exploited by the receiver and would probably be worse off. This means that both the sender and the receiver should simply hang on to their initial $10 endowment and not engage with one another any further.

However, there is an alternative way to think about this situation. Suppose the sender decides to trust the receiver and sends him or her all of the $10. The $10 gets tripled to $30. Now the sender has nothing while the receiver has $40 (remember both senders and receivers get $10 to start with). Suppose the receiver, knowing full well that he or she can exploit the sender's trust by returning nothing, decides to *reciprocate* the sender's trust by sending back $20. Then the sender ends up with $20 while the receiver ends up with ($40 – $20) = $20 as well. (Or maybe the receiver sends back $18, in which case the sender ends up with $18 and the receiver ends up with ($40 – $18) = $22.) In both of these instances, the sender and the receiver are better off than they would have been if no money had changed hands. If no money changes hands, then both the sender and the receiver make only $10. There are numerous other splits possible. What is worth noting is that in all instances where the sender *trusts* the receiver and the receiver turns out to be *trustworthy* and *reciprocates* the sender's trust, both the sender and the receiver end up with more money than if the sender had not trusted the receiver in the first place.[10]

This game provides an easy way of measuring trust and trustworthiness. It excludes a number of aspects that would characterize transactions in real life, such as communication, word-of-mouth, face-to-face interaction, handshakes and promises, but that is the beauty of this game. It tries to measure trust in a purely abstract way. The factors mentioned above would most likely lead to *increased* trust. If we can document the existence of trust in this very abstract and context-free situation, then we can really claim that trust is a *primitive* in many human transactions. We can always add layers of complexity once we know what happens in the simplest possible (and most abstract) scenario.

Berg and her colleagues recruited 64 participants to take part in this game and divided them into 32 pairs of senders and receivers with each participant getting $10. All decisions taken by senders and receivers were completely anonymous. How did these senders behave? Out of the 32 senders, five senders sent all $10, one sent $8, three sent $7 each, four sent $6 each, six senders sent $5 each and all but two sent positive amounts. Only two out of 32 senders sent nothing; that is, out of 32, only two (about 6 percent) decided not to place any trust in the receiver. Thirty out of 32 senders (94 percent) sent positive amounts and 20 out of 32 senders (63 percent) sent $5 or more. This seemed to suggest that a majority of the senders were willing to place substantial amounts of trust in strangers. Across all 32 senders, the average sent was $5.16, a far cry from the $0 that the untrusting model of human behavior would suggest. If people really cannot be trusted, then why are all these people sending money, willing to trust anonymous strangers even when it means doing so could result in substantial losses? And no, before you make the argument, it is not the small sums involved that make it so. There is massive evidence that this type of behavior persists even if the stake size is multiplied many times.[11]

Is this trust reciprocated? The evidence for this is more diffuse; at least in this first study. Above I noted that there were five receivers who received $30. Of these five, receiver 1 sent back $20. This meant that the sender and the receiver in this pair ended up with exactly $20 each. Receivers 2 and 3 sent back $15. Remember that the receiver got $10 at the beginning of the game. This meant that in each case, the sender in the pair ended up with $15 while the receiver ended up with $25. The receivers made out better than the senders, but the senders still ended up with $5 more – $15 as opposed to $10 – than if they had not trusted the receiver at all. However, two of these trustors were less fortunate and got back a lot less. On average, adding up money not sent and that received back from the receivers, the senders ended up with $9.50. So on average, the senders made less than $10 and would have been better off if they had kept their initial $10. The receivers were certainly better off and made a lot more than $10. So there is a lot of trust, but it seems that it may not pay off all the time.

Berg and her colleagues realized that participants in their study were placed in a relatively novel environment and it might take them a while to work out the appropriate course of action. So they decided to run a second experiment where they recruited 56 participants (28 pairs) who had *not* participated in their first study. Except here, these people were told about what happened in the first study in relation to amounts sent and returned. This should go some ways towards reducing the novelty and uncertainty of the situation and allow participants to make more deliberative decisions. Suppose that, in the first experiment, senders failed to anticipate that the receivers had no incentive to return any money. Then, providing the history of prior plays might make the senders in the second experiment more aware that some of the receivers in the first experiment did not reciprocate, and this may make the senders in the second experiment wary of sending money. Surprisingly (or not surprisingly for those of us who undertake this line of work), participants in this second treatment exhibited higher levels of trust and reciprocity. Only three out of 28 senders (11 percent) sent nothing. On average, the senders here sent $5.36 and ended up earning $11.10 overall, a return of 11 percent on top of the initial endowment of $10. Investments of $5 had an average payback of $7.14 (more than 40 percent return on investment) while investments of $10 had an average payback of $13.17 (13 percent return). As before, the receivers also made more than $10.00 on average. Thus history, instead of teaching participants the folly of being trusting and trustworthy, seemed to have reinforced both of these responses.

Subsequently, a group of researchers led by Andreas Ortmann (currently at the University of New South Wales) showed that this trusting and trustworthy behavior is not impacted by various different ways of presenting the information or asking questions such as (a) *How much money do you think you will send?* (b) *How much money do you think will be returned to you?* (c) *How much money would you return if you were the receiver?* In the words of Ralph Waldo Emerson (and excusing the sexism): "*Trust men and they will be true to you; treat them greatly and they will show themselves great.*"

DOES TRUST PAY?

An astute reader may be thinking: well, it is clear that a lot of people are willing to trust, but it is not so clear that this trust really pays. After all, it seems that on average the senders are either not better off (end up making less than $10) or even if better off, not by much (10 percent or so). Is this enough evidence that trust pays? It turns out that the answer is yes. First, it is important to understand that as with many other similar studies, the original Berg, Dickhaut and McCabe study never used words such as "trust" and "reciprocity". Instructions to the participants are always couched in neutral terms. For example, senders are told that they can choose to *transfer* money to another person if they so wished. If they did transfer a positive amount, then this amount will be tripled and given to the paired receiver. The latter then has the choice of keeping that entire amount or returning some or all of it to the paired sender. However, we know already that framing and context matter. One way such framing may matter is that when asked to take part in a game such as this and provided instructions are written in neutral and non-emotive terms, it is not clear that all the participants interpret the game in the same way as everyone else. Also, although the experimenter may think of this game as measuring trust and reciprocity, perhaps the participants interpret the game in a totally different way.

Lee Cronk, an anthropologist at Rutgers University, looks at these framing effects in the Berg et al. trust game played by Maa-speaking pastoralist Maasai in Kenya. In a control treatment, subjects play the game with neutral instructions. The experimental treatment utilizes a framing that invokes *osotua*, which literally means umbilical cord but refers to "gift-giving relationships based on obligation, need, respect and restraint". The results suggest that compared to games with neutral framing, in the *osotua* frame, there is reduced trust (measured by average amount sent by senders) and reciprocity (measured by average proportion returned by receivers).[12] Senders also expect lower returns in the *osotua* frame. Cronk suggests that the *osotua* framing seems to have shifted gameplay away from the logic of investing and towards mutual obligations to respond to genuine needs. Since the perceived need is assessed to be less in the framed game, transfers are also lower.

Together with my students, Sherry Li and Tirnud Paichayontvijit, I look at a different form of framing by making sure that all the participants interpret the game the same way and that their interpretation coincides with that of the experimenter. We do this by changing the standard instructions and explaining the incentives of the game to the participants in the following way:

> Paragraph 1: One way to think about this situation is as follows: the receiver has no incentive to send any money back to the sender because the round ends immediately after that. Anticipating that, the sender should hang on to his/her $10.00 and send nothing to the receiver. This means they will both end the round with $10.00 each.

> Paragraph 2: But suppose the sender decides to transfer $10.00 to the receiver. Then the receiver will get $30.00. If the receiver sends back an amount more than $10.00 then it is easy to see that both the sender and the receiver can make more money than if they simply hung on to their $10.00 in each and every round.

We implement multiple different treatments each making incremental changes. For example, in some treatments we provide an explanation of the game but replace words such as "trust" with words such as "transfer". In others, we reverse the order of the two paragraphs so that, at times, the arguments about the benefits of trusting appear first, while in others, it appears second. There are also baseline treatments where no explanation is provided. Did trust pay? Across the different treatments where participants were provided with an explanation of the game, the amount transferred shifted towards showing complete trust; that is, towards sending all $10. On average, senders earned returns of 16 percent, with returns ranging from 14 percent to 28 percent. This suggests that when the underlying contingencies implicit in the transaction are made clear to subjects, and all participants interpret the game in the same way and this interpretation coincides with that of the experimenter, trust does pay.

IS A TRUSTING DECISION ANALOGOUS TO A RISKY DECISION?

Anytime the sender in the investment game decides to place trust in the receiver, he or she is implicitly taking a chance. There is a chance that the recipient of that trust will turn out to be trustworthy and repay that trust, making both parties to the transaction better off, but there is also a chance that the receiver will renege and keep the entire amount, leaving the trustor worse off than if he or she had not trusted at all. Thus, the decision to trust *may* be thought of as being similar to buying a lottery ticket. With some chance, you will make a lot of money, but with some chance, you will earn nothing and lose the amount you spent buying the ticket(s). Do people who are confronted with a situation where they have to place their trust in a stranger behave as if they are buying a lottery ticket? The answer turns out to be in the negative. The mental algorithm that is called upon when asked to place trust in a stranger is different from that which is called upon when people buy a lottery ticket.

How can we go about testing to see if senders make a distinction between trust and risk in making their decisions? A group of researchers led by Ernst Fehr of the University of Zurich adopted a novel approach.[13] Each sender in their game has $12 each and can choose to send $0, $4, $8 or all $12 to a paired receiver. This amount is tripled, which means that the receiver will get $0, $12, $24 or $36, respectively. The receiver can then send back any amount up to the maximum received. For instance, if the sender sends $8, then the receiver gets $24 and he or she can return any amount between $0 and $24. In a second treatment, the sender faces the same choices as in the investment game except a random mechanism, rather than a human being, decides how much money the sender will get back. Thus, this second treatment is analogous to participating in a lottery, with good and bad outcomes both possible.

Here is the novel part of this study. In both the trust game as well as the lottery-choice game, some of the participants receive a single intranasal dose of oxytocin while the rest receive a placebo. Oxytocin is a neuropeptide which plays a central role in social interactions. In addition to its well-known physiological functions in milk-letdown in mothers, oxytocin receptors are distributed in various brain regions associated with pair-bonding, maternal care, sexual behavior and the ability to form normal social attachments. Oxytocin has at times been referred to as the "hug hormone" or the "moral molecule".[14]

There are 58 senders in the trust game, half of them (29) were administered oxytocin while the other half received a placebo. The data show that oxytocin increases senders' trust considerably. Out of the 29 senders who received oxytocin, 13 (45 percent) showed maximal trust by sending their entire endowment to the paired receiver.

However, in the placebo group, only six out of 29 (21 percent) did so. The average transfer in the oxytocin group is $9.60, which is significantly higher than that in the placebo group ($8.10). The median transfer in the oxytocin group is $10 while the median for the placebo group is $8. No similar difference is seen in the lottery-choice game; both the oxytocin group and placebo group behave similarly. The average or median amount sent by those in the oxytocin group is no different to that sent by the participants in the placebo group. Thus, administration of oxytocin leads to increased trust in the trust game but does not affect behavior in the lottery-choice game, suggesting, yet again, that the decision to trust is fundamentally different from the decision to accept a risky gamble.

Catherine Eckel of Texas A&M and Rick Wilson of Rice compare behavior in the trust game with other responses designed to mimic decision-making under risk. One measure is the Zuckerman Sensation Seeking Scale, which asks participants to choose their preferred alternative from a pair of statements about risky activities. For example, one pair of statements is:

Option 1:   *skiing down a high mountain slope is a good way to end up on crutches*; or

Option 2:   *I think I would enjoy the sensations of skiing very fast down a high mountain slope.*

Participants also make choices in a series of lotteries that vary in their mean and variance. What Eckel and Wilson find is that none of the risk measures (neither the Zuckerman Sensation Seeking Scale nor the lottery choices) have any significant correlation with the decision to send money in the trust game (that is, the decision to trust). While it seems to be a logical inference that the decision to trust a stranger may be caused by the same mental processes that induce people to engage in risky gambles, the results presented above suggest that the decision to trust is fundamentally different from making choices under risk.

The insights from this chapter can be summed up in the following anecdote told by Robyn Dawes (of Carnegie Mellon) and Richard Thaler (of Chicago):

In the rural areas around Ithaca it is common for farmers to put some fresh produce on the table by the road. There is a cash-box on the table, and customers are expected to put money in the box in return for vegetables they take. The box has just a small slit, so money can only be put in, not taken out. Also, the box is attached to the table, so no one can (easily) make off with the money. We think that the farmers have just about the right model of human nature. They feel that enough people will volunteer to pay for the fresh corn to make it worthwhile to put it out there. The farmers also know that if it were easy enough to take the money, someone would do so.

Faced with a request from their government, most people will comply; they will wear a mask or other personal protective equipment; they will engage in physical distancing as far as practicable. Some will flout the rules. But they are likely to be a small minority. If and when this happens, the rule-flouters can and should be punished, but to design a gigantic government bureaucracy on the belief that everyone will violate rules unless compelled to follow them on fear of punishment is just not borne out by the evidence.

DOES THIS WORK IN REAL LIFE?

Yes, it does. In 2015, Afzaal Deewan and his partner Natalie, set up the restaurant Der Wiener Deewan, serving buffet-style Pakistani food in Vienna.[15] The restaurant came with a twist. The owners decided to do away with prices. Instead, their motto was "*eat all you want, pay as you wish*". At the conclusion of the meal, patrons can pay based on what they thought their meal was worth. Self-interest would suggest that unless there are people who live close by and intend to engage in repeat business, many others, particularly visitors to the city who are unlikely to go back, should eat a lot and only pay a small amount. Soon, the restaurant should be struggling. However, contrary to what we may think, the restaurant has been thriving.

EXTRINSIC INCENTIVES CAN CROWD OUT INTRINSIC MOTIVATIONS

The idea that human beings can be relied on to do the right thing comes from the work of Edward Deci of the University of Rochester and

Richard Ryan of the Australian Catholic University and the University of Rochester (quite a bit of this in conjunction with Richard Koestner of McGill University). This line of work is known as "cognitive evaluation theory", which arose out of a larger body of work in psychology known as "self-determination theory" first explored in the 1970s. To an extent, self-determination theory came about as an oppositional response to the emphasis on behaviorism in the early part of the twentieth century. Most readers will be aware that a key assumption of behaviorism is that human (or even non-human) behavior can be modified by rewarding desirable behavior and/or punishing undesirable behavior (often known as "operant conditioning").[16]

Deci and Ryan proposed that intrinsic motivations are powerful enough, and excessive reliance on external rewards and punishments may even be counter-productive and make people less inclined to follow the rules. Three crucial features of this intrinsic motivation that Deci and his collaborators highlighted are autonomy, competence and relatedness; related concepts that emphasize to what extent people have control over their own destiny. The importance of these in the context of government exhortation to follow instructions is obvious. Do we trust people to follow instructions to self-isolate or do we force them into compulsory managed isolation? Do we trust them to wear protective gear or fine and prosecute them for every infraction? When we talk about being part of a team and doing what is right, do we then back up those words with actions or do we pass and/or enforce laws that severely curtail personal autonomy? If and when we rely excessively on external rewards and punishments it is not surprising that there may be a backlash. People may well be willing to engage in voluntary self-isolation when they feel a large degree of autonomy. When those same people are forced to endure compulsory isolation, at moments of bereavement and personal trauma, people feel they are no longer in control of their own lives. This is where the external cues have completely crowded out any intrinsic desire to do the right thing.

In an early study, Deci asked a group of college students to work on solving puzzles. Half of the group were paid and the other half not, but the payment was not conditional on them solving puzzles. Deci found that the unpaid group kept working on the puzzles for much longer than did the students who were paid.

We met Mark Lepper of Stanford University in an earlier chapter, where I wrote about his work on the confirmation bias. Lepper teamed up with David Greene of the University of Northern Colorado and Richard Nisbett of the University of Michigan to look at behavior of children. They asked preschool-aged children to take part in a drawing activity. The children were divided into three groups. One group was told that they would get a certificate at the end of the activity. A second group also received the same certificate but were unaware of this beforehand. The certificate came as a surprise to them. A third group received no reward. Lepper and his colleagues find that children who were told about the reward beforehand and therefore expected to receive the reward for undertaking the task were significantly less interested in continuing the activity, whereas the children in the other two groups continued to engage in the activity for a much longer period.

* * *

Situations involving trust and reciprocity arise in myriad contexts in day-to-day life, often in employment relationships. Many, if not most, employment relationships give rise to what is known as an "agency problem". An owner of a café, a bar or a retail business has hired a manager to run his or her business. The owner pays the manager a fixed salary that is independent of the profit earned from the business. The owner wishes the place to do well and make a big profit. In order to do so, the manager needs to work hard. But if the manager does not receive a share of the profit generated by the business, then the manager does not have much of an *extrinsic incentive* to work hard. Extrinsic incentive is when the manager is materially not better off even if the business does well, since the manager does not share in any of the profit. The manager may still work hard as a result of *intrinsic incentive*. Intrinsic incentive is when the manager works hard because it is the right thing to do, otherwise the manager will feel guilty. It is important for the manager to work hard so that he or she can feel the satisfaction of having completed a good job. These latter motivations are referred to as intrinsic motivations, since they are internal; they come from within us and are not extrinsic, that is, not driven by external carrots and/or sticks.

In saying that the high-trust model does not work, the worldview of the talk-show host (and many others) is that, left to themselves, people will do what is in their self-interest. That is, the managers of the world will slack off and not work hard. This view says that intrinsic motivation is worthless and, in order to make people do the right thing, they need to be compelled in some form or the other. Often, this may be carrots (rewards), such as merit increases, bonuses, promotions or at least a pat on the back (in the form of an "Employee of the Month" plaque on the store wall). However, equally often, this can be guaranteed by sticks, such as fines, penalties and punishments for violating the prevailing rule or norm. In sentencing the woman for violating quarantine to attend her husband's funeral, the judge was not merely punishing her for rule-breaking. He was also making an example of her, for her supposed selfishness, so that others got the message. If you break our rules, we will impose harsh penalties on you. This view of humanity is unduly cynical and misguided.

Many of us donate blood and undertake sundry other acts of charity. Why? What is in it for us? We do this not for the money or the glory but because it makes us feel good, gives us a warm glow of having done something good, something that will help someone else. Is there some vanity involved? Possibly, but that is not the entirety of the story since there are many other easier ways of stoking our vanities than parting with a pint of blood. This behavior is primarily driven by intrinsic motivation. However, suppose you believe that intrinsic motivation is all hokum and no one does anything unless compelled to do so. Then there is an obvious answer in order to get people to donate. How about offering to pay people to donate blood? As Richard Titmuss (1907–1973) of the London School of Economics argued, paying people to donate blood turns out to be highly counterproductive and leads to fewer people donating blood. Why? This is because here is a situation where the extrinsic incentive crowds out the intrinsic incentive. I was donating blood because it gave me a warm glow. But now that donating blood is being reimbursed, maybe others will think that I am donating blood for the money, even if I turn this money down. All of a sudden, my motives do not appear so lofty any more or, even if they are, others may not think so.[17]

This attitude of mistrust, in turn, leads to the following dictum: *employment relationships must be governed by explicit contracts which are incentive compatible, meaning that they must clearly specify the incentives involving the rewards for performing well and the punishments for performing poorly.* In the absence of a well-designed, incentive-compatible contract providing both carrots and sticks, employees have no incentive to work hard and will inevitably shirk, leading to lower profits for the owner. However, a great deal of evidence suggests that we are over-emphasizing the need for explicit incentives. Often a system relying on the mutual trust and reciprocity between owners and workers (or governments and citizens) performs as well as, if not much better than, a system based on explicit rewards and punishments.

GIFT EXCHANGE IN EMPLOYMENT RELATIONSHIPS

In the mid-1950s, the sociologist George Homans looked at the behavior of "cash posters" at Eastern Utilities, located on the east coast of the United States. Homans studied a group of ten young women whose job was to record customers' payments on ledger cards at the time of receipt. The company's policy for this cash posting was 300 per hour. Careful records were kept of the speed at which various workers worked, and those who fell below the quota received a mild rebuke from the supervisor. Homans found that the average number of cash postings per hour was 353, 18 percent greater than the required number set by the employer.

Theories of human behavior that proceed from the assumption of mistrust and the need for external carrots and/or sticks have a hard time explaining why (1) the faster cash posters did not reduce their speed to just meet the required standard of 300 and (2) the firm did not increase the speed expected of the faster workers? All cash posters were paid the same hourly wage rate and it was not that the faster workers could expect to earn more in the form of performance bonuses. Since the hourly wage was fixed and did not depend on effort, and the reward of future promotions was rarely a consideration, the mistrust theory suggests that the workers should adjust their work habits to just meet the quality standard set by the company. However, it was obvious that the workers were putting in effort far in excess of what was expected of them.

This led George Akerlof (who shared the Nobel Prize in Economics with Joseph Stiglitz in 2001) to propose a new model of employment relationships based on "gift exchange" between the employer and the employee. According to Akerlof, as part of their interactions, employees acquire sentiments for each other and for the firm. As a consequence of sentiment for the firm, the workers derive utility (satisfaction) from an exchange of "gifts" with the firm where the level of satisfaction depends on the norm of gift exchange. On the workers' side, the gift given is work in excess of the minimum work standard; on the firm's side, the gift given is wages in excess of what these women could receive if they left their current jobs.

* * *

While there seems to be ample evidence to support Akerlof's idea of gift exchange, such as the Homans study of cash posters at Eastern Utilities, still, these are non-replicable one-off observations. Ernst Fehr at the University of Zurich together with his collaborators, Simon Gächter, Urs Fischbacher, Georg Kirchsteiger and Arno Riedl, among others, set off on an ambitious research project to test the validity of the gift-exchange model in employment relationships using a series of well-crafted experiments.[18] Once again, the big advantage to these experiments was that Fehr and his associates could change the experimental design in a number of ways to understand what the impact is on behavior. This allows for teasing out the effects of various causal factors on the efficacy of employment contracts.

Fehr and his associates examine these issues at length using a variety of different setups, which, however, share some common features. The idea is to look at an employment relationship between firms and workers that rely on either extrinsic incentives or intrinsic incentives. Participants are assigned to the role of a firm or a worker at the beginning of the session and these roles remain unchanged for the entire time. The worker needs to expend effort to generate revenue. Effort imposes costs on the worker. The higher the effort, the greater the revenue generated. Higher effort also imposes a larger cost on the worker. The firm receives the revenue. The worker is paid a wage. The firm's profit is the difference between the revenue that it earns and the wage that it pays the worker. The worker's profit is the difference between the wage and the cost of his or her effort. It is important to understand that the effort involved here is not real effort, in that the employee is not doing actual work. All of this is implemented via the concept of imputed cost, discussed previously. Any given level of effort has an associated cost, which is explained to the worker, and when the worker puts in a particular level of effort, then he or she incurs that associated imputed cost.

The firm is better off the higher the effort put in by the worker, since that generates higher revenue for the firm. However, since effort is costly, putting in more effort imposes a larger cost on the worker; therefore, if he or she is paid a fixed amount of money for his or her effort, then the worker is better off putting in low effort. Thus, there is a dichotomy between the goals of the firm and those of the worker. The firm wants the worker to work hard and put in a lot of effort, which will create more revenue. The worker has little incentive to do so if he or she is paid a fixed amount, and should put in the smallest amount of effort that he or she can get away with (one that will not get him or her fired from the job).

The intrinsic incentive-based employment contract is simple. The employer offers to pay the worker a wage and asks the worker to put in a certain amount of effort. There is no enforcement whatsoever. If the worker accepts the wage then he or she is free to put in any effort level he or she wants, not the effort the employer requested. So, in offering a particular wage and asking for a given effort, the employer is implicitly trusting the worker to put in that effort.

The extrinsic incentive system allows the employer to explicitly monitor the worker on top of paying a wage. (Think of closed circuit television (CCTV) cameras.) If and when the worker shirks and is discovered shirking, the employer can impose a penalty on the shirking worker. Shirking is not caught with certainty. The idea is that the worker may shirk but this may not always be picked up by the CCTV cameras and so cannot be held against the employee in that case. The employer may have his or her suspicions but is not able to prove it.

If we adopt the viewpoint that trust does not pay, then the former intrinsic motivation-based employment relationship should lead to massive amounts of shirking. None of the workers should put in much effort. This, in turn, should generate very little revenue for the employer. In order to elicit effort, we must rely on the second type of employment contract that specifies explicit penalties for shirking. This means that effort and profit should be much higher in the second, penalty-based, employment contract.

The other common feature of this line of work is that in most situations, there are more workers than there are employers, that is, some of the workers will be left unemployed and not be able to earn any money. The employers have market power and they can afford to pay relatively lower wages to the workers because if a worker does not accept this wage, then his or her alternative is to be unemployed.

By now you probably have an idea of where this is headed. The results are strongly supportive of the gift-exchange model. The researchers find that even in the absence of any explicit enforcement mechanism, on average, firms offer wages which are considerably higher than the market clearing wage even though they do not have to, especially in light of there being more workers than jobs and therefore workers should be willing to work for relatively low wages. Workers, in turn, respond with effort levels which are much higher than the minimal level of effort.

Furthermore, Fehr and his colleagues find that, on average, worker effort increases in line with the wage offered; that is, when the firms offered the workers a higher wage (which is analogous to a trusting move, since the worker can simply take the wage and put in the lowest possible effort in return), the workers reciprocated with higher effort levels. In the intrinsic incentive-based employment relationships, firms offer higher wages and ask for higher effort from the workers compared with the situation where the worker can be penalized for shirking. Further, the average effort level put in by the workers under the contract with monitoring is lower than that put in by the workers in the trust contract. This finding is driven by the evidence that even with explicit fines for non-compliance, a number of workers shirk given that the monitoring technology is imperfect and does not catch shirking with 100 percent accuracy.

Finally, what is striking is that in the extrinsic incentive system, once we net out the cost of some workers shirking (given the less than certainty of getting caught) as well as the cost of installing the monitoring technology, the employers' profits are *lower* than the situation where the employer chooses to trust the employee. Fehr and his associates go on to argue that such high-wage/high-effort strategies are better from the point of view of both the firms and workers, and that mutual trust and reciprocity between firms and workers lead to better outcomes for them. Fehr and his collaborators comment: "exclusive reliance on selfishness and, in particular, the neglect of reciprocity motives may lead to wrong predictions and to wrong normative inferences".

* * *

Additional evidence about the downside of extrinsic incentives comes from further work by Ernst Fehr, this time in collaboration with Bettina Rockenbach. Two hundred and thirty-eight participants were divided into sender–receiver pairs and asked to play the trust game devised by Joyce Berg and her colleagues. The sender and the receiver have $10 each. The sender can send any or all of this $10 to the receiver. Any amount sent to the receiver is tripled by the experimenter. The receiver is then given the option of keeping all the money given to him or her, or sending some back to the sender. The game ends at that point. However, Fehr and Rockenbach add a twist to the game. They ask each sender to specify a "back transfer". The sender, if and when sending money to the receiver, can ask the latter to send back a specific proportion of the tripled amount. For instance, suppose the sender sends $5. In that instance the receiver would be given $15. Then the sender can specify a back transfer of any amount between $0 and $15 (that is, any amount less than or equal to the maximum amount received by the receiver). For instance, the sender could say that I want the receiver to send back $8 out of the $15 that the receiver will get.

Fehr and Rockenbach look at a *trust treatment* and a *penalty treatment*. In the trust treatment, the receiver is under no compulsion to adhere to the sender's desired back transfer and can return any amount, which can be less than what the sender asked for. In the penalty treatment, in addition to specifying a desired back transfer, the sender has a punishment option. If the sender so chooses, he or she can impose a fine of $4 on the receiver if the receiver returns an amount which is less than what the sender asked for. However, the sender can decide not to impose the fine, even though the option is there.

Surprisingly, across all transfers by the sender, the receivers return more money *when the sender had the option of imposing a fine but chose not to do so*, and the receivers return much less when *the sender imposes the fine at the outset*. On average, the receivers return 41 percent of the tripled amount received in the trust treatment (where no fine is available to the sender), 30 percent of the tripled amount in the incentive treatment where the sender chooses to impose the fine and *48 percent of the tripled amount when the sender could have imposed the fine but chose not to do so*.

Let me assure you that none of this is dependent on the fact that these games do not involve real effort. Plenty of researchers have tried out replications using both cognitive and physical effort. Cognitive effort is where participants have to undertake mental work, such as solving complex mathematical problems. Physical effort involves, for example, cataloguing library books, typing sentences, stuffing envelopes, finding mistakes in typed sheets or raising money for charity. John List of Chicago and Uri Gneezy of University of California San Diego show that even when it comes to physical effort, as described above, the basic results remain unchanged. Relationships based on mutual trust and reciprocity outdo those based on enforcement. I have done work with collaborators (Tony So, Paul Brown, Linda Cameron and Dmitry Ryvkin) showing a similar result for cognitively challenging mathematical tasks, where the right answer is hard to find and the idea is to see whether people can come close to the correct answer. (Think people throwing darts and trying to come as close to the bull's eye as possible and getting rewarded or penalized for how close to or far away from the target they are.) We find that performance-dependent payment schemes are not necessarily better at motivating people to get closer to the correct answer. Andrew Schotter of New York University and Antonio Merlo of the University of Pennsylvania show that this result can be partially explained as follows. When payment is performance dependent (extrinsically motivated), we often tend to adopt a more myopic focus of whether we are winning or losing. For tasks that are cognitively challenging, this myopic focus can be detrimental to learning about the core aspects of the task. At times, intrinsic motivation facilitates better performance of these tasks since it allows us to adopt a broader perspective.

There is a key lesson here that everyone ignores. The enforcement technology and the MIQ facilities may lead to fewer people breaking out, but when you look at it from the viewpoint of social welfare, you need to subtract the cost of implementing this enforcement mechanism. When you do that, the costs no longer outweigh the benefits; society as a whole is worse off. You have wasted a large amount of taxpayers' money with minimal returns. You are far better off trusting people, assuming that most of them will repay that trust. Then you can go after the minority who will flout the rules. This is a far more cost-effective and humane system.

FROM THE LAB TO SILICON VALLEY

James Baron and Michael Hannan of Stanford University and Diane Burton of the Massachusetts Institute of Technology, working under the aegis of the Stanford Project on Emerging Companies (SPEC), examine the impact of organizational practices on employee turnover in a sample of high-technology startups in California's Silicon Valley. Baron and his colleagues ask the question: given that different high-technology startups in Silicon Valley seem to have implemented distinctive types of contractual relationships between the owner(s) and the workers, what are the implications of these human resource practices on the propensity of employees to quit? Baron and his colleagues trained MBA and doctoral students to conduct semi-structured interviews with the chief executive officers or chief finance officers (CEOs/CFOs) of 173 firms with at least ten workers.

Based on their extensive surveys and interviews, the researchers classify the organizational structures of the high-technology startups into two broad models (albeit with some degree of overlap between them): (1) *the commitment model*, which entails reliance on emotional-familial relationships based on mutual trust and reciprocity between management and workers and among workers themselves; (2) *the autocracy/bureaucracy model*, which emphasizes monetary considerations but also greater control and coordination through close personal oversight of line managers.

The commitment model most closely resembles the gift-exchange model we discussed previously, while the autocracy/bureaucracy model relies primarily on explicit rewards/punishments. If you accept the tenet that it is essential to provide workers with extrinsic motivations in order for them to put in high effort, then the organizations relying on the commitment model should perform worse than the others.

What Baron and his colleagues find is that firms whose CEOs/CFOs rely on the autocratic/bureaucratic model experience far greater turnover than the firms which implement the commitment model. How about firm profitability? Given that young high-technology startups incur significant setup costs which might dampen profitability at least initially, a better measure of success is revenue growth. Baron and his colleagues find that there is a strong negative relationship between employee turnover and revenue growth, implying that firms which experience excessive labor turnover (such as those relying on extrinsic motivation and the autocracy/bureaucracy model) also experience much slower revenue growth compared with firms which rely on the commitment model.

FURTHER IMPLICATIONS OF TRUST AND INTRINSIC INCENTIVES

Bruno Frey and Felix Oberholzer-Gee at the University of Zurich look at people's responses to what are termed NIMBY (not in my backyard) problems. This refers to a community's willingness, or lack thereof, to accept the location of noxious or undesirable facilities (such as nuclear power plants, prisons, airports, electrical pylons and chemical factories) in their neighborhoods. One response by governmental agencies is to offer financial compensation to communities in return for their willingness to accept these facilities. Frey and Oberholzer-Gee argue that in some cases, offering monetary payments may be counter-productive because they crowd out any intrinsic motivation that the community may have felt in accepting the facility. Consequently, monetary incentives may become less effective and, in some instances, may lead to a lower willingness to accept the facility in question.

Working with a professional survey company in 1993, Frey and Oberholzer-Gee first asked respondents about the location of a nuclear waste facility in their locality. 51 percent of respondents said that they would vote in favor of having the nuclear waste repository in their community, 45 percent opposed the facility, while 4 percent did not care. Next, the researchers repeated the exact same question asking the respondents whether they would be willing to accept the construction of a nuclear waste repository if the Swiss Parliament offered to compensate the residents of the community. Surprisingly, while 51 percent of the respondents agreed to accept the nuclear waste repository when no compensation was offered, the level of acceptance dropped to 25 percent when compensation was offered. Everyone who rejected the first compensation was then made a better offer raising the amounts offered significantly. Despite this marked increase, only a single respondent who declined the first compensation was now prepared to accept the higher offer.

These findings are not unique to Switzerland. Howard Kunreuther and Douglas Easterling carried out a similar survey regarding the location of a nuclear waste facility in Nevada, USA, and found that increased tax rebates failed to elicit increased support for such a facility. Other researchers have reported similar findings; that support for noxious facilities often decline when people are offered compensation.

One possibility as to why citizens' acceptance levels decline when offered compensation is that the offer of a generous compensation might be taken as an indication that the facility is more hazardous than they previously thought. A higher compensation, then, might indicate higher risk associated with the facility, which in turn leads to a lower level of acceptance. Frey and Oberholzer-Gee test this by directly asking respondents whether they perceived a link between the size of the compensation and the level of risk. Only 6 percent agreed with this connection, which indicates that it is not the perception of higher risk with higher compensation that is driving these responses.

INTRINSIC MOTIVATIONS, SUSTAINABILITY AND CLIMATE CHANGE

While Frey and Oberholzer-Gee use surveys, Juan Camilo Cardenas (of the Universidad Javeriana), and John Stranlund and Cleve Willis (of the University of Massachusetts, Amherst) provide behavioral evidence of the same phenomenon. Cardenas and his colleagues carried out their experiments in three rural villages in Colombia. Their experiments were designed to approximate an environmental quality problem that villagers in developing countries routinely face.

Specifically, participants were asked to decide how much time they would spend collecting firewood from a surrounding forest, given that the collection of firewood has an adverse effect on the water quality of the region owing to soil erosion. Next, the researchers confront their participants with a government-imposed quota on the amount of time that can be spent collecting firewood. The quota, however, is enforced imperfectly, in that there is only a small chance that someone exceeding the quota would be detected and punished, which is typical of these command-and-control environmental problems. This poses what is often termed a "social dilemma". Collectively, everyone is better off if everyone abides by the quota, but as long as everyone else obeys the quota, then one individual can make himself or herself better off by collecting more than the quota, since increased collection by one individual does not make a big difference. So it is in each individual's self-interest to exceed the quota. However, if it makes sense for one person to exceed the quota, then it is rational for everyone to do so. In that case, everyone exceeds the quota and, collectively, everyone is worse off.

These social dilemmas are commonplace. All countries are better off if we all abide by limits on our greenhouse gas emissions. If every other country is doing their best to minimize emissions, it does not make a big difference if one country emits more than it should. So, individual self-interest dictates that each country has an incentive to emit more. However, if one emits more, then it is in the interest of everyone to do so. Therefore, every country emits more and collectively we are all worse off.

This tension between cooperating for the common good and behaving in our self-interest is captured eloquently by Joseph Heller in the following passage from *Catch-22*. Here, the book's intrepid hero Yossarian is talking with Major Major Major Major:[19]

> "Suppose we let you pick your missions and fly milk runs," Major Major said. "That way you can fly the four missions and not run any risks."
> "I don't want to fly milk runs. I don't want to be in the war anymore."
> "Would you like to see our country lose?" Major Major asked.
> "We won't lose. We've got more men, more money and more material. There are ten million people in uniform who can replace me. Some people are getting killed and a lot more are making money and having fun. Let somebody else get killed."
> "But suppose everybody on our side felt that way."
> "Then I'd certainly be a damned fool to feel any other way. Wouldn't I?"

For the sake of the country and the war effort, these soldiers need to be willing to fly missions but, individually, most do not wish to fly these dangerous missions over enemy territory, particularly because Colonel Cathcart keeps raising the number of missions they must fly to meet their quota. Everybody refusing to fly missions is the least desirable outcome in this case – at least from Major Major's and the country's perspective – but if one person does not fly missions while others do, then the person not flying is better off, and eventually, the others will stop flying as well.

In the Cardenas et al. study, the participants are confronted by a social dilemma very similar to those they face in their day-to-day lives. Collect more firewood in our self-interest or abide by the quota which is good for the collective? What Cardenas and his colleagues find is that the outcome, in time spent collecting firewood, was worse in the presence of the imperfectly enforced government-imposed regulation, because when confronted with the external regulation, the behavior of the participants became significantly more self-interested, while in the absence of any regulatory control, their choices were more group orientated. When there is no regulation, but participants are allowed to communicate with group members between rounds, individuals make more efficient choices, that is, choices that generate more social welfare. Cardenas, Stranlund and Willis suggest that recognizing this trade-off between self-interested and group-regarding behavior can have profound implications for many social dilemmas including environmental policy design and evaluation.

Work by Elinor Ostrom (1933–2012) and her colleagues associated with the "Workshop in Political Theory and Policy Analysis" at Indiana University corroborate these findings on the basis of thousands of written cases about irrigation systems in Nepal.[20] Some of these are managed by government agencies (agency-managed irrigation systems, AMIS) while some are managed by the farmers (farmer-managed irrigation systems, FMIS). Ostrom and her colleagues find that compared with AMIS, FMIS are able to achieve a higher agricultural yield, more equitable distribution of water and better maintenance of the irrigation systems. There are striking differences in the way the two systems are managed. Under AMIS, infractions are recorded by government officials, while under FMIS, they are recorded by the farmer-monitors. Furthermore, the AMIS tend to rely more on fines for infractions than do the FMIS. Rules and quotas are followed 65 percent of the time in FMIS compared with only 35 percent of the time in AMIS. Thus, rules and sanctions designed by the farmers themselves tend to be more effective than those imposed by government officials.

TRUST IN ACTION: THE GRAMEEN BANK EXPERIENCE

A pervasive problem in less developed countries (or even for the less well-off in some developed countries) is the lack of credit; that is, an inability to borrow money to finance entrepreneurial activities. Let me stick with the problems of the less developed world for now. In rural areas of these countries, there are people who are engaged in agriculture or handicrafts and often work for others for a pittance. Some of them might be able to work on their own; till their own land or start their own basket-weaving or wood-carving enterprise. These activities, however, require some startup money, which is very small but still pose a significant barrier. Formal banks are unwilling to lend money to them because of a lack of collateral.

The recourse is often to borrow money from local moneylenders at exorbitant interest rates, sometimes landing the borrower into lifelong debt. It is easy to see why the banks are reluctant to lend money to the rural poor; it is difficult to monitor these loans. The bank manager is not well placed to corroborate whether a loan default is owing to pestilence or a natural event beyond the borrower's control, or whether the borrower spent the money somewhere else. As a consequence, default rates can be high and many rural credit schemes have a poor track record of loan recovery. Economists had been aware of this problem faced by the rural poor but the first truly innovative solution was offered by an enterprising economist named Muhammad Yunus, who in the early 1980s started an enterprise named *Grameen Bank* (or *Rural Bank*; *grameen* means rural in Bangla, the language spoken in Bangladesh).

The Grameen Bank makes small loans to the rural poor without requiring any collateral. Borrowers must belong to a "solidarity group", typically consisting of five members. One member of the group receives a loan and must repay it before another member can receive a loan. The group is not required to pledge any collateral. Repayment responsibility rests solely on the individual borrower, while the group's job is to ensure that the borrower behaves in a responsible way. The system relies on two principles: (1) *peer monitoring*, where members of the group who live in the same village monitor the debtor and make sure that the money is spent appropriately; and

(2) *mutual trust and reciprocity* between the bank and the borrowers, on the one hand, and between the group members, on the other hand.

Grameen Bank's track record has been notable, with loan repayment rates of close to 100 percent. More than half of its borrowers in Bangladesh (close to 50 million) have risen out of acute poverty thanks to these loans. In 2006, Muhammad Yunus and the Grameen Bank together were the recipient of a Nobel Prize "for their efforts to create economic and social development from below".

* * *

In the preceding pages, I have tried to convince you that the model of humanity which proceeds on the basis of mistrust is not accurate. It is far easier to trust people and then pursue the minority of rule violators than it is to implement expensive and labyrinthine mechanisms for enforcing compliance. In the words of Lin Ostrom, covenants do not always need swords to be enforced; sometimes appeals to human goodwill achieve the same goals at much lower cost to society.

Appeals to human goodwill may not be costless, but it is not a stretch to suggest that any of these costs – monetary, psychological and/or societal – would be considerably less than those associated with punishments. Antanas Mockus, ex-Mayor of Bogota, Colombia, provides an argument along these lines in an op-ed article in the *New York Times*. Mockus argued that we need to dispense with the model by which, in order to attain compliance, we need to resort to elaborate enforcement mechanisms.

> As a professor of philosophy, I had little patience with conventional wisdom. ... Bogotá's traffic was chaotic and dangerous when I came to office. We decided the city needed a radical new approach to traffic safety. Among various strategies, we printed and distributed hundreds of thousands of "citizens' cards", which had a thumbs-up image on one side to flash at courteous drivers, and a thumbs-down on the other to express disapproval. Within a decade, traffic fatalities fell by more than half.[21]

A reader of a draft of my book said to me: okay, fine, I understand that trusting people may work but while this may be true for New Zealand and other high-trust societies, this can never work in less developed countries such as India. In New Delhi, they have had to impose heavy fines for not wearing masks.[22] This is a valid point. The willingness to obey rules is crucially dependent on the strength of the rule of law. In countries that are highly corrupt and where rule-breaking is normal, it is certainly more difficult to get people to follow instructions. However, I draw the reader's attention to the following three points.

First, recall Lin Ostrom's work showing that FMIS based on mutual trust and peer monitoring perform better than government-managed systems. Also recall Muhammad Yunus's success in providing small loans without collateral in Bangladesh. These are less developed countries too. So, prima facie, it does not seem that trust is impossible in less developed countries.

Second, we often tend to focus excessively on those who are violating a rule rather than the large numbers who are not. Remember, safety is like the pile on the floor; the more we wear masks the more safety we add to the pile. Not everyone has to wear a mask as long as enough others do. However, it may be okay to trust people to do the right thing and then penalize the rule violators, which is what the New Delhi example is suggesting.

Third, there is yet another aspect to this story that is not always immediately obvious. Just as we sometimes do the right thing even when no one is watching, there is an intrinsic aspect to punishment as well. Punishments can take explicit forms such as a fine for disobeying a rule, but it can also take more subtle forms, such as being observed by our peers and being judged. Remember the priming example about the watching eyes from a previous chapter.

When it comes to mask-wearing or obeying similar other rules, we are being constantly monitored by others around us. If I go to the supermarket and find that everyone else is wearing a mask, I feel out of place for not wearing one and worry that others are judging me. So, being observed by our peers often acts as subliminal monitoring. In less developed countries with larger populations, people are constantly being watched by lots of other people.

Jeff Carpenter of Middlebury College was also interested in this question. What happens to our willingness to abide by rules or act selfishly when groups get larger and we are surrounded by lots of people? On the one hand, when there are more people, it becomes harder for each individual to monitor others. This makes it easier to act selfishly and the act of being observed may matter less. On the other hand, in larger groups with more people, there are also many watching eyes, monitoring you and passing judgment on the appropriateness of your actions. Carpenter finds that it is the latter effect that predominates. When there are many people watching you, you are less likely to act in a selfish manner.

This is not straightforward. If there are many people watching you, there is an incentive to act in a less selfish manner. Equally, if many people around you are behaving in a selfish manner, then you might be inclined to do so too. It is not so much the *people* in less developed countries who cannot be trusted. It very much depends on the strength of the rule of law; on prevailing norms and customs. People are the same everywhere. What makes the difference is the type of institutions we put around them and the values we inculcate in them. However, if someone says that trust-based mechanisms have a better chance of success in developed nations such as New Zealand, I would not argue too much; except to hope that in the not too distant future, countries such as India, Nepal or Bangladesh would also see the evolution of institutions that lead to higher mutual trust.

With some appropriate caveats then, the evidence suggests that people are more likely to behave in a cooperative way when we appeal to their goodwill, but forcing compliance on the basis of punishments makes people more self-regarding and can be counter-productive. The evidence presented in this chapter suggests that the model of humanity based on mutual trust and reciprocity (particularly in societies that display high levels of social capital) yields better outcomes than a model which proceeds to make policy on the basis of general mistrust.

NOTES

1. NZ Herald. (2020). In awe of NZ: How world media reacted to New Zealand eliminating Covid-19. *New Zealand Herald*, 9 June. (No byline.) https://www.nzherald.co.nz/nz/in-awe-of-nz-how-world-media-reacted-to-new-zealand-eliminating-covid-19/MMOWHK3HHQCYU3TWV7G3TSJJK4/.
2. An Official Information Act filed by Covid Plan B requesting results from serological testing elicited the following response from the Ministry of Health: "Currently there are no Ministry sanctioned seroprevalence studies being performed."
3. Smith, A. (2020). Woman given 14-day jail sentence for escaping isolation facility. *New Zealand Herald*, 28 August. https://www.nzherald.co.nz/nz/covid-19-

coronavirus-woman-given-14-day-jail-sentence-for-escaping-isolation-facility/M
VVSAPJWOYTG5MOHQMDPD4H334/.

4. Dillane, T. (2020). Booze run vs father's funeral: questions of systemic racism over quarantine escapees' contrasting sentences. *New Zealand Herald*, 29 August. https://www.nzherald.co.nz/nz/booze-run-vs-fathers-funeral-ques tions-of-systemic-racism-over-quarantine-escapees-contrasting-sentences/FLG5 GV3EXGPNU4HY35KWTBU23A/. As noted from the headline, this article also makes a point about the respective ethnicities of the violators involved. As I have tried to highlight in various places in this book, times of stress bring out all types of conscious and unconscious biases in humans. I am going to sidestep this issue since it is not immediately relevant for our purposes here.

5. Talk given by Sunetra Gupta at Covid-19 Science and Policy Symposium organized by Covid Plan B, 17 August 2020. Her presentation, together with those of others, such as Jay Bhattacharya and David Katz, are available at: https://www. covidplanb.co.nz/videos/.

6. Chaudhuri, A. (2020b). Don't make Kiwis pay for Covid-19 quarantine. *Newsroom*, 29 June. https://www.newsroom.co.nz/ideasroom/1256268/dont-m ake-kiwis-pay-for-quarantine.

7. Davison, I. (2020). Stateless: New Zealanders working overseas struggle to return home. *New Zealand Herald*, 23 November. https://www.nzherald.co.nz/ nz/stateless-new-zealanders-working-overseas-struggle-to-return-home/AYPH3 OTMDMMH7MJJNZYMHTZCPI/.

8. Akoorie, N. (2020). Covid 19 coronavirus: Tangiwai Wilson's whānau desperate to take her body through Auckland to Northland for tangi. *New Zealand Herald*, 19 August. https://www.nzherald.co.nz/nz/covid-19-coronavirus-tangiwai-wil sons-whanau-desperate-to-take-her-body-through-auckland-to-northland-for-ta ngi/OKPMXTLUFGC5ILYYCB5YUD5E6E/.

9. See, for instance, my article: Chaudhuri, A. (2020d). Election 2020: Why the Nats fared so poorly. *Stuff*, 20 October. https://www.stuff.co.nz/opinion/123135666/ election-2020-why-the-nats-fared-so-poorly. "Nats" refers to the right-of-center party, the National Party. New Zealand's main left-of-center party led by Prime Minister Jacinda Ardern is the Labour Party. As I have noted previously, Stuff is a syndicated news service that provides content on its own as well as via a number of other newspapers owned by their parent company, Nine Entertainment.

10. An astute reader may be thinking: yes, by engaging in trust and reciprocity, both the sender and the receiver are better off, but this is at the expense of the experimenter who has to pay out more money. This is not the time and place to go into this issue. Suffice to say that the basic results would remain unchanged even if participants were playing with money they had earned by taking part in another activity prior to the trust game. I provide many other examples in the following pages to demonstrate that these trusting and reciprocal motivations arise in many different situations. This allows us to be confident that these results are generalizable.

11. Lisa Cameron of Monash University has carried out pioneering work showing that raising the monetary stakes does not make a big difference. Cameron, L. A.

(1999). Raising the stakes in the ultimatum game: Experimental evidence from Indonesia. *Economic Inquiry*, *37*(1), 47–59. My book, *Experiments in Economics: Playing Fair with Money*, provides a more comprehensive discussion of this topic.

12. Since different receivers receive different amounts from the paired sender, in order to compare across receivers, we need to compare the proportion returned rather than the absolute amount returned. For instance, one receiver may receive $18 while another receives $30. Suppose the former sends back $9 while the latter sends back $10. We would typically refer to the former as being more reciprocal than the latter. This is because even though the former sends back a smaller absolute amount ($9), proportionally, this amount is larger ($9/$18) = 50 percent. The latter sends back a larger absolute amount ($10), but proportionally, this is smaller since ($10/$30) = 33 percent. The idea is that if both these receivers received $30, then the former would return 50 percent of $30, which is $15, while the latter would return 33 percent of $30, or $10.

13. Kosfeld, M., Heinrichs, M., Zak, P. J., Fischbacher, U., and Fehr, E. (2005). Oxytocin increases trust in humans. *Nature*, *435*(7042), 673–676.

14. Resnick, B. (2019). Oxytocin, the so-called "hug hormone," is way more sophisticated than we thought. *Vox*, 13 February. https://www.vox.com/science-and-health/2019/2/13/18221876/oxytocin-morality-valentines.

15. Gneezy, A., Gneezy, U., Riener, G., and Nelson, L. D. (2012). Pay-what-you-want, identity, and self-signaling in markets. *Proceedings of the National Academy of Sciences*, *109*(19), 7236–7240.

16. My family members and I are big fans of *The Big Bang Theory*, about a group of nerdy physicists at Caltech. In one memorable episode of this show, Sheldon rewards Penny with a chocolate every time Penny behaves in a way that satisfies Sheldon. This continues until Leonard, Penny's boyfriend and Sheldon's roommate, figures out that Sheldon is applying operant conditioning to Penny's behavior. Leonard subsequently realizes that Sheldon has been using the same technique on Leonard too. If you have not watched the show, I highly recommend it. Mayim Bialik, who plays Amy, Sheldon's girlfriend on the show, actually has a PhD in neuroscience and would be conversant with much of what is discussed in this book.

17. Often, if you pay people for donating blood, then the type of person who shows up is one whose blood we do not want. Economists refer to this as an "adverse selection problem". I am going to avoid a more detailed explanation and let readers figure this out on their own. Another example of adverse selection is provided by the supposed Groucho Marx saying that he (Groucho) did not want to be a member of any club that would have him as a member.

18. In this section I am summarizing research results reported in a multitude of papers including the following. Fehr, E., Gächter, S., and Kirchsteiger, G. (1997). Reciprocity as a contract enforcement device: Experimental evidence. *Econometrica*, *65*(4), 833–860. Fehr, E., Kirchler, E., Weichbold, A., and Gächter, S. (1998). When social norms overpower competition: Gift exchange in experimental labor markets. *Journal of Labor Economics*, *16*(2), 324–351.

Fehr, E., Kirchsteiger, G., and Riedl, A. (1993). Does fairness prevent market clearing? An experimental investigation. *Quarterly Journal of Economics*, *108*(2), 437–459. Fehr, E., Kirchsteiger, G., and Riedl, A. (1998). Gift exchange and reciprocity in competitive experimental markets. *European Economic Review*, *42*(1), 1–34.

19. This gentleman's first name is Major, last name is Major, middle name is Major and he has the rank of Major. If you have not read *Catch-22* then you must rectify this omission at the earliest opportunity, preferably as soon as you have finished reading this book.

20. Elinor Ostrom (better known as Lin to her many admirers) received the Nobel Prize in Economics in 2009 but unfortunately passed away in 2012.

21. Mockus, A. (2015). The art of changing a city. *New York Times*, 16 July. http://www.nytimes.com/2015/07/17/opinion/the-art-of-changing-a-city.html.

22. Sanyal, A. (2020). 2,000 fine for not wearing mask in Delhi, up from 500, to tackle Covid. *NDTV*, 19 November. https://www.ndtv.com/india-news/coronavirus-rs-2-000-fine-for-those-not-wearing-masks-in-delhi-up-from-rs-500-says-arvind-kejriwal-2327352.

5. Politics, pathogens and party lines

During the pandemic, a popular narrative was that conservatives were anti-lockdown while liberals were in favor. In this chapter, I show that:

- this unidimensional view of politics is incomplete, if not inaccurate;
- both conservatives and liberals come in two types: social conservatives and social liberals, as well as economic conservatives and economic liberals; these groups differ in their policy stances;
- when it came to support for lockdowns there was a concordance in the views of social conservatives with economic liberals but for very different reasons;
- there are evolutionary reasons behind why these political ideologies came to exist.

* * *

Early in the pandemic, a popular perception took hold, both among regular people and the media, that conservatives were anti-lockdown while liberals were in favor. This also implied that anyone who opposed lockdowns must necessarily be conservative and, in order to be a bona fide liberal, one must provide full-throated support for lockdowns. It turns out that this perception is incorrect on many levels.

First, this was not true in most countries other than the US (and possibly to a smaller extent in the UK and Canada). In most other countries, there was general agreement among large sections of the population with widely differing viewpoints. I have noted repeatedly in the preceding pages the striking degree of agreement between New Zealand's center-left and center-right parties. This agreement among opposites, rather than strong disagreements between the left and the right, is a more accurate depiction of the popular mood. Indeed if there was so much disagreement between the left and the right in most countries, then it becomes very difficult to explain and/or understand the general uniformity in policy responses across the globe. The bulk of the countries around the world, whether liberal or conservative, were eager adopters of stringent lockdowns.

Second, the conservative–liberal breakdown in Covid-19 responses made little sense, as the country that has steadfastly refused to implement lockdowns is Sweden, a liberal bastion. Sweden is often the favorite target of US conservatives for its liberal policies. In contrast, conservative countries such as Saudi Arabia, or countries such as India or Israel, led by governments that are far from liberal, adopted strict lockdowns.

Third, this usual approach of dividing political ideology along a unidimensional liberal–conservative spectrum is, at best, highly incomplete, if not totally incorrect. This is because this unidimensional view of politics misses a lot of nuances, which are important in understanding popular responses in times of stress. Conservatives come in two types, economic conservatives and social conservatives, and the two do not necessarily agree on everything. The same is true of liberals, or to use my preferred sobriquet, "progressives". There are social progressives and there are economic progressives, with often divergent views. I have more to say on this topic below.

Fourth, a large body of research led by John Jost of NYU and John Hibbing of the University of Nebraska-Lincoln have shown that conservatives, particularly social conservatives, are much more sensitive to threats and averse to pathogens (disease-causing bacteria or viruses) than liberals. Research led by John Hibbing suggests that not only are conservatives much more threat sensitive, they also have more pronounced startle responses to sudden, sharp and loud sounds, which again bears testimony to their greater threat sensitivity.[1] Given that Covid-19 was a deadly pathogen that threatened lives and livelihoods, it then becomes very difficult to understand why and how conservatives, or at least social conservatives, could be so blasé about it.

This line of research, particularly that initiated by Hibbing, also suggests that, contrary to prior beliefs that political ideology and positions are molded primarily by our societal circumstances and influences, that is, our political ideology is almost exclusively driven by nurture, many of our values are indeed heritable and therefore attributable to nature. So, being a liberal or a conservative may not be so much a matter of which friends you have, but who your parents are and what they believe in.

In her book *The Nurture Assumption*, Judith Rich Harris argued that parents should not worry too much about how their children will turn out because, while parents do make a difference in their children's lives, peers matter a great deal more in forming our core values and beliefs.[2] Recent evidence suggests that this view is incomplete. Parents, in passing on their genes, do seem to matter a great deal and more than thought before. Also, our parents often determine who our peers are. They get to choose which neighborhoods we grow up in and which schools we attend. We often end up being friends with the children of our parents' friends. Therefore, the argument that peers matter more than parents is incomplete in that our peers are often chosen for us by the actions of our parents.

However, conservatives were neither as unconcerned about the Covid-19 threat nor as opposed to lockdowns as popularly believed. Some conservatives (mostly social conservatives) were concerned, while others (economic conservatives) were less so. The same is true of liberals; not all of them were as worried or as pro-lockdown as generally portrayed. Social liberals (social progressives) were less supportive of lockdowns compared with economic liberals (or as I term them, "economic progressives"). In order to understand who responded in what way, we need to talk more about politics, political ideology as well as some basic evolutionary theory to understand how beliefs and attitudes are formed.

It is also worth noting that Covid-19 was the first pandemic in the era of social media. While 24-hour news channels were in existence during earlier pandemics, such as avian or swine flu, Covid-19 was the first pandemic in an era dominated by Facebook, Twitter, Google, Snapchat, Instagram and TikTok with the associated pressures for clicks, likes, tweets and retweets. Views and opinions, whether correct or incorrect, safe or dangerous, benign or offensive, spread around the world at the press of a computer key. This all made decision making, whether at the level of governments or at the level of individuals, all the more complicated.

SINGLE-DIMENSIONAL VIEWS OF POLITICS AND MORAL FOUNDATIONS THEORY

What does being conservative or liberal mean? Readers will appreciate that this question forms the basis of voluminous research papers, books, monographs and university courses. A facile response is that conservatives are traditionalists; in favor of upholding traditional norms and customs, and opposed to change. Liberals desire systemic change. The idea that conservatives are right-wing while liberals are left-wing dates back at least to the French Revolution and to the 1791 French legislative assembly, where those supportive of constitutional monarchy, and therefore opposed to radical change, the Feuillants, sat on the right, while the revolutionary Jacobins, Girondins and Cordeliers (led by Jacques Pierre Brissot and the philosopher and mathematician Nicolas de Condorcet) sat on the left.[3]

In recent times, the concept of political ideology has enjoyed a resurgence in the social sciences. This is, at least partly, owing to the highly polarized atmosphere in the US since the election of Donald Trump in 2016. The US occupies a large role in the psyche of the rest of the world and tends to dictate cultural values and ideological arguments around the globe. If and when the US president expresses authoritarian views or support for authoritarian leaders, leaders of that ilk feel emboldened all over. Equally, when the US president speaks out in favor of democracy, equality, diversity and inclusivity, proponents of those values all over the world feel empowered. If and when the US president challenges long-established social norms and democratic precepts, those who are inclined to do the same rejoice. So, it is not surprising that when the US found itself in a highly polarized political atmosphere, the rest of the world felt itself equally polarized even though the same is not true of other countries, or at least not to the same extent. Mostly these other countries are merely reflecting US-style polarization, what may be thought of as empathic polarization.[4]

Political ideology can be thought of as a set of connected beliefs and attitudes that organize our views on specific political and social issues. So, how should we understand liberals and conservatives, particularly in the US context? An eloquent answer to this comes from Jonathan Haidt (of NYU) in his book *The Righteous Mind* where Haidt puts forward his "moral foundations theory". Haidt suggests that humans care about five different aspects of morality:

1. *Care/harm* – the importance of caring for and protecting others; that is, not harming them even if this is personally costly;
2. *Fairness/cheating* – embodied in notions of fairness, reciprocity and proportionality; along the lines of "from each according to one's ability; to each according to one's needs". It is not as if Karl Marx came up with this idea *de novo*; the ideas of proportionality and sharing rules are well ingrained in religious principles; in ideas such as the Golden Rule and the dictum in Leviticus that "as a man does so shall be done to him; eye for eye, tooth for tooth, fracture for fracture";
3. *Ingroup loyalty* – this is straightforward and would make immediate sense to all of us. This implies looking out for my family, my clan, my friends, my tribe, my country, my gender and my race. This is why we wave team and country flags, wear team jerseys and shout ourselves hoarse cheering for the home team;
4. *Authority or respect* – submitting to tradition and to authority figures; accepting the dictates of authority and believing that questioning authority leads to social disintegration; and finally (probably most relevant in the context of Covid-19)
5. *Sanctity or purity* – abhorrence for disgusting things, foods, pathogens, diseases and so on.

Together with Jesse Graham and Brian Nosek (both of the University of Virginia) and other collaborators, Haidt asked thousands of people their views on a multitude of questions related to these five moral foundations. I list some of the questions asked by Haidt and his colleagues to give you an idea:

- Compassion for those who are suffering is the most crucial virtue. (Care/harm)
- When the government makes laws, the number one principle should be ensuring that everyone is treated fairly. (Fairness/cheating)
- I am proud of my country's history. (Ingroup loyalty)
- Respect for authority is something all children need to learn. (Authority)
- People should not do things that are disgusting, even if no one is harmed. (Sanctity)
- One of the worst things a person could do is hurt a defenseless animal. (Care/harm)

- Justice is the most important requirement for a society. (Fairness/cheating)
- People should be loyal to their family members, even when they have done something wrong. (Ingroup loyalty)
- I think it's morally wrong that rich children inherit a lot of money while poor children inherit nothing. (Fairness/cheating)
- It is more important to be a team player than to express oneself. (Authority)
- If I were a soldier and disagreed with my commanding officer's orders, I would obey anyway because that is my duty. (Authority)
- Chastity is an important and valuable virtue. (Sanctity)

On each question, respondents need to state whether they strongly disagree (rated 0), moderately disagree (1), slightly disagree (2), slightly agree (3), moderately agree (4) or strongly agree (5). Participants are also asked to indicate their political orientation from "Strongly Liberal" to "Strongly Conservative". Figure 5.1 summarizes the crux of Haidt's findings. In keeping with tradition, the liberals appear on the left of this figure while conservatives appear on the right; this means that the respondents are getting more conservative or right-wing as moving from left to right. According to Haidt, both liberals and conservatives care about all five moral foundations, but to different degrees. Liberals care far more about "individualizing" foundations, about not causing harm and ensuring fairness. Conservatives care about these too, but not as much as liberals. Conservatives care proportionally more about "binding" or "group-orientated" foundations, such as authority, ingroup loyalty and sanctity. Again, it is not that liberals do not care about any of this, but they care about harm/care and fairness more than they do about ingroup loyalty or obedience to authority.

To liberals, burning the flag is a perfectly legitimate act protected by fundamental rights of free speech and expression; to conservatives, this is an act of complete insubordination, a violation of the oath to protect and defend their country, a marker of disloyalty and, therefore, a complete sacrilege. Each side holds its position with conviction and completely fails to understand how and why the other side can feel differently about this. Similarly, to conservatives, obeying authority, say in the form of an order from a superior, is essential, while for liberals, it is imperative to use their judgment and ask about care/harm or fairness/cheating when deciding to obey orders.

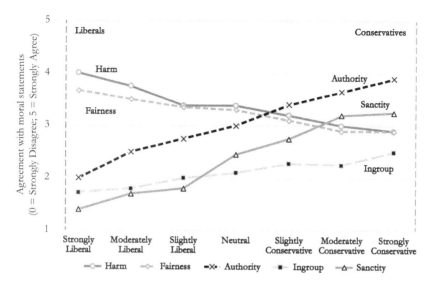

Source: Figure recreated by author on the basis of data from Haidt (2012).

Figure 5.1 *Differences between liberals and conservatives in the five moral foundations from Haidt (2012)*

According to researchers, for example, John Hibbing, these are not casually held beliefs or simply a matter of opinion; a great deal of this is hardwired. Conservatives feel a visceral sense of disgust when they see a flag being burnt. Liberals, similarly, are outraged if they believe that personal liberties and freedom of expression are being sacrificed at the altar of the common good or to safeguard the interests of the larger group. Liberals and conservatives do see the world differently.[5]

One of the best examples of this dichotomy in allegiances comes from Rob Reiner's movie *A Few Good Men* (based on a play by Aaron Sorkin). In the movie, US Marines Lance Corporal Harold Dawson and Private First Class Louden Downey stand accused of murdering fellow Marine William Santiago at the Guantanamo Bay Naval Base in Cuba. Santiago had repeatedly complained about various issues at the camp which had earned him the ire of the Base Commander Colonel Nathan Jessup (played by Jack Nicholson, whose bravura performance in the role earned him a best supporting actor Oscar nomination; the Oscar went to Gene Hackman for the Clint Eastwood directed movie *Unforgiven*). If some of you have not seen the movie, which also received a best motion picture Oscar nomination, you should watch it as soon as possible and I will try not to spoil it for you. Suffice to say that, in the movie, Jessup directs Lieutenant Jonathan Kendrick (Kiefer Sutherland) to teach Santiago a lesson. Kendrick, in turn, instructs Dawson and Downey to do so, which unfortunately results in Santiago's death. Kendrick, Dawson and Downey are each bothered to a greater or lesser extent by the order from Jessup, which appears to contravene the Marines' written rules. However, disobeying an order from a superior is also anathema to their oath.

As Jessup states in one memorable scene: he eats breakfast a stone's throw away from the enemy and the only way he can provide the protection he does to US citizens is that his soldiers follow orders; otherwise, people die. Tom Cruise, Demi Moore and Kevin Pollack are Navy lawyers who are entrusted with defending Dawson and Downey only to realize very quickly that the only way to provide a vigorous defense means proving that Dawson and Downey were merely following orders from their superiors (Kendrick and Jessup). I have not given much away because the movie is about what transpires once Tom Cruise et al. set out to try to prove that Dawson and Downey were acting under orders from Kendrick and Jessup. The movie also features Kevin Bacon as the lawyer prosecuting Dawson and Downey in military court.

Incidentally, it is now generally conceded, possibly in a win for liberal sensibilities, that soldiers have a moral obligation to refuse to carry out immoral orders. This conclusion came out of the verdicts rendered by the Nuremburg trials for Nazi officers accused of war crimes following the Second World War. Officer after officer in those trials resorted to the defense: *"Eine Bestellung ist eine Bestellung"* ("An order is an order"). The Nuremberg justices soundly repudiated this defense and sentenced most of the officers for the crimes they were charged with.[6]

UNIDIMENSIONAL POLITICAL APPROACHES TO UNDERSTANDING COVID-19 RESPONSES

If conservatives are so focused on sanctity and aversion to disease and pathogens, how is it they were supposedly so unconcerned with

Covid-19, at least in the US? The answer is, at least, twofold. First, conservatives pay attention to a very different set of media outlets and/or authority figures than liberals do. Second, when it came to Covid-19, sanctity and pathogen aversion ran into conflict with the authority and ingroup loyalty foundations. A group of researchers at the University of California San Marcos and the Naval Postgraduate School in Monterey, including Abraham Rutchick, Dustin Calvillo and others, set out to try to understand the apparent lack of concern among vast swaths of conservatives in the US. In a way, their findings are not hard to anticipate. Yes, many of these people are averse to diseases and sensitive to such threats, but they were also receiving a completely different message from the President and his acolytes, including the anchors on Fox News, such as Sean Hannity.

It is well documented that Fox News was at the forefront of minimizing Covid-19 related risks.[7] This was problematic since typical Fox News viewers tend to be older, a group that was significantly more at risk than younger viewers. However, even among Fox News viewers, there were significant differences in behavior as to who they were getting their information from. A group of researchers led by Leonardo Bursztyn of the University of Chicago have shown a distinct difference between the fans of two highly popular shows on Fox, one anchored by Tucker Carlson and the other by Sean Hannity. Carlson started highlighting risks associated with Covid-19 in February 2020, while Hannity only started doing this later, around mid-March 2020. Bursztyn and his colleagues find that when it came to changes in behavior in response to the coronavirus, such as washing hands more often, practicing social distancing and canceling travel plans, primary viewership of Hannity is associated with these changes in behavior four days later than the average Fox News viewer, while viewers who are primary consumers of Carlson changed behavior three days earlier than the average Fox News viewer.

However, let us get back to what Rutchick and his colleagues did. Three hundred and forty-six participants in their study were asked to indicate their party affiliation (Republican/Democrat/Other) and their political orientation, from extremely liberal to extremely conservative. They also answered questions about their perception of how vulnerable they were to Covid-19 and the severity of the disease. They were asked about whether they thought Covid-19 was a conspiracy and whether the media was exaggerating its dangers. Participants were also shown news headlines and asked how trustworthy they thought those headlines were. Some of these headlines were real; others were fake. The latter were taken from websites such as Snopes.com or Factcheck.org.[8] Finally, Rutchick and colleagues asked another 609 participants about the extent of their approval of Donald Trump. The participants in these follow-up studies were also asked to answer a series of questions to test their cognitive abilities. (I discussed these problems previously, in Chapter 2. For example: a bat and a ball together cost $110. The bat costs $100 more than the ball. How much does the ball cost?)

Rutchick and his colleagues find that those who are politically conservative (identify as Republican) tend to minimize their own vulnerability to Covid-19 and the severity of the disease. They are much more likely to believe that the pandemic is a conspiracy and highly exaggerated by the media. Conservatives are more likely to fall for fake news, in that those who profess themselves to be liberal are more likely to be able to distinguish real headlines from fake headlines. Further, Rutchick and his colleagues find that the more news participants received from Fox News, the less vulnerable they felt, and the more they agreed that the pandemic was a conspiracy and that the media was exaggerating the danger. Those who got their news from CNN believed the opposite; they believed more in the severity of Covid-19 and did not agree that this was a conspiracy or an exaggeration.

Conservatives typically were more approving of the job Donald Trump was doing but these higher levels of approval, possibly coupled with the downplaying of the danger by the President himself, also implied that conservatives were less informed about Covid-19 and the science behind viruses. Rutchick and his colleagues argue that while conservatives do tend to be more sensitive to threats, it appears that this tendency can be overcome with sufficient ingroup pressure, contextual framing of the problem by political leadership and media exposure. However, these researchers do not find much effect for people's responses in the cognitive ability questions. It is not the case that conservatives or liberals were better or worse on those questions. This is an issue that I will come back to shortly.

This leads me back to the point I made previously that, when it came to Covid-19, threat sensitivity ran headlong into the "ingroup loyalty" and "authority" moral foundations. When we are faced with a threat, our natural instinct is to avoid it. Once again, threats such as Covid-19 or others create a sense of uncertainty. How deadly is the threat and what is the best way to deal with it? Evolutionary theory suggests that one way of combating threats may be to fall back on cultural traditions and adhere more closely to the ingroup. Sometimes these traditions and adherence to the ingroup require rituals and practices that are personally costly. For instance, orthodox Jews wear elaborate black suits even in the heat of summer, while devout Muslims go without food or drink from sunrise to sunset during the month of Ramadan.[9]

These ritualistic practices are sometimes referred to as "hard to mimic" signals, since it is personally costly to engage in such rituals. This guarantees that dilettantes will not be able to engage easily in similar signals and will, therefore, not be able to assimilate themselves within established groups. However, these costly signals also became ways of indicating ingroup status, and this status, by advertising the member's affiliation with the group, can be useful in receiving aid during times of trouble. This is one way in which threat sensitivity and pathogen aversion conflicted with ingroup loyalty among conservatives. If the ingroup is saying that the threat is not real, then what do you do? Do you listen to the emotion processing parts of the brain that are asking you to take the threat seriously? Or do you listen to another message, which says that, in spite of the perceived threat, it is important to stay close to the herd in times of trouble to make sure that you have friends to provide aid when needed? Many conservatives, even if they were personally repelled by the Covid-19 threat, ended up listening to that part of their brain, which suggested following the dictates of the ingroup.

This does not really solve the puzzle. If threat sensitivity is a primary distinguishing feature of conservatives, then why this lack of concern about Covid-19? Why should ingroup loyalty necessarily triumph over pathogen aversion? Another evolutionary argument helps us understand this type of behavior. Situations of uncertainty cause fear, stress, apprehension and a sense of losing control. It would be good if we could find out more about the problem at hand but finding out this information is often neither easy nor quick, especially if you cannot boot up your laptop and start searching on Google immediately. So, what do you do? We turn to our friends and family for advice. However, those friends may or may not know more than us. Therefore, we turn to authority figures, those we respect, those with prestige, who most likely know more than us, and who are worthy of emulating. They may be our elders, with more experience, or those occupying high office, a leader, a chief or a priest. Then we follow their instructions. A number of anthropologists, such as Joe Henrich of Harvard and Francisco Gil-White of the University of Pennsylvania, have shown that this "prestige biased" learning about problems, where we look to figures of authority and follow their direction, is a key feature of human cultural evolution.

In collaborative work with Andrew Schotter of NYU, Barry Sopher of Rutgers and others, I have shown that advice-giving over generations, where each generation provides advice to a successive generation about the correct course of action based on the experiences of the former generation, can help future generations figure out solutions to a variety of social dilemma problems. In their book, *Not By Genes Alone*, Pete Richerson of University of California, Davis, and Rob Boyd of University of California Los Angeles (UCLA) document how these intergenerational norms become part of the evolutionary process via a process of cultural transmission of social knowledge; it is not only genes that evolve, culture and social learning does too. Both of these forces, genetic evolution as well as cultural and social evolution, play a crucial role in who we are, what we do and what we believe in.[10]

So, when it came to Covid-19, it was no wonder that many conservatives took their lead from Donald Trump and his supporters, including the anchors of Fox News, just as liberals took their lead from Democratic leaders and other media outlets such as CNN or MSNBC. In this example, taking cues from the dominant group personality (which may be thought of as a form of prestige-biased transmission) reinforced feelings of ingroup loyalty, which in turn suppressed conservatives' threat sensitivity.

* * *

Assuming for the time being that it is the liberals, with their emphasis on lockdowns, who got the response right, and the conservatives who had no clue about the right course of action, why do conservatives hold the views that they do? Are the conservatives cognitively less sophisticated and does this make them more prone to be misguided and/or misinformed? The findings of Rutchick and his colleagues do not provide support for this conjecture, since those researchers find no differences along party lines in cognitive abilities. These cognitive tests are not definitive and do not necessarily capture essential elements of cognitive sophistication or smartness. The less sophisticated are more likely to fall for fake news, suffer from misperceptions about the true severity of Covid-19 and/or believe that this is all a hoax or a conspiracy. Nevertheless, prima facie it does not seem that there is a party line breakdown in this cognitive sophistication.

David Rand at MIT has been working for a while on understanding our susceptibility to fake news and "bull**it".[11] Rand, together with Gordon Pennycook and other colleagues, decided to delve deeper into this issue regarding the wide chasm in responses along party lines. It is possible that conservatives minimize the threat of Covid-19 because they are cognitively less sophisticated and hence more susceptible to fake news and therefore have incorrect beliefs and information about the disease. Alternatively, it may have nothing to do with cognitive sophistication but simply a desire to blend in with the ingroup whose leaders were actively downplaying potential risks of Covid-19. This desire to blend in is often referred to as (politically) motivated reasoning. I may be reasonably sure that something is true (say that Covid-19 can be a virulent disease) but I adopt a contrary position because that helps me stay in line with the ingroup's position on the matter. As we have seen previously from the work by Solomon Asch, disagreeing with or acting against the majority view can be psychologically painful. It may also get us kicked out of the group. Here, our political ideology and our cognitive sophistication may be in strong disagreement.

Dan Kahan, a professor of law and psychology at Yale, together with his collaborators, proposes what he terms a theory of "identity protective cognition". Kahan proposes that when it comes to events that are probabilistic, ideology and cognitive sophistication may interact to predict attitudes about such events. People with the most cognitive sophistication often occupy the farthest points on the spectrum. According to Kahan, Democrats who are more numerate and cognitively sophisticated are much more convinced about the perils of climate change. For Republicans, the opposite holds true. Cognitively sophisticated Republicans are less likely to hold beliefs that climate change is a pressing threat.

So, which is it? Are all conservatives misinformed or are some of the more informed conservatives hiding their true views in order to blend in? To answer this question, Rand and his collaborators carry out a study that is similar in spirit to the Rutchick study discussed previously. They recruit around 750 participants each in three countries: the US, the UK and Canada. Participants answer questions regarding their political affiliation from "Strongly Liberal" to "Strongly Conservative"; about behavior changes in the aftermath of Covid-19 (social distancing, hand-washing, mask-wearing, and so on) and about their perceptions of Covid-19 risk, such as how vulnerable they think they are to the disease. Participants are queried about various misperceptions regarding Covid-19.[12] They also take the cognitive reflection test (the cost of the bat and the ball and similar questions), as in Rutchick. There are also a battery of other questions designed to measure participants' level of numeracy or their trust in government and/or other sources, such as news media. They were also tested for their receptivity to bull**it.

As before, conservative attitudes were correlated with greater misperceptions in all three countries; but far more so in Canada and the US than in the UK. This suggests that the political polarization in the US seems to find a degree of resonance across the border as well. However, while there were similarities across the US and Canada in Covid-19 misperceptions, this was not true about the job approval for Donald Trump and Justin Trudeau. There was greater divergence in the views of conservatives and liberals when it came to approving or disapproving of Trump but closer alignment in views when it came to rating Trudeau. Again, viewers of Fox News report greater misperceptions about the disease and a stronger belief in the efficacy of Donald Trump's handling of the virus.

What about the key question posed earlier? *Did conservatives minimize the threat of Covid-19 because of cognitive limitations or because they did not want to stray from the party line on the topic?* Although political ideology predicted the stance that respondents took on their threat perceptions of Covid-19 (Democrats more cautious compared with Republicans), Rand and his colleagues found no evidence for any interaction between ideology and cognitive sophistication in any of the three countries. They argue that the result is unequivocal. Greater cognitive sophistication implies decreased misperceptions about Covid-19 for liberals and conservatives alike in all three countries. However, cognitive sophistication did not correlate with risk perceptions and/or the desire to change behavior appropriately to deal with the threat.

Rand et al. conclude with a point that I will explore in more detail below. Being reflective, numerate and having basic science knowledge is important for the ability to identify false information about the virus, but it may not be enough to determine what behaviors are most effective or to motivate someone to change their behaviors. The only measures in Rand et al.'s data that correlated with changing behavior were a lower number of misperceptions and a greater perception of risk. This, in turn, suggests that, given the complexity and the level of uncertainty regarding the risks and dangers from Covid-19, political ideology predicted different responses *not owing to misinformation or susceptibility to fake news but because the diversity of responses is not captured by this unidimensional perspective on politics.* Political ideology predicted differential responses because people differed across more than one dimension; conservatives can be socially conservative and/or economically conservative, who do not necessarily perceive risk in the same way and do not necessarily agree on the appropriate response to threats. The same is true of liberals. There are social progressives and economic progressives, and they did not or do not agree on everything either. In relation to Covid-19, there was a trade-off between threats; the threat of disease and the loss of lives and livelihoods from it, but also the threat of economic damage and the consequent loss of lives and livelihoods. Even within conservatives and progressives, different groups with distinct worldviews responded differently. In order to understand this dichotomy, we need to turn once more to some evolutionary ideas. This is what I discuss next but I make one small detour on the way there.

DOING TOO MUCH VERSUS DOING TOO LITTLE

As I noted in Chapter 1, economists have their flaws, but trade-offs, scarcity and opportunity costs are their stock in trade. So, even if economists disagreed on the risk from Covid-19 and/or the resulting policy implications, generally they all understand and appreciate the opportunity–cost argument; the trade-off between identified lives and statistical lives. While the rest of the world fretted that some people, primarily conservatives, were not doing enough, most economists appreciated that while not doing enough was surely a problem, doing too much could be a problem as well. Not doing enough would lead to too many lives lost from Covid-19, while doing too much would save those lives but at the expense of shutting down the economy and thereby causing loss of lives elsewhere.[13] At some point, the additional benefit of devoting more resources to minimizing the threat of Covid-19 would simply not be worth the extra cost.

Evidence to this effect was provided by a group of economists from Harvard and MIT but led by Hunt Allcott of NYU. As in the other studies, Allcott and his colleagues also collect voluminous survey data on participants' exposure to news media, their threat perception and threat sensitivity, as well as political affiliation. However, the most innovative part of this study is that they combine this survey data with Global Positioning System (GPS) location data from smartphones to understand the partisan divide. Access to this GPS data allows the researchers to track travel patterns of those with divergent political affiliations. Did they stay home or did they make visits to points of interest, such as movies, restaurants and malls, particularly at the height of the pandemic in late March and early April 2020?

Allcott et al. put the question of trade-offs front and center by highlighting that social distancing may save lives from Covid-19 but could end up taking lives elsewhere by reducing economic activity. They add that in the presence of these trade-offs, differential responses to the threat may not necessarily be inefficient. According to Allcott et al., "One group might engage in less social distancing because their cost of distancing is greater (e.g., they will lose more income) or because their benefit of distancing is smaller (e.g., they are at lower risk of infection)". But as long as everyone concerned has the same beliefs regarding the actual threat posed by Covid-19, they will or should be able to equate the marginal benefits and marginal costs of social distancing. This is not exact but, collectively, people should be able to arrive at a reasonable solution along the lines of the "wisdom of the crowd" paradigm I discussed previously.

The problem is that exposure to different news media, different leaders and different messages may well lead to divergent beliefs regarding the true underlying threat. If that happens, then there is scope for serious inefficiencies, as it is no longer a question of how much social distancing is optimal. The question now becomes: how much social distancing is being undertaken (or not) by Republicans and Democrats? Given the underlying trade-offs between saving Covid-19 lives and keeping the economy going, should they be doing more or less or about the same?

In order to answer their question, Allcott and his colleagues build on the standard SIR epidemiological model, which I discussed briefly in Chapter 1. Allcott and his colleagues start with a theoretical model that relies on the underlying disease susceptibility probabilities. Too much social distancing means more lives saved from Covid-19, but greater reduction in economic activity resulting in greater losses of lives and livelihoods elsewhere. Alternatively, too little social distancing and too much risky behavior in visiting points of interest leads to greater infection transmission and to greater loss of lives from Covid-19. Ideally, as a society, we want to reach a point where we have established a reasonable balance between the two: sacrificing lives from Covid-19, on the one hand, and sacrificing lives elsewhere, on the other. Allcott and his colleagues go on to find that Republicans were engaging in too much risky behavior and not enough social distancing. So, while they were contributing to keeping the economy going, they were also responsible for large-scale community transmission of Covid-19 infections. Democrats, however, were engaging in too much social distancing; they were certainly preventing the spread of Covid-19, but they were doing so at proportionally higher levels of economic damage.

I illustrate these trade-offs in Figure 5.2. The vertical axis provides a composite measure of total benefits in terms of saving identified lives (that is, lives that would be lost to Covid-19) as well as saving statistical lives (that is, lives that would be lost owing to economic slowdown). Ideally, we want to maximize this total benefit at the peak of the curve. Therefore, if everyone is similar in relation to infection risk and has the same beliefs, then both Republicans and Democrats should situate themselves at point O. This is where the aggregate benefit is maximized. However, the Republicans are stopping at point R; they are engaging in too much risky behavior and not enough social distancing. By doing this, they are keeping the economy going but creating higher chances of infection transmission, thereby increasing deaths from Covid-19. Democrats are erring on the side of excessive caution. They are engaging in too much social distancing, but this, in

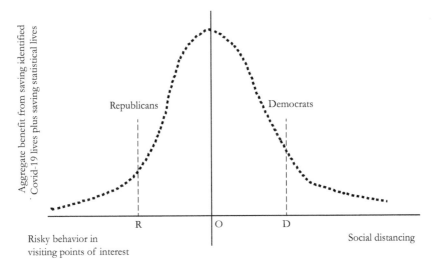

Figure 5.2   Differences in the degree of social distancing between liberals and conservatives in Allcott et al. (2020)

turn, means that while Democrats are keeping Covid-19 deaths down, their actions are leading to excessive levels of economic damage leading to a loss of lives elsewhere.

A TWO-DIMENSIONAL APPROACH TO UNDERSTANDING POLITICAL IDEOLOGY

The studies discussed so far take a unidimensional view of political ideology by placing people on a single liberal–conservative spectrum. I argued previously that this view of politics is at least incomplete, if not incorrect. I alluded to there being two distinct dimensions to both conservatism and progressivism: an economic dimension and a social dimension. It is important to understand and highlight these distinctions if we are truly going to understand the differential responses. This is also essential for good, well-informed policy making. Let me now turn to the dual dimensions of political ideology.

Quentin Atkinson and Chris Sibley are political psychologists at the University of Auckland. Atkinson and Sibley have long been aware of the fact that the unidimensional view of politics was not quite satisfactory.[14] For instance, in the 2016 US Presidential elections we witnessed significant internecine warfare within both the Democratic and the Republican parties. On the left, supporters of Hillary Clinton and Bernie Sanders clashed sharply, with Clinton taking a more free-market view while Sanders espoused a more populist position. A similar schism was apparent within Republicans, with significant opposition to Donald Trump from the more moderate segments. It is no exaggeration to say that moderate Republicans, such as Jeb Bush, had more in common with the centrist Democrats such as Clinton than he had in common with Trump; while on a number of issues, such as opposition to free trade, the supporters of Donald Trump were not that far away from the supporters of Bernie Sanders. Libertarians, for instance, are conservative in the sense of being pro-free market and pro-business, but typically hold progressive views on drug legalization or abortion.

This line of work suggests that, in contrast to the traditional unidimensional view of politics, there is voluminous evidence for two different dimensions of political ideology. One of these dimensions can be thought of as being economic in nature and posits a conflict between economic conservatism and economic progressivism. This dimension predicts how we view issues such as taxation or the welfare state. Economic conservatives are typically in favor of free markets and opposed to redistributive policies. They tend to view the world as a competitive jungle; they are happy to live with economic hierarchies and inequalities, and believe this to be a natural order of things. The converse of economic conservatism is economic progressivism; those who abhor inequality and favor redistributive policies, such as higher taxes or higher social welfare benefits, in order to reduce the gap between the haves and the have-nots.

The second dimension can be thought of as a social dimension where those who are socially conservative are typically in favor of harsh treatment of criminals and strong national security, and opposed to same-sex marriage and the separation of the church and the state. Social conservatives view the world as threatening and dangerous. Social conservatives value adherence to established cultural norms. They tend to place the interests of the collective over individualistic concerns. Social progressives are those who value individual rights and liberties, such as freedom of speech, and are wary of restrictions on the same.

Haidt's moral foundations theory in some ways conflates these two distinct dimensions where the individualizing foundations of care/harm and fairness/cheating can be thought of as a version of economic progressivism, while the binding group-minded foundations of ingroup loyalty, obedience to authority and sanctity are proxies for social conservativism. The difficulty is that the obverse of economic progressivism is not social conservatism or vice versa. At the other end of the spectrum from economic progressivism lies economic conservatism, a competitive worldview. Similarly, social conservatism is open to subjugating/sacrificing individual rights and liberties to serve the interests of the collective. The opposite of this is social progressivism; upholding individual rights and liberties. Moral foundations theory misses some of these nuances, and it does not address how humans came to possess these two distinct dimensions to their politics, especially since these two dimensions of ideology are observed in a wide range of cultures, suggesting a degree of universality.

Atkinson and Sibley teamed up with Scott Claessens, Kyle Fischer and I to develop an evolutionary explanation of why these two distinct dimensions exist and how they came about as part of human evolution. I explain this first and then go on to discuss how this dual dimensional view can better explain the differential responses we observe to Covid-19.

DUAL EVOLUTIONARY FOUNDATIONS OF POLITICAL IDEOLOGY

It is probable that these two distinct dimensions to our political views arose as a consequence of two key challenges to human group living. In his book *Chimpanzee Politics*, the primatologist Frans de Waal documents that the social groups of chimpanzees, who are close genetic kin of humans, are also characterized by dominance hierarchies. Those at the top enjoy greater mating benefits, and chimpanzee society is also marked by Machiavellian political machinations and leadership changes.[15]

Atkinson, Claessens and their co-authors (2020a) note:

> Human group living shares much of this complexity. However, the ancestral human hunter-gatherer communities that emerged over the course of the Pleistocene age (roughly 2.5 million years ago to about 12,000 years ago) were vastly different from those of other great apes. They were

characterised by contact and trade between extended networks, relatively egalitarian socio-political structures and deeply embedded cultural norms, conventions and institutions.

What were the two key shifts that allowed humans to move beyond great ape society toward creating more complex networks and cultures? The first shift required humans to cooperate more, often over a wider network including cooperating with strangers who were not genetically related; for instance, the cooperation required for hunting big game. Cooperation acted as a leveling mechanism that led to less rigidly hierarchical societies and a human mind that was predisposed toward cooperating with non-related kin. This cooperation also requires the development of other-regarding (instead of self-regarding) preferences and empathic concerns. Developing a reputation for being cooperative or sustaining cooperation over repeated interactions became essential if humans were to enjoy the benefits of these cooperative ties among strangers. Otherwise, they were likely to be excluded from cooperative bonds, which would have meant access to far fewer resources.

However, cooperation alone is not enough. In an earlier chapter, I introduced the concept of a social dilemma. These are situations where there is a conflict between cooperation and self-interest. If everyone else in a group is working together, then it is in an individual's self-interest to free-ride on the effort of others. For example, if all my other group members are working all night to finish a report for presentation due in the morning, then it probably does not matter if I go out for a drink or get some sleep, because the work will get done even without me; maybe not as well, but well enough for anyone not to notice any difference. This makes me better off because the report is completed and I have not paid the same cost as the others in lost sleep. Most collective action problems are subject to these free-riding incentives. However, if it is in my individual self-interest to free-ride, then it must be the same for everyone else in the group. So, no one does any work and the whole project falls through. All those of you who have engaged in group activities will understand this.

Society is better off if all commercial fishing boats abide by their quota. It does not make a big difference if an individual boat cheats a little and takes more than its quota, but if it is rational for one, then it is rational for everyone else. The end result is over-fishing

and seriously depleted marine stocks. In order to sustain cooperation over time, societies must develop mechanisms for deterring
free-riding and punishing free-riders. In the second key shift,
humans became more group-minded, conforming to social norms
in culturally marked groups and punishing norm-violators. To deal
with the tension between cooperation for the common good and
self-interest, groups started creating social norms and conventions,
traditions and rules; that is, a group culture that clearly delineated
who belonged and therefore was worthy of receiving aid from the
group, and who did not and therefore should be excluded from these
cooperative networks. These changes lead to a group-minded human
psychology underpinned by emotions such as shame, pride, anger
and disgust.

Considerable evidence suggests that, unlike other great apes,
humans are more willing to abide by group-specific social norms.
They establish elaborate markers in the form of hard-to-mimic costly
rituals to identify those who belong or to advertise their allegiance to
the group, and they punish (or are apt to punish) those who violate
the norms established by the group. These group norms serve multiple purposes. At one level, they act to reduce free-riding tendencies
but, beyond that, and as previously noted, these norms also help distinguish members of the ingroup from others. This facilitates ingroup
cohesion, which is valuable in the event of intergroup competition
and other threatening or uncertain circumstances. Atkinson and his
colleagues argue that these two fundamental human responses to
the challenges of group living – cooperation and group conformity –
explain why scholars have repeatedly identified a two-dimensional
structure of political ideology.

The first domain, cooperation, is concerned with cooperating
more across wider interdependent networks and sharing the spoils of
cooperation more evenly. This is the domain that has molded our attitudes regarding cooperation and competition. Is it really a cut-throat
world where competition and inequality reign supreme? Or could
we achieve more equitable outcomes with greater equality and access
to resources? Are we more similar to chimpanzees, fighting over our
share and preserving what is ours, or to bonobos (who are genetically
as close to humans as chimpanzees), willing to share newly found
food? Do we believe in a winner-take-all society, or do we believe in
creating social safety nets that look out for the least well-off? Should

government and society cater primarily to the well-off or should we enact redistributive policies to help those less fortunate?

These are, broadly, economic questions, and our attitudes on these relate to our degree of economic conservatism or economic progressivism. Economic conservatives believe in the forces of the free market even if that leads to inequality and hierarchy, since they consider these inevitable and nothing to worry unduly about. Economic progressives believe in egalitarianism; they argue for redistributive policies to take care of the most vulnerable. This is the first dimension of our dual dimensional foundation of political ideology. Where do we situate ourselves on the spectrum? Competition or cooperation? Winner take all, or redistribution of some of the gains of the winners to protect the losses of the losers?

The second dimension is concerned with group conformity, maintaining adherence to group norms and punishment and/or ostracization for those who violate those norms. For early humans, it was vital to sanction norm-violators because they threatened the viability of the group and made it vulnerable to threats from outsiders. They believe that the collective should always supersede the individual. This is the conflict between Nathan Jessup (Jack Nicholson) and Daniel Caffey (Tom Cruise) in *A Few Good Men*. Jessup wants to protect the sovereignty of the group and its viability, at all costs; Caffey wants to make sure that no unjust act goes unpunished, since each individual is important and their inherent rights to freedom of thought, speech, religion or sexual orientation are sacrosanct and should not be sacrificed at the altar of group conformity.

In Figure 5.3, I present a graphical overview of these two dimensions of politics. This is laid out in a standard North–East–West–South grid. The vertical North–South line measures variation in economic conservatism versus economic progressivism. If we move up and to the North, then individuals are becoming more economically conservative. These are people who have a "the-world-is-a-competitive-jungle" worldview. However, if we move down and to the South, then people are becoming more progressive; they have a more egalitarian worldview and are strongly supportive of redistributive policies to help the downtrodden. The horizontal axis going from West to East measures the degree of polarization along the social dimension. Here, those to the left (or West) are social progressives who champion individual rights and liberties, even if that comes at the detriment of the

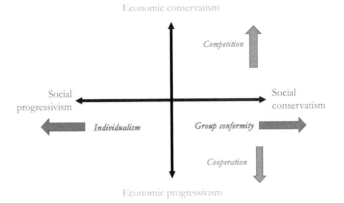

Source: Figure created by author on the basis of arguments in Claessens et al. (2020a).

Figure 5.3   Graphical overview of the dual dimensions of political ideology

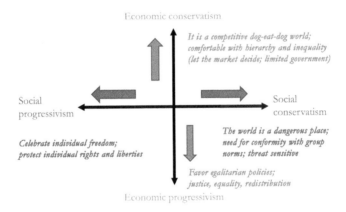

Source: Figure created by author on the basis of arguments in Claessens et al. (2020a).

Figure 5.4   Worldviews underlying the two-dimensional foundation of politics

group as a whole. As we move right (or to the East), individuals are becoming more socially conservative; they believe that the "world is a dangerous place" and, therefore, that it is important to stick closely to the ingroup and obey that group's established norms and customs.

In Figure 5.4, on the basis of arguments provided by Claessens et al. (2020a), I provide a little bit more information about the contents of the worldviews that underpin these two dimensions. I believe this makes it easier for the reader to quickly grasp the trade-offs that I have discussed.

WHY SO MUCH VARIATION?

The next logical question is, of course: why is there so much variation? Why are we all so different from one another? Why can we not agree and all get along? More broadly, why can't we all be progressives or conservatives? Why don't we converge at one or the other extreme of these two spectrums or even one single point where everyone is of the same type and has the same beliefs and attitudes? As Atkinson, Claessens and others note, this variation occurs owing to two other related biological concepts: "fitness trade-offs" and "behavioral plasticity". If you are willing to persevere with me for a while and look behind the jargon, then both these concepts are simple and easy to follow, and appeal to most of us in a wide variety of ways as we go about our lives.

What is fitness trade-off? In order to better understand this concept, let us now go back to the animal world. Bull elephant seals can exceed 20 feet in length and weigh 6000 pounds, while female elephant seals weigh only 800 to 1200 pounds. Why are bull elephant seals so much bigger? The evolutionary explanation is that elephant seals are polygamous, so males must compete for females. Bull elephant seals pummel one another on the beach for hours until one finally retreats, battered and bloody. The winners of these battles command nearly exclusive sexual access to harems of as many as 100 females. This explains why males are so much bigger.

A male with a mutant gene for larger size would be more likely to prevail in fights with other males, and this gene would proliferate in the population. That is, the males are big because small males seldom gain access to females. However, although the large size is beneficial for access to sexual mates, size becomes a disadvantage also, since a large size makes it more difficult to escape from the great white shark, their principal predator. Larger size means greater mating opportunities and so natural selection would favor those with a gene for larger size, but those with this gene are also slower moving and, therefore, more vulnerable to predators. This means that natural selection should also benefit those who are smaller and better able to get away. In the end, nature will strike a balance in terms of size; those larger than this size will tend to be killed disproportionately more by predators, while those of smaller size will be unable to gain access to females and mate. Both of these two types, too large and too small, will be unable to procreate, and those genes will gradually die out.

A similar argument applies to the peacock's tail and the stag's antlers. A larger tail for a peacock signifies better genetic quality and is useful for attracting mates. A peacock with a larger tail will do better in the mating market than a peacock with a smaller tail. So, there will be an incentive for peahens to look for larger and larger tails, or a peacock with a mutation for a larger tail will attract more mates and have more progeny. But larger tails make it more difficult to run away from predators, implying that peacocks with larger tails will also be more vulnerable.

This applies to stags' antlers also; bigger antlers means victory in more fights and therefore access to more females. Equally, bigger antlers make it harder to escape from predators. This is the basis of fitness trade-offs in the process of natural selection; some peacocks with larger tails attract more mates and leave behind more progeny; but some peacocks with larger tails are more vulnerable to predators and, therefore, leave behind fewer progeny.

These fitness trade-offs apply to humans as well; free-riding on others' effort can be a good strategy, but only to an extent. If that free-riding leads to complete ostracism from the group, then my access to resources becomes limited, resulting in my death and consequent inability to pass on the complete free-riding gene. Similarly, cooperating with others and accommodating everyone else's needs all the time may be fine, but this will probably make me vulnerable to cheating from others who take advantage of my good nature. So, erring too far in this direction is problematic as well.

Being excessively group minded and conformist may provide a degree of protection against external threats, but it does not allow for creativity and innovation. Similarly, too much independence isolates me from the group and makes me more vulnerable to threats, especially if my group does not come to my rescue. Fitness trade-offs prevent humans from going off to one extreme or the other.

The other force preventing convergence to extreme outcomes is behavioral plasticity. This is the simple idea that not everything is hardwired; both nature and nurture matter. In addition to heritable individual differences, our values and attitudes are often an adaptive response to the social environment. It is easier to be cooperative and charitable in times of plenty, much less so in times of scarcity. Most of us are not Philip Sidney, and how cooperative we are may well depend on the times we grew up in.[16]

Daniel Nettle, an evolutionary psychologist at Newcastle, provides a few more illuminating examples of how heritability of traits (and fitness trade-offs) interact with environmental pressures (behavioral plasticity). We have met Nettle in a previous chapter when we discussed the priming effects of watching eyes on generosity. The common predator for the Trinidadian guppy (*Poecilia reticulata*) is the fish, pike. Guppies that come from populations living upstream of a waterfall where no predators are present tend to be bolder and less cautious in the presence of the pike. These effects are heritable and are not based on individual experience with predators. If and when predators are introduced into a previously predator-free environment, the population distribution changes rapidly towards greater caution, but equally, removing predators from an environment quickly leads to more guppies who lose their sense of caution around predators.

However, as Nettle notes, even within the same environment, there is no obvious reason for everyone to converge to one specific type. There could easily be situations where multiple different types coexist, a situation referred to as "polymorphism". In the coho salmon, *Oncorhynchus kisutch*, there are two male morphs (types): "hooknose" males, who reach maturity later, grow to a large size and compete with other males to fertilize female egg deposits. Then there are the rarer "jacks", smaller in size, who hide near the nests and sneak in to fertilize eggs. It has been shown that the fitness of the large and small types is roughly equal while those of intermediate size are at a fitness disadvantage. The intermediate-sized fish are too small to fight with the larger hooknoses but are too large to hide like the jacks in order to sneak in and fertilize eggs.

Similar polymorphism is seen among humans. A common human personality trait is extraversion. Those who are extraverts (and/or open to new experiences) are more likely to seek out greater numbers of sexual partners and therefore will tend to have more progeny. However, extraverts are also likely to engage in risky explorations including sensation and thrill-seeking activities that can cause injury and death. So, we can end up with at least two types: a highly extraverted type, who has more sexual unions but is also likely to have lower life expectancy owing to greater thrill seeking; and another type who has fewer sexual encounters but also does not suffer injury or death owing to thrill seeking and therefore has greater potential chances of finding sexual partners.[17]

In reality, though, we end up with a continuum of types ranging from high to low extraversion with cut-offs at either end; those who are excessively extraverted do not survive long enough to mate, while those who are excessively introverted seldom find partners in order to leave behind progeny. Think of it this way: all of us have two dials in our brains, one for the degree of economic conservatism versus progressivism, and a second for the degree of social conservatism versus progressivism.[18] Depending on our genes and our environment, these dials are set at different readings for different people. For someone such as Martin Shkreli,[19] the competitive dial is turned all the way up, while for Mother Teresa, this is turned all the way down. Equally, for Shkreli, the social dial may be set towards the left (West); he may or may not care much about people's religious values or their sexual orientation. But for Pat Robertson or for Ayatollah Khomeini, the social dial is turned all the way up (to the East) and any deviation from accepted social or religious norms, such as blasphemy or homosexuality, needs to be punished harshly. Their competitive dial, however, may be set at an intermediate level. Figure 5.5 provides an illustration of these two dials in our brain.

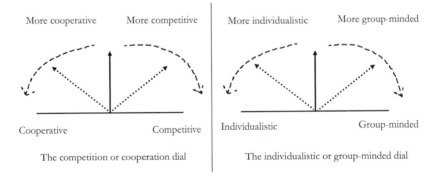

Figure 5.5   The two dials in our brain

DUAL FOUNDATIONS OF POLITICAL IDEOLOGY AS AN EXPLANATION OF DIFFERENTIAL RESPONSES TO COVID-19

Having shown that both conservatism and liberalism have two distinct components, one economic and the other social, and explaining how and why these two dimensions came about as part of human evolution, Quentin Atkinson, Kyle Fischer and I turned our attention to figuring out how these two dimensions matter when it came to Covid-19 responses.

In late 2019 and early 2020, we were undertaking work to try to understand differences in political ideology using UK residents on an online platform named Prolific, which has thousands of registered participants interested in taking part in surveys. Participants are reimbursed for their time. When Covid-19 hit, we realized that this presented us with an excellent natural experiment. Since we already had a great deal of data from respondents about their political attitudes prior to the pandemic, we could now go back and poll those respondents again to see how their attitudes may (or may not) have changed owing to the pandemic. We have data for more than 400 respondents, both before and after the pandemic hit, representing a large cross-section of UK society, in gender, age, ethnicity and socio-economic status.

Our first prediction was that the response of economic progressives to Covid-19 will be driven by cooperative and empathic attitudes, while social conservatives will display conformist and norm-enforcing policy preferences. Thus, while both types may be in favor of lockdowns, this will be for distinctly different reasons. Economic progressives will view the pandemic as a social dilemma where social distancing is akin to cooperating, while not doing so is analogous to free-riding. Therefore, they will support lockdowns since they believe that this is the compassionate and empathic course of action. Social conservatives, however, are sensitive to threat and averse to pathogens, and will support lockdowns owing to that threat aversion. Economic conservatives who are in favor of free-market policies will be averse to shutting things down and so would be opposed to lockdowns. Finally, given the well-known aversion to pathogens from social conservatives, we expected that the degree of social conservatism will increase following the Covid-19 pandemic as compared to before. We did not expect the pandemic to make any difference to people's degree of economic conservatism.

The first thing we needed to do was to figure out how to measure things, that is, scales that will allow us to measure degrees of economic conservatism (or progressivism) and social conservatism (or progressivism). For economic conservatism (versus progressivism), which represents the trade-off between competition and cooperation, respectively, we decided to adopt the *social dominance orientation* (SDO) scale developed by Jim Sidanius of Harvard and Felicia Pratto of Connecticut. This scale asks respondents to answer statements such as:

- It is OK if some groups have more of a chance in life than others.
- Inferior groups should stay in their place.
- To get ahead in life, it is sometimes okay to step on other groups.
- We should have increased social equality.
- It would be good if groups could be equal.
- We should do what we can to equalize conditions for different groups.

In answering these statements, respondents can choose integer values between 1 (strongly disagree) and 7 (strongly agree). For instance, on "Inferior groups should stay in their place", or similar statements, we expect economic conservatives to choose 7 (strongly agree), or similar, while we expect economic progressives to choose 1 (strongly disagree), or similar. Some are "reverse scored". For instance, for a statement such as "We should do what we can to equalize conditions for different groups", choosing 1 (strongly disagree) is the most competitive response while choosing 7 (strongly agree) would be the most cooperative response. So, on a statement such as this, the scores are reversed for subsequent analysis; a 1 is replaced by a 7, a 2 by a 6, a 3 by a 5, and so on.

An economic conservative, with a cut-throat mindset, will have higher scores on the SDO scale, while lower scores imply economic progressivism. The choice of 1 and 7 is arbitrary and we could choose other values, with the caveat that in most of these studies a higher value implies a more competitive person while a lower value implies someone who is more cooperative. This is certainly not the only feasible scale for measuring a competitive worldview. There are others, but all of them suffer from one drawback or another. Researchers need to choose a scale knowing full well that any measure is not exact. The SDO scale may not be the ideal, but it is probably as good as any; in any event, it is likely that other scales used to measure competitive (or cooperative) tendencies will yield similar results.

In measuring social conservatism, we turned to the right-wing authoritarianism (RWA) scale devised by Bob Altemeyer of the University of Manitoba. Altemeyer's scale was derived from an earlier scale named the Fascism or F-scale designed by Theodor Adorno of University of California Berkeley and his colleagues in the 1950s. Similar to Solomon Asch, whose work I discussed in a previous chapter, Adorno's work was also undertaken in the aftermath of the Second World War and was aimed toward understanding the fascist mindset.[20] The term "right-wing authoritarianism" is unfortunate because it is a bit of a misnomer, representing the historic origins of this scale. This scale is better thought of as measuring the tension between group conformity and individualism. Consequently, it is better to think of this as a scale measuring *authoritarianism* in general, whether left-wing or right-wing. As I note in the associated footnote, there are plenty of examples of left-wing authoritarians and left-wing authoritarianism. However, for the time being, I am going to stick with the right-wing authoritarianism terminology since this is the currently used nomenclature in the literature.

Here are some examples of the statements posed:

- It is always better to trust the judgment of the proper authorities in government and religion than to listen to the noisy rabble-rousers in our society who are trying to create doubt in people's minds.
- It would be best for everyone if the proper authorities censored magazines so that people could not get their hands on trashy and disgusting material.
- Atheists and others who have rebelled against established religions are no doubt every bit as good and virtuous as those who attend church regularly.
- Some of the best people in our country are those who are challenging our government, criticizing religion, and ignoring the "normal way" things are supposed to be done.

As with SDO, responses to the RWA scale are also typically measured on a 1 (strongly disagree) to 7 (strongly agree) scale. Again, as in the case of SDO, some questions are reverse scored. For example, a group-minded person is expected to strongly agree with a statement like: "It would be best for everyone if the proper authorities censored magazines so that people could not get their hands on trashy and disgusting material." So this person is expected to choose 7, while a less group-minded person is expected to choose 1. Alternatively, a conformist, socially conservative personality is expected to strongly disagree with a statement such as: "Atheists and others who have rebelled against established religions are no doubt every bit as good and virtuous as those who attend church regularly." This person is expected to choose 1 on this type of statement, while a less conformist person is expected to choose 7. In the latter, the score of 1 will be changed to 7 for further analysis. So, the higher the participant scores on the RWA scale, the more socially conservative and group-minded this person is. Social progressives are expected to score low on this scale.

In addition to our measure of political ideology, we also measure other things. For instance, we measure empathic responses to the pandemic via a set of statements such as:

- The government should waive all insurance costs and hospital fees for testing and treating Covid-19.
- Paid leave should be granted to anyone diagnosed with coronavirus Covid-19.
- I am very concerned about those most vulnerable to Covid-19.

In order to measure conformist (group-minded) responses to Covid-19, we asked participants to consider statements of the following type:

- It is important to follow the UK government's rules regarding Covid-19.
- Because of Covid-19, it is very important that others take physical distancing very seriously and limit all social contact.
- I support government measures to restrict the movement of UK citizens to limit the spread of Covid-19.
- It is vital right now that the government strongly enforces social distancing measures.

- It is vital right now that the government strongly punishes people who do not engage in social distancing.
- Strict entry restrictions should be imposed at all borders while the Covid-19 pandemic is ongoing.
- The army should be mobilized to enforce quarantines and rules regarding Covid-19.

As in the case of SDO and RWA, these questions are also rated on a scale from strongly agree to strongly disagree. Similar to Rutchick and Rand and their collaborators, we also ask a series of questions about how vulnerable people thought they were to Covid-19; whether they knew of others who had the disease or succumbed to it; how worried they were about health outcomes as well as the financial fall-out. In the interests of parsimony, I am going to provide only our headline results.

We find that people became more socially conservative (as measured by scores on the RWA scale) following the pandemic. Those who are more socially conservative exhibit a preference for stricter enforcement, such as border restrictions, involving the military to enforce social distancing rules and harsh punishments for violators of those rules.

Also, in keeping with our prior conjecture, people with low scores on the SDO scale (economic progressives) preferred empathic responses to the pandemic and, similar to social conservatives, were in favor of strict enforcement of social distancing measures. This means that those who score high on the SDO scale (and, therefore, have a competitive mindset) are much less likely to support heavy-handed government restrictions since they are much more invested in maintaining normal economic activity. However, this also meant that those economic progressives who scored low on this scale were much more likely to support stringent social distancing rules since they considered this to be the empathic course of action. Contrary to the conventional conservative–liberal story, there were sections of conservatives, social conservatives, who are in favor of lockdowns. Equally, economic conservatives were opposed to lockdowns. Similarly, among supposed liberals, economic liberals (progressives) were strongly in favor of lockdowns while social liberals who emphasize individualistic values and are opposed to state control were opposed to lockdowns.[21] So, we had concurrence on the issue of lockdowns from two very different and disparate groups who would, in the normal course of events, find it hard to agree on anything.

Working independently, a group of researchers at UCLA and University of California Merced, led by Theodore Samore and Colin Holbrook, arrive at very similar conclusions to ours, that it was social conservatives driving the strong support for lockdowns. However, in their analysis, which was carried out in the US, the results are driven almost entirely by self-identified democrats with very little effect on self-identified Republicans, where support for lockdowns was minimal.[22]

* * *

Where does this leave us? What I have shown in this chapter is that the popular perception suggesting that all conservatives were opposed to lockdowns while liberals were in favor is incomplete at best, if not downright incorrect. There are nuances here that are important to understand. One type of conservatives, social conservatives, were strongly in favor of lockdowns, while another type, economic conservatives, were opposed. Similarly, economic progressives were strongly supportive of lockdowns and perceived this to be the empathic and compassionate course of action. Social progressives were not in favor, given their emphasis on and preference for individual rights and liberties.

If economic conservatives and social progressives were opposed to lockdowns, then what explains the nearly unanimous support for the same? This is where political institutions, political leaders and the media came into play. In a country like Sweden where social progressives dominate, lockdowns were anathema. The Freedom of the Press Act and the Fundamental Law on Freedom of Expression are two of the four fundamental laws underpinning the Swedish constitution and take precedence over all other laws.[23] Therefore, it was no wonder that heavy-handed government restrictions were never going to be popular in Sweden.

At the expense of engaging in some generalities, in most other countries, such as Canada, the UK, France, Germany, Australia, New Zealand or Israel, the strong agreement between social conservatives and economic progressives meant that there was little opposition to stringent restrictions on mobility. Social progressives who support individual rights and liberties are generally not the type to take to the streets and were at peace conceding to the demands of the economic progressives that lockdowns were the empathic course of action in order to save precious lives, even if that came at the expense of serious restrictions on rights and freedoms. Social progressives are generally comfortable with a live-and-let-live policy. They may have been concerned that some conservative voices were being drowned out, but the economic conservatives are not part of the social progressives' ingroup or ecosystem and therefore, social progressives saw little benefit or reason to find common cause with economic conservatives. Similarly, economic conservatives who believe in free markets may have been opposed to lockdowns, but they also tend to be less ideological than their socially conservative counterparts, implying that when the social conservatives demanded lockdowns as a means of averting the pathogen threat, economic conservatives, generally, fell in line.

One place where the situation was different was the US, which saw a significantly greater battle. This is most likely attributable to economic conservatives constituting a more vocal and empowered faction in the US. In spite of Donald Trump's reputation as a germaphobe,[24] Trump is first and foremost an economic conservative, someone with a competitive "dog eat dog", "devil take the hindmost" mindset. As President, Trump pandered endlessly to the social conservatives in multiple ways, such as appointing socially conservative judges to the Supreme Court, but for a long time he donated money to the Democrats; Bill and Hillary Clinton attended his third marriage to Melania Knauss and his daughter Ivanka used to be close friends with Chelsea Clinton. In 2000, during the Mayor's Inner Circle Press Roast, Trump's lawyer and former New York City Mayor, Rudy Giuliani, dressed up in drag, and he and Trump engaged in behavior that was termed "bizarre" by the UK's *Independent* newspaper.[25] Trump's multiple marriages and serial philandering also do not sit well with social conservatives. It is arguable that Trump is not and was not a social conservative though he often played one on television. Faced with the pandemic, Trump's instincts as an economic conservative took over, so he downplayed the risk of the pandemic in order to maintain normal economic activity. Here, as we have discussed previously, the US was also different given the pre-eminent role of Fox News in its political and popular discourse. Economically conservative commentators, such as Lou Dobbs, Maria Bartiromo or Sean Hannity, amplified the anti-lockdown message coming from Trump.

It is highly probable that, as in the UK, even in the US the social conservatives were in favor of lockdowns. The work by Samore, Holbrook and their colleagues show that this is true among those who identify as Democrats. Samore et al. fail to find a difference among self-identified Republicans. This is almost certainly because, given the unique socio-political climate in the US, this was one of the few countries were the social conservatives struggled to carry the day, partly owing to the relative strength of economic conservatives and partly owing to the social conservatives' deference towards an autocratic ruler, whose message was often amplified by the megaphone of Fox News. It was only the highly polarized atmosphere of the US that saw more of a struggle, with economic conservatives leading the way and social conservatives following. In most other places, the social conservatives, especially when joined by the economically progressive, won the battle and provided strong and unquestioning support for lockdowns and other stringent restrictions on daily activities. Equally, the higher threat sensitivity on the part of social conservatives in the US often drove them to seek solidarity with their ingroup; but the ingroup was dominated by economic conservatives who were often downplaying that same threat.

NOTES

1. I note that this particular finding about greater startle response on the part of conservatives has been challenged by Bert Bakker at the University of Amsterdam and his colleagues. However, there are important distinctions between the two studies. The original study by Hibbing and his colleagues measured *Orbicularis oculi* startle response. *Orbicularis oculi* are the muscles around the eyes, and here, what is being measured is the extent to which people blink when presented with a sudden sharp noise through headphones. In contrast, the Bakker et al. study looked at galvanic skin response (or electrodermal response). These measure changes in sweat gland activity on the skin. However, while the differences in startle response may or may not be borne out, there is currently a significant body of evidence regarding the greater threat sensitivity and particularly pathogen aversion on the part of conservatives. It is possible that the relationship between threat sensitivity and political ideology may be more nuanced and that this link may vary across types of political beliefs, different types of threat, and different countries. See Brandt, M. J., Turner-Zwinkels, F. M.,

Karapirinler, B., van Leeuwen, F., Bender, M., van Osch, Y., et al. (2021). The association between threat and politics depends on the type of threat, the political domain, and the country. *Personality and Social Psychology Bulletin, 47*(2), 324–343. https://doi.org/10.1177/0146167220946187.

2. Harris, J. R. (1998). *The Nurture Assumption: Why Children Turn Out the Way They Do.* Macmillan.

3. Among his many other contributions, Condorcet is probably best known for the Condorcet paradox, which suggests that in elections, majority preferences may exhibit what are known as "intransitive" cycles with three or more candidates. For example, suppose in a head-to-head match-up, a majority prefer Bernie Sanders over Elizabeth Warren in one pair but prefer Elizabeth Warren over Joe Biden in another pair. Rationality suggests that if people prefer Sanders over Warren and Warren over Biden then in any head-to-head match-up between Sanders and Biden, the majority must now prefer Sanders over Biden. This is the fundamental idea behind transitivity. However, it often turns out that in the Sanders–Biden pair, people prefer Biden over Sanders. This implies that these preferences are intransitive. Sanders is preferred over Warren, Warren is preferred over Biden, Biden is preferred over Sanders … these preferences may generate a cycle with no clear winner.

4. In spite of all the talk about political polarization in the US, it is worth bearing in mind that none of this is of as recent a vintage as people seem to think. In 1800, Thomas Jefferson was accused of fathering children with one of his slaves, Sally Hemmings, but still managed to prevail over the incumbent President John Adams. It was only two centuries later that DNA evidence proved that the accusations had been true all along and that Jefferson did father children with Hemmings. In 1804, Jefferson's Vice President, Aaron Burr, had a duel with another founding father, Alexander Hamilton, who had been Treasury Secretary under President George Washington. The duel took place in Weehawken, New Jersey. Hamilton missed but Burr shot Hamilton, who died two days later. Burr was later charged with murder in both New York and New Jersey, but the charges were written off. Both Jefferson and Burr represented the Democratic-Republican Party while Hamilton and Adams represented the Federalist Party. The 1800 elections saw both Burr and Jefferson take on the incumbent President Adams, except they ended up with a tie in the Electoral College. This moved the election to the House of Representatives, which was controlled at the time by the Federalists. Hamilton, a leader of the Federalist Party, worked hard to make sure that the House elected Jefferson President rather than Burr, with the latter becoming Vice President. The duel was not directly related to this but came as a culmination of long simmering tensions between the Democratic-Republicans and the Federalists.

5. There is some evidence that conservatives and liberals may have different brain structures. A group of researchers including Ryota Kanai and Geraint Rees (Kanai et al., 2011) found, in a sample of young adults, that "greater liberalism was associated with increased grey matter volume in the anterior cingulate cortex, whereas greater conservatism was associated with increased volume of

the right amygdala". The anterior cingulate cortex (ACC) can be divided into two components, dorsal (top) and ventral (bottom). The dorsal part is connected with the prefrontal cortex and parietal cortex, and plays a major role in cognitive processing, problem solving, resolving conflicting emotions and making executive decisions. By contrast, the ventral part of the ACC is connected with the amygdala, nucleus accumbens, hypothalamus, hippocampus, and anterior insula, and is involved in assessing the salience of emotion. The amygdala is part of our limbic system, the oldest part of the brain, which we share with many other life-forms. The amygdala is primarily implicated in processing emotions including the well-known fight-or-flight response. An interesting side note: a co-author on this paper is the famous actor Colin Firth, who won the 2011 Best Actor Oscar for *The King's Speech*, though some readers may instantly think of him as Mr Darcy in the BBC television series *Pride and Prejudice* or Mark Darcy, Bridget Jones's boyfriend. How he came to be a co-author on an academic paper on brain structures is a story that I will leave readers to investigate on their own.

6. The first set of Nuremberg Trials were held in Court Room 600 of the Palace of Justice on Fürtherstrasse in Nuremberg, Germany. This is a fully functional courthouse, which also houses a museum providing an enormous amount of information about the trials. Court Room 600 has undergone significant renovations but it is still possible to see the doorway through which the Nazi accused were brought in for trial or where people such as Göring, Frick, Kaltenbrunner and Hess were seated; where the prosecution and defense tables were, where the judges sat and where the witness box was. The alignments are different now. If you happen to find yourself in Nuremberg or the vicinity, I strongly recommend a visit to the Palace of Justice. Given that this is also a fully functional courtroom in use today, I recommend visiting on a Sunday when there are no cases scheduled and you can spend as much time sitting in the room as you want.

7. Rubin, J. (2020). Fox News has succeeded – in misinforming millions of Americans. *Washington Post*, 1 April. https://www.washingtonpost.com/op inions/2020/04/01/fox-news-has-succeeded-misinforming-millions-americans; Swisher, K. (2020). Fox's fake news contagion. *New York Times*, 31 March. https://www.nytimes.com/2020/03/31/opinion/coronavirus-fox-news.html.

8. For example, real headline: "Trump: US Won't Close Border with Mexico as Coronavirus Spreads"; fake headline: "Sales of Corona Beer Drop Sharply Because Consumers Associate the Beer with the Coronavirus".

9. These traditions become ingrained in the popular culture even if, at times, the meaning of the traditions are quite opaque. For example, what explains the prohibition against eating shellfish or pork in Judaism? One argument is that these prohibitions came about because shellfish are more likely to contain parasites, and pork may lead to a disease such as *Trichinosis*. However, this is disputed, and it is possible some of these prohibitions in Mosaic law are merely a way of setting the Jewish tribe apart from the Philistines. The latter ate pork but pigs were largely absent among the Jewish herding community. Regardless, it remains the case that adhering to and endorsing these traditions can be personally costly but

they are also a way of signaling group allegiance and advertising your member-ship of the group.

10. Those who are deeply involved in this area will recognize that I am engaging in some simplifications of the complex and passionate debate on individual, group and multi-level selection. This is neither the time nor the place to engage in that debate. My defense is that the evidence in favor of cultural evolution is overwhelming, and so appealing to this in making my arguments should not be controversial.

11. The latter involves our willingness to provide a high rating to a sentence such as "The invisible is beyond new timelessness" on a scale from 1 (not at all profound) to 5 (very profound).

12. For instance, they are asked to rate the validity of statements such as: Warm weather stops the coronavirus from spreading; the coronavirus is not airborne; the coronavirus will kill most people who contract it; vitamin C can cure corona-virus; the coronavirus was created in a laboratory; the coronavirus is probably a hoax. Pennycook, G., McPhetres, J., Bago, B., and Rand, D. G. (2020). Attitudes about COVID-19 in Canada, the U.K., and the U.S.A.: A novel test of political polarization and motivated reasoning. Unpublished manuscript. University of Regina, Saskatchewan.

13. Among others, this argument was made eloquently by the 2018 Nobel Prize Winner in Economics, Paul Romer, and Harvard University Provost, Alan Garber. Romer, P., and Garber, A. (2020). Will our economy die from coro-navirus? *New York Times*, 23 March. https://www.nytimes.com/2020/03/23/opinion/coronavirus-depression.html.

14. For more than a decade now, Sibley has been tracking the values and attitudes of ordinary Kiwis, through his project on the New Zealand Attitudes and Values Study (NZAVS). More information about the study can be found at the University of Auckland's https://www.psych.auckland.ac.nz/en/about/new-zealand-attitudes-and-values-study.html website. Sibley knows the answers to all types of questions regarding where Kiwis stand on various fraught debates, such as legalized marijuana, assisted dying, same-sex marriage or immigration. On any given weekday, Sibley can be found in the older section of the University of Auckland's Science building supervising an army of postgraduate students and research assistants pouring over the latest data from their studies. Some of Sibley's work in this area was undertaken with John Duckitt, a now retired Professor of Psychology also at Auckland.

15. Fans of Frans de Waal would be justified in asking at this stage why we have chosen to use chimpanzees (*Pan troglodytes*) as the benchmark. After all, humans are as closely related to bonobos (*Pan paniscus*) as they are to chim-panzees. This is a valid criticism. My response is that compared to bonobos, we know a lot more about chimpanzee social structures since they have been studied more, both in captivity and in the wild. Second, while bonobos are certainly far less aggressive than chimpanzees and are well-known for diffusing conflicts quickly via both heterosexual and homosexual intercourse, it appears that bonobo society is also hierarchical. Except among bonobos, the hierarchy

is female-centered and female dominated. This makes the structure of bonobo society different from the current structure of human society. *Ex post*, given the current primarily patriarchal structure of human society, the comparison to chimpanzee society seems more apt than a comparison to bonobo society. But as De Waal writes:

> Just imagine that we had never heard of chimpanzees or baboons and had known bonobos first. We would at present most likely believe that early hominids lived in female-centered societies, in which sex served important social functions and in which warfare was rare or absent. In the end, perhaps the most successful reconstruction of our past will be based not on chimpanzees or even on bonobos but on a three-way comparison of chimpanzees, bonobos and humans.

16. Sir Philip Sidney (1554–1586) was an English poet, courtier, scholar and soldier who is remembered as an important figure of the Elizabethan age. Sidney died in the Battle of Zutphen, which was fought in September 1586, near the town of Zutphen in the Netherlands as part of the Eighty Years' War. It was fought between the United Provinces of the Netherlands with the help of the English, against the Spanish. According to legend, as he lay mortally wounded, he gave his water to another wounded soldier, saying, "Thy necessity is yet greater than mine". This information is taken from Wikipedia (n.b.b.).

17. A similar argument applies to those with an openness to new experiences. When it comes to personality types, there is strong positive correlation between extraversion and openness. See Aluja, A., Garcia, O., and Garcia, L. F. (2003). Relationship among extraversion, openness to experience and sensation seeking. *Personality and Individual Difference*, *35*(3), 671–680. Aluja et al. show that the correlation between extraversion and openness is driven to a large extent via sensation seeking, as documented in Zuckerman (1979).

18. I thank Kyle Fischer for providing this analogy regarding the two dials in our brain.

19. Among his other activities, Martin Shkreli was the co-founder and former CEO of the pharmaceutical firm Turing Pharmaceuticals. In September 2015, Turing obtained the manufacturing license for the antiparasitic drug Daraprim and raised the price of one tablet from $13.50 to $750, creating understandable controversy and revulsion. In 2017, Shkreli was charged and convicted in federal court on two counts of securities fraud and one count of conspiring to commit securities fraud. This was not related to the Daraprim controversy. He was sentenced to seven years in federal prison and forced to pay millions of dollars in fines.

20. Adorno was focused on right-wing authoritarianism as adopted by the Nazis. However, later in the century, people would come to realize that Stalin or Mao were no less of a blood-thirsty autocrat. This led to scholars making a distinction between left-wing and right-wing authoritarianism, with Edward Shils of the University of Chicago being the pioneer. Arguably, left-wing and right-wing authoritarianism measure different things. In our study, we measured both types. But, in the context of modern-day USA or the UK, it is likely that it is right-wing

authoritarianism that is more of a pressing issue than left-wing authoritarianism. Therefore, I have focused on the former in my discussion here.

21. As I noted earlier, social distancing is a collective action problem. If everyone else is engaging in social distancing and one person does not, then this person is better off since he or she can go about his or her own life without increasing the risk of spreading infection too much. However, if it is rational for one person to do so, then this applies to everyone else. In that case, no one engages in social distancing, which, in turn, means that the only way to achieve this goal is to enforce strict lockdowns. As I have explained in the previous chapter, this view of humanity, that is, no one will engage in social distancing or mask-wearing even when implored to do so, is just not borne out by the evidence. Thus, the progressive view that lockdowns were the only way to achieve compliance is misguided.

22. With apologies to Samore and his colleagues, I have modified and adapted the innovative title of their paper for the heading of this chapter. I hope that the authors will consider this to be a compliment rather than plagiarism. I like the alliterative nature of their title.

23. The other two laws are the Instrument of Government and the Act of Succession.

24. Lippman, D. (2019). The Purell presidency: Trump aides learn the president's real red line. *Politico*, 7 July. https://www.politico.com/story/2019/07/07/donald-trump-germaphobe-1399258.

25. Oppenheim, M. (2018). Bizarre video of Rudy Giuliani dressed in drag while being seduced by Donald Trump resurfaces. *Independent*, 10 May. https://www.independent.co.uk/news/world/americas/rudy-guiliani-donald-trump-drag-video-seduce-new-york-mayor-us-president-a8344921.html.

6. Irrational exuberance in the midst of Covid-19

At the height of the pandemic, while the global economy headed into recession, share and house prices boomed. In this chapter, I discuss:

- the concept of an asset bubble where the price of a financial asset deviates from its true underlying value;
- how cognitive biases played a role in such price bubbles;
- what economists mean when they talk about expansionary fiscal and monetary policy as a way of fighting recessions;
- how such monetary and fiscal policies exacerbated such price bubbles, which in many cases will lead to lasting wealth inequality.

* * *

By April 2020, as increasingly more countries placed curbs on economic activity as well as domestic and international mobility, it became clear that we were looking at a global recession with shrinking gross domestic products and rising unemployment; a recession that was going to be at least as bad as the Global Financial Crisis (GFC) of 2008–09, if not worse. Yet, following a sharp, albeit brief, drop in March, share and real estate prices in most developed nations kept booming.[1] This is surprising since, with economies going into recession, we would expect corporate profits and therefore their share prices to fall. How did this come about? To a large extent, these soaring share and real estate prices represented market bubbles and were brought about by expansionary fiscal and monetary policies adopted by governments and central banks all over the world. In order to understand the "how" and the "why" of this, we first need to look at what an asset bubble is and how fiscal and monetary policies operate.

WHAT IS AN ASSET BUBBLE?

An asset or price bubble is a situation where the price of an asset far exceeds the asset's fundamental value. "Fundamental value" is what the asset is truly worth, not what it may be currently trading for. For instance, consider a house. The price of the house should reflect the value of the land on which the house stands as well as the total cost of the building itself. The value may not be exact and may lie within a range, but we would not expect a house to sell for too much more than its true value. Deviations are possible but should not persist over time. A similar argument applies to shares in a company. The current price of the share should reflect the stream of future dividends that we expect to receive. This price should incorporate relevant information about the business (and the market) and should not change unless something fundamental changes about the company, people's expectations or the market conditions. This, in turn, implies that prices should track the fundamental value closely and that it should be difficult to beat the market consistently by buying and selling such shares. If all traders are perfectly rational and equally well-informed about the market conditions, then they should all price the share in a similar way. This idea that prices of financial assets should track the fundamental value is the essence of the *efficient markets hypothesis* as proposed by Eugene Fama of the University of Chicago in the 1970s.

However, working with Gerry Suchanek of the University of Arizona and Arlington Williams of Indiana University, Vernon Smith, who won the 2002 Nobel Prize in economics, showed that contrary to the postulates of the efficient markets hypothesis, large and persistent bubbles arise regularly in markets for financial assets, with prices hovering far above any feasible fundamental value for long periods. Their work is interesting and important enough that it is worth going into in more detail; all the more so since financial asset bubbles profoundly affect many of us.

Suppose you own a financial asset in the form of shares in a company. If you hold on to these shares, then you can earn dividends from the company. To keep things simple, I use the term "share" to indicate one unit of this financial asset. Further, suppose that these shares last for a finite amount of time after which they become valueless.[2] Let us say that because company earnings are not certain, the dividend payments are uncertain too. However, you know for certain that, for each share you hold, in any given period there is a one-quarter chance that this dividend payment will take one of four values: $0, $0.08, $0.28 or $0.60. This implies that in any period, the expected dividend is $(1/4) \times (0 + 0.08 + 0.28 + 0.60) = \$0.24$. Therefore, in any given period, on average, you would expect to earn $0.24 in dividend payment for each share held.

Smith et al. then set up a large number of decision-making market experiments with students (and at times even experienced stock traders) at the University of Arizona.[3] Typically, each market consists of between nine and 12 traders, who interact for 15 periods and are paid their earnings in cash at the end of the session. Each trader is given some cash money and some shares. The cash held earns interest, but it can also be used to buy shares. Remember that each share earns you an expected dividend of $0.24 per period. This means that if you hold on to one share for the entire 15 periods, your expected earnings from that share is $(\$0.24) \times (15) = \$3.60$. A trader's total earnings from the entire session is given by cash endowments to start with, plus any interest earned, plus any dividends received, plus any profit from selling shares, minus any payments made for buying shares. In any period, traders can buy and/or sell shares. They are free to not do anything and simply hang on to their cash endowment, which earns interest, and their share endowment, which earns dividends.

Two issues are worth noting at the outset. First, unlike real-life markets where there are many things happening at the same time and the degree of uncertainty is high, the variables within the experiment are controlled tightly. Also, all the experimental parameters are known to all the participants. They know what the expected dividends and interest rates are; they know how many periods they will interact for; and they know exactly who has how much cash and/or shares. This is vastly different from real markets where not all participants are aware of relevant opportunity costs. For instance, if Isha decided to do some day-trading in shares, she may or may not know the opportunity cost involved. Would she be better off investing in gold or trading currency? The advantage of the stylized markets set up by Smith et al. is that it allows us to identify specific mechanisms at work behind the formation of bubbles. If bubbles arise in the sanitized confines of the laboratory where all information is common knowledge, then we can plausibly expect them to arise in situations where there are many more potential confounds.

Second, the fundamental value of a share should also be commonly understood by all. Given that each share becomes valueless at the end of the fifteenth period and yields an expected dividend payment of $3.60 per share, it would seem unlikely that the price at which these shares are bought and sold should deviate significantly from the underlying fundamental value. At the beginning of the session, the expected value of a share is $3.60, which is the sum of the expected dividends over time. With ten periods left, the expected value of the share is $2.40; with two periods left, the share is worth only $0.48 in expectation, and so on.

Figure 6.1 shows what typically happens in this type of market. The graph is adapted from a survey article by Stephan Palan of the University of Graz, where he provides an overview of what occurs in these markets. The horizontal axis shows time (consecutive periods of trading in the market) and the vertical axis shows what is happening to the average price of the share over time. For the sake of convenience, I have multiplied all numbers by 100, so that $3.60 is shown as 360. The thick dotted line that slopes downward from left to right shows the declining fundamental value of the share over time.

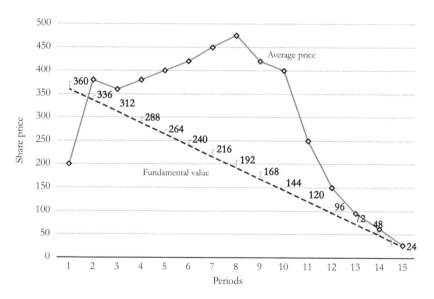

Source: Figure recreated by author on the basis of data from Palan (2013).

Figure 6.1   Asset bubble with declining fundamental share value

Suppose traders are rational and markets are efficient, then we expect the average trading price to track this dotted line. Individual prices may be dispersed but, generally, if we take averages over the actual prices at which each share trades, then this average should be close to the fundamental value. The path of actual average prices in each of the 15 periods is shown by the solid line with diamonds. A look at Figure 6.1 suggests that the average prices are nowhere near the fundamental value for most of the periods. The average price starts at $2.00, but from that point, the average asset price starts climbing until it reaches a value of $4.75 in period 8. The price then stays far above the fundamental value line until it crashes dramatically following period 10, and is virtually equal to the fundamental value of $0.24 in the final period.

This inverted U-shaped path of the actual average asset prices is typically referred to as a "price bubble". Note, for instance, that at the beginning of period 6, with ten periods left in the market (including period 6), the share is worth $2.40 but it is changing hands at an average price between $4.00 and $4.50. The same is true of period 7 (nine periods left) and period 8 (eight periods left) where the share is worth $2.16 and $1.92, respectively, but is being traded at average prices of around $4.50 to $4.75. So, if Isha does buy a share at (say) $4.75 at the beginning of period 8, then with eight periods left, the expected dividend from the share is only $1.92, which implies that Isha is most likely looking at a loss of $2.83 on this share unless she manages to find another trader who is willing to buy at an even higher price. In this particular market, a trader such as Isha will find that she is the "last sucker", the one who paid top-dollar for the share, where the price starts an inexorable decline towards the fundamental value beyond this point.

If you are wondering whether this is an artifact of the declining fundamental value of the share, let me assure you that it is not. Figure 6.2 shows what happens if the fundamental value is constant over time. This figure is reproduced from work I did with David Dickinson of Appalachian State University and my Auckland colleague Ryan Greenaway-McGrevy. Here, traders play for 15 periods as in the original Smith et al. experiments. The fundamental value of the share is always equal to $7.00. This means that any shares held in the fifteenth, and final, period can be redeemed for $7.00. As is evident from Figure 6.2, this market also shows a strong bubble pattern, with the

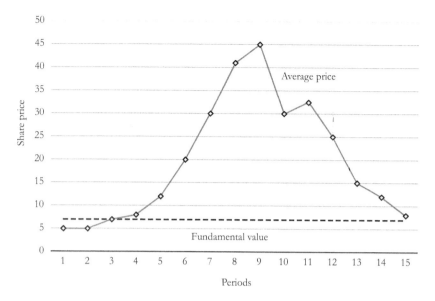

Source: Figure recreated by author on the basis of data from Dickinson et al. (2020).

Figure 6.2   Asset bubble with flat fundamental share value

average price of a $7.00 share going as high as $45.00 in period 9. In general, the average price is substantially higher than the fundamental value of $7.00 for ten of the 15 periods, the exceptions being periods 1, 2, 3, 4 and 15.

ASSET BUBBLES IN REAL LIFE

Asset bubbles such as those found in the laboratory occur often in real life, except they are not always as easy to perceive. At times, people realize the existence of a bubble only after the bubble crashes; when house-owners may find that they have gone under with negative equity, implying that the price of the house they own is valued at much less than the amount they owe on it to the bank. One conclusion is inescapable: when a bubble crashes, it destroys a lot of wealth, and in recent times bursting bubbles have often set off severe economic recessions.

Possibly the earliest recorded bubble is the so-called "tulip mania" that infected the Netherlands in the seventeenth century. In 1637,

there was a huge speculative bubble in the price of tulip bulbs
as recorded in the book *Extraordinary Popular Delusions and the
Madness of Crowds* by the British journalist Charles Mackay. Tulips
were probably introduced to Europe in the middle of the sixteenth
century from Turkey. They were different from other European
flowers and quickly became a status symbol. As the flowers grew in
popularity, professional growers paid higher and higher prices for
bulbs, and prices rose steadily. By 1636, tulip bulbs became one of the
Netherlands' leading exports. The price of tulips skyrocketed because
of speculation in tulip futures among people who never saw the bulbs.
Tulip mania reached its peak during the winter of 1636–37, when
some bulbs were reportedly changing hands ten times in a day. The
collapse began when buyers refused to show up at a tulip bulb auction
in Haarlem, which was suffering from an outbreak of bubonic plague.
This outbreak might also have helped to burst the bubble.

Another notable bubble is that involving the share prices of the
South Sea Company in the UK, which supposedly had a permit to
trade slaves in the South Seas, implying South America and the surrounding waters. In reality, this meant very little because this particular trade was dominated by Spain, with whom Britain was at war at the
time.[4] A great deal of insider trading and questionable practices[5] saw
share prices of the company more than quadruple during the course of
1720, before crashing down to earth. Many investors were ruined by
the share-price collapse, and as a consequence, the national economy
reduced substantially. A parliamentary inquiry was held after the
bursting of the bubble to discover its causes. A number of politicians
were disgraced, and people found to have profited immorally from
the company had personal assets confiscated proportionate to their
gains. An interesting side note: it appears that Sir Isaac Newton also
held stocks in the South Sea Company. When asked about the price
bubble, he is rumored to have said: "I can calculate the movement of
the stars, but not the madness of men." It is not known how much
money Newton may have lost or gained.

Closer to our times, in the early 2000s, there was the "tech-stock"
bubble where the prices of information technology companies, many
of which had yet to turn a profit, increased sharply before crashing.
This is the bubble that led to the coining of the term "irrational
exuberance" by the then Governor of the US Federal Reserve, Alan
Greenspan. The term later became the title of a best-selling book

by the Yale economist Robert Schiller. I have used the term as the heading for this chapter since it is appropriate in the current context.

Then there was the defining bubble of our lifetime; the US housing-market bubble whose crash set off the GFC, or the Great Recession, in 2008–09, the biggest economic crisis we have experienced in recent times prior to the Covid-19 pandemic. A great deal has been written about the GFC and there is no point in my elaborating on that here. Interested readers can read the book *The Big Short* by Michael Lewis (or watch the movie directed by Adam McKay and starring Brad Pitt and Steve Carrell) and the chapter on asset bubbles in my book, *Behavioural Economics and Experiments*.

RATIONAL SPECULATION?

Why do people often buy assets at an inflated price? The answer seems obvious: the opportunity for speculative gains. Different traders enter the market with different expectations and information. Isha may well decide to buy a share at an inflated price if she is certain that another trader, Ana, is willing to pay an even higher price for the share. However, a part of this bubble phenomenon is also caused by the "bounded rationality" of traders, where traders both in the laboratory and in real life, confronted with a cognitively demanding environment, fail to anticipate that bubbles will eventually crash. Instead, many traders engage in naive behavior based on their (often myopic) forecasts of what they expect the price to do. When an asset price starts to deviate from the fundamental value, traders seem to believe that the fundamental value is no longer the primary concern but base their future forecasts on current prices. They fail to take into account salient information, such as the fundamental value or the length of the time horizon.

Evidence for this bounded rationality is provided by Vivian Lei of the University of Wisconsin-Milwaukee, Charles Noussair of the University of Arizona and Charles Plott of the California Institute of Technology (Caltech). These researchers conducted a study where they turned off the speculative channel. Here, as in Smith et al.'s work, traders start with both shares and money, but are divided into buyers who can only buy but not sell any shares and sellers who can only sell but not buy any shares. There is no scope for capital gains by adopting buy-low-sell-high strategies. This should get rid of speculative bubbles, but it does not, mostly because both buyers and sellers make mistakes and force prices up from their fundamental value. These bubbles are smaller in magnitude than those in the Smith et al. study, but they exist nonetheless. A lack of speculative profit opportunities does not succeed in completely eliminating these bubbles. Indeed, in the presence of traders who do make mistakes, speculation, especially on the part of more seasoned traders, becomes even more of a possibility. If someone is an experienced trader and is aware of the presence of numerous inexperienced traders, then the former may be more inclined to engage in speculative trades to take advantage of those with less experience. Traders who are better at predicting the movements of prices, often because they have more experience, consequently earn higher profits.

In many instances, lack of experience is coupled with a lack of self-control. When some traders see other traders buying, even at inflated prices, the urge to buy becomes overpowering. Sometimes this type of behavior is referred to as "momentum trading", a type of herd mentality where traders feel the urge to trade because everyone else is doing so. Andrew Lo at MIT's Sloan School of Management and colleagues examine the behavior of 80 anonymous day-traders. They find that subjects who possess worse self-control, that is, those traders who exhibit far more emotional reactions to both gains and losses, perform worse than those who exercise greater self-control.

Martin Kocher (of the University of Vienna), Konstantin Lucks (of the University of Munich) and David Schindler (of Tilburg University) provide *causal* evidence that it is the lack of self-control that leads to bad trades, rather than bad trading outcomes leading to stronger emotional responses. Prior to any trading, Kocher et al. had some of their participants take part in a mentally demanding task. Following this, all participants take part in an asset trading market where the fundamental value of the asset is declining over time. Those participants who have completed the mentally demanding task are expected to possess less self-control than those who did another task. There is abundant evidence that mentally demanding activities drain self-control[6] and data collected by Kocher et al. via post-study questionnaires provide ample evidence that the relevant set of participants did indeed experience reduced self-control.

Kocher and his colleagues find that those traders depleted of self-control generate bigger bubbles than those who are not so depleted. Indeed, not even all traders have to be depleted of self-control. Even a market with half depleted and half non-depleted traders generates significant bubbles in comparison with markets where all traders are depleted of self-control. Kocher et al. conclude that: "Together, these findings suggest that self-control depleted traders become more reliant on heuristics, are much more emotion driven, and rely less on their cognitive skills to find optimal trading strategies."

Over many studies, the only thing that reliably leads to attenuated bubbles is greater experience with the task at hand. Charles Noussair of the University of Arizona, together with colleagues Ernan Haruvy and Yaron Lahav, has shown that only extensive experience with market trades leads to an elimination of bubbles. Those traders with significant experience with market bubbles are also better at avoiding them.

The soaring asset prices during the pandemic reflected the entry of large numbers of new and therefore inexperienced traders into markets for financial assets, driven to a large extent by seeking higher returns in the face of unprecedented low interest rates. The implications of this lack of experience on the soaring prices should be evident on the basis of the previous discussion. Let me now turn to discussing the role of government fiscal and monetary policies behind this.

THE COVID-19 RECESSION; FISCAL AND MONETARY POLICY

As it became clear in early 2020 that the decision to implement restrictive measures to combat Covid-19 were inevitably going to lead to lower incomes and unemployment around the world, governments and central banks responded by enacting expansionary fiscal and monetary policies, respectively. Most readers will have some understanding of what this means, but just to be sure, it is worth explaining this a little more.

Expansionary fiscal policy simply implies that the government starts running budget deficits. At the most basic level, the government earns revenue via a variety of taxes. When it decides to spend more than it earns in taxes, we term that a budget deficit. (The converse would be a budget surplus, where taxes exceed spending.) In recessions, faced with declining output and employment, governments often run deficits. Here, the aim is to create extra jobs since businesses may not be hiring enough people. At times, these deficits may go directly toward providing expanded unemployment benefits to those who lose their jobs. The government could also support individuals and households via tax cuts, thereby letting people keep more of their money. These are standard economic methods of fighting recessions since the Great Depression of the 1930s, as suggested by the "father of modern macroeconomics", John Maynard Keynes.[7]

What happens when the government wants to spend more than it raises in tax revenue? It needs to borrow money (often termed deficit financing). The terms vary from one country to another but, broadly, the government instructs the Treasury about the magnitude of the borrowing it wishes to undertake. The Treasury, in return, issues three main types of debt: Treasury bills, Treasury notes and Treasury bonds. These are all essentially IOUs of different types that have to be paid back sometime in the future. Treasury bills typically have the shortest maturity (less than a year), while Treasury bonds have maturities of ten years or more. Who holds this debt? Typically banks or institutional investors. Many large retirement funds such as KiwiSaver (in New Zealand), Vanguard (in the US) and other similar retirement accounts invest part of their funds in government bonds. The same is true for those individuals who invest in managed funds where government bonds constitute a component of that fund.

So far so good; the government's deficit financing alleviates some of the economic misery. Contrary to what some deficit hawks suggest, there is nothing particularly good or bad with budget deficits. Both deficits and surpluses come with some advantages and disadvantages; as with everything else, there are trade-offs. Also the magnitude of these budget deficits may or may not mean all that much. There are countries in the world whose total debt exceeds their total national income. At the time of writing, Japan's total debt is more than double the size of its national income, while for Italy the debt is more than 1.5 times its income. Other countries, such as Greece, in recent times have run into serious difficulty even with a smaller level of government debt. Many factors in addition to the debt level matter. My father smoked more than 20 cigarettes a day for nearly 40 years but lived until the age of 90. Many others would have succumbed much sooner.

However, when the government starts running large deficits, it is yet another debtor in the market and starts to compete with businesses in order to raise money from capital markets. Standard economic analysis suggests that this will lead to a rise in interest rates, because interest rates are a price, the price of borrowing money. When demand for borrowing money increases, particularly with the government also trying to borrow funds, the price of this borrowing, in the form of interest rates, also goes up. Note again, that even in this instance, there is nothing particularly good or bad about higher interest rates. If interest rates go up, then those who have money deposited in banks (such as retirees who live off the interest income from their savings) are better off, but the young couple who wants to borrow to buy a new house are worse off. The opposite is true when interest rates go down.[8]

However, in recessions, when incomes fall, businesses are less willing to expand. Therefore, they are not creating many new jobs. Business investments are typically funded out of credit, that is, borrowed money, rather than out of retained profit, which is typically paid out in dividends to shareholders. When the interest rate goes up, borrowing money becomes even more difficult for businesses. Economists term this "crowding out" of private investment; that is, the government's attempt to borrow large sums of money to finance its deficit is pushing out private firms from being able to borrow those sums.

To address these two issues, that is, the potential increase in interest rates and the consequent lack of credit for businesses, governments (and central banks) turn to monetary policy. The aim is to prevent interest rates from rising too much. At the same time, the government wants to make sure that these businesses have adequate credit available to keep going. The policies that are adopted to combat these are typically termed "quantitative easing", whereby a country's central bank, for example, the Federal Reserve (in the US) or the Reserve Bank (of New Zealand), starts buying up government-issued bonds. Sometimes, the central bank may even buy bonds issued by private companies in order to provide liquidity to those businesses. For instance, during the 2008–09 GFC, the US Federal Reserve, under the Troubled Asset Relief Program (TARP), bought up not only government-issued bonds but also privately issued mortgage-payment backed securities.[9]

In return, central banks print currency to pay for the bonds and this currency goes into circulation in the form of a larger money supply. Quantitative easing floods the system with liquidity, which in turn should put downward pressure on the interest rates and provide much needed credit to cash-strapped businesses. This is over and above lowering other key rates such as the overnight lending rates at which banks can borrow money from the central bank. (See note 12 of this chapter for a more detailed discussion about such overnight lending rates.) These moves are designed to push retail interest rates, such as mortgage rates, or deposit rates down. The aim in both instances is to make borrowing easier (cheaper) in the hope that businesses will borrow money and invest, and that this will create additional jobs. They are also intended to provide much-needed credit to businesses.

THE LIMITS OF PRINTING CURRENCY

Faced with the Covid-19 recession, governments and central banks set off on massive programs of deficit spending and quantitative easing. The latter resulted in very low interest rates; for a while New Zealand considered taking interest rates negative, where depositors would actually have to pay banks to hold their money. In many ways, it is this policy of printing currency and flooding the system with liquidity in an attempt to keep interest rates low that led to inflated asset prices. However, a quick detour before I get to that.

I have already noted that large-scale government deficits coupled with quantitative easing may well be justified in some circumstances, but I also noted that many factors are in play and countries need to be aware of potential pitfalls. What works for a large open economy, such as the US, may or may not work for Australia and may work even less well for a small open economy, such as New Zealand. I noted previously that New Zealand quadrupled its debt from roughly NZ$50 billion to nearly NZ$200 billion during the course of 2020. I will discuss potential difficulties of this approach shortly. However, as with lockdowns, there was general agreement across the economic and political spectrum about the validity of expansionary government policies. To an extent, this support was predicated on standard Keynesian arguments but, during the pandemic, a radically new idea took hold: that governments could pile up as much debt as they wished with impunity and then could simply repay this debt by printing more money. This idea is known as Modern Monetary Theory (MMT) and had strong support from progressive politicians such as Bernie Sanders and Alexandria Ocasio-Cortez. Stephanie Kelton of Stonybrook University, one of the main proponents of this theory, was an advisor on the Sanders Presidential campaign during the 2020 Democratic primaries.

To a large extent, the tenets of MMT are not that different from policies espoused by traditional Keynesians; that governments should engage in expansionary monetary and fiscal policies during recessions in order to save jobs, even if this means over-stimulating the economy and creating inflationary pressures. Many left-leaning economists, such as Paul Krugman, espouse these views.[10] Among others, support for this view was expressed elegantly in the book *Hard Heads, Soft Hearts* by Alan Blinder, a Princeton Professor and Vice Chair of the Federal Reserve Board of Governors of the Federal Reserve System under President Bill Clinton. Similar to Keynesians, MMT proponents argue that, faced with a recession, central banks should print large amounts of money to finance public infrastructure projects, thereby generating jobs. However, the proponents of the theory go much further than Keynesians, by arguing that governments can continually engage in these policies of deficit financing and money printing with impunity since no sovereign government that issues its own currency can ever go bankrupt. It can always print more money to pay off that debt.

This view of economics is wrong on multiple levels.[11] For instance, if and when the Federal Reserve or Reserve Bank of New Zealand (RBNZ) buys up government debt from bond holders and the creditors have been paid off, that does not imply that the government debt has been canceled. The government's debt now is the additional amount of money floating around the economy. The money that the central banks print will end up in the banking system as reserves,[12] and the government (via the central bank) will need to pay interest on those reserves. This money is also legal tender backed by the authority of the government. If there comes a time where no one else wants to accept this money, then holders of this money should be able to sell it back to the RBNZ for something of value in return. (Though this is not exactly what happens. If you need to show up at the RBNZ or the Federal Reserve to get your money's worth, then things are already in bad shape, as I explain below.)

Government borrowing is not a one-off event but a long-term game. This entire system, whether deficit financing or money printing, is based on trust; that the government will honor its debt. No government in the world can satisfy all their creditors if one day all those creditors came calling to get their money back. However, as long as the government keeps making the interest payments on the loans, or at least has the capacity to pay back part of those creditors (sometimes by borrowing even more), the economy remains stable; the juggler's balls keep going around in the air.

If for some reason, that trust in the government is lost, then watch out for the juggler's balls to come crashing down. Any hint of default or not honoring its debt obligations will lead to long-term damage to the government's reputation and its future ability to borrow. No one will want to hold the government's debt in the form of government bonds in the future.

When that happens, money starts flowing out of the country via capital flight as people desperately seek to invest their money elsewhere in an attempt to earn a return. In turn, the value of the currency falls drastically. This typically has catastrophic effects on the economy. An example of this is the Asian Financial Crisis in 1997. The crisis started in Thailand with the financial collapse of the Thai baht. Capital flight ensued almost immediately, beginning an international chain reaction that caught up Hong Kong, Laos, Malaysia, the Philippines and, to a lesser extent, Singapore, Taiwan and Vietnam. There are other examples of similar capital flight.

Further, as Sebastián Edwards, an international economist at UCLA, notes:

> MMT, or some version of it, has been tried in several Latin American countries, including Chile, Argentina, Brazil, Ecuador, Nicaragua, Peru, and Venezuela. All had their own currency at the time. Moreover, their governments – almost all of which were populist – relied on arguments similar to those used by today's MMT supporters to justify huge increases in public expenditure financed by the central bank. And all of these experiments led to runaway inflation, huge currency devaluations, and precipitous declines in real wages.

Four episodes in particular are instructive: Chile under President Salvador Allende's socialist regime from 1970 to 1973; Peru during President Alan García's first administration (1985–1990); Argentina under Presidents Néstor Kirchner' and Cristina Fernández de Kirchner from 2003 to 2015; and Venezuela since 1999 under Presidents Hugo Chávez and Nicolás Maduro.

In all four cases, a similar pattern emerged. After the authorities created money to finance very large fiscal deficits, an economic boom immediately followed. Wages increased (helped by substantial minimum-wage hikes) and unemployment declined. Soon, however, bottlenecks appeared and prices skyrocketed, in some cases at hyperinflationary rates. Inflation reached 500% in Chile in 1973, some 7,000% in Peru in 1990, and is expected to be almost ten million percent in Venezuela this year. In Argentina, meanwhile, inflation was more subdued but still very high, averaging 40% in 2015.[13]

THIS RECESSION IS UNLIKE OTHERS

During the Covid-19 recession, it was soon evident that the ability of quantitative easing to stimulate business spending was going to be limited since, during this recession, what was holding back business spending was not a lack of credit but an acute uncertainty about what the future held. Why may businesses not expand even with lower interest rates? This is because in deep recessions, it is not the lack of credit that holds them back. In these situations, businesses and households get caught in a low-level coordination trap. No business wants to expand unless others do so. Firms cannot sell their goods at prevailing prices and this reduces demand for labor; in turn, demand for goods is inadequate because many customers are unemployed. This creates a vicious cycle of insufficient demand where the key issue is not credit or liquidity but a crisis of confidence.

The Covid-19 recession was different in other ways. In the past, governments were fighting recessions caused by shocks that had already happened. In the pandemic, the governments were fighting a recession that they were exacerbating, if not causing in the first place. I have noted that a great deal of evidence suggests that the lockdowns had a negative effect in the aggregate. So, it is debatable whether and how much expansionary policies we really needed. Yes, Covid-19 would probably have led to a recession in any event, but arguably, government policies exacerbated this recession. Whatever the net impact of creating recession with one hand and fighting it with the other, an inevitable conclusion is that there will be distributional consequences from such low interest rates. The expansionary monetary policies will certainly create further wealth inequality and, so, the unadulterated support for the same from progressive politicians seems anathema.

This is because the soaring asset prices were directly the result of the very low interest rates and there are, at least, two ways that this will impact wealth inequality. Investors looking for returns (or yield) realized that putting money into bank accounts or term deposits was futile since these were yielding interest rates close to zero. This set off a quest for other investments that would yield a higher return, causing investors to gravitate toward houses and equities, furiously bidding up prices and fueling speculative bubbles.

For most households, their main source of wealth is the house they own. In previous recessions such as the GFC, house prices had taken a beating, making investments in real estate a losing proposition. Not so this time around. Also, the lockdowns disproportionately affected blue-collar workers often working for hourly wages. White-collar workers who could work from home were not particularly affected; at least, not to anywhere near the same extent. Generally, these white-collar workers did not suffer adverse shocks to their wealth. Therefore, these households whose income and/or revenue streams were not impacted were free to invest in financial assets. In his book *Capital in the Twenty-First Century*, Thomas Piketty notes that the primary means of achieving wealth is to own financial assets. Property owners who have equity accumulated in their properties are best placed to cash in on the low interest rates by investing in more properties and other assets. Data from New Zealand suggests that residential property owners are among the largest beneficiaries of government-related support provided during this pandemic. Mortgage holders will receive around $2.3 billion of relief on their repayments over the course of 2020, thanks to the low interest rates. However, these benefits can only accrue to those who already own property and/or other assets, or have the financial means to invest further. Low interest rates were a massive boon to the asset-owning class, to the detriment of those with little collateral.[14]

There was a second contributing factor to soaring asset prices, primarily share prices. With countries in lockdown and people working from home, most people found themselves with plenty of time on their hands. They now decided that, given the very low prevailing interest rates, it would be worth entering the stock market. In the meantime, technological advances have made it possible for platforms such as Robinhood in the US or Sharesies in New Zealand to make it extremely easy for retail investors to take part. This influx of new investors also had an impact on share prices.[15]

This is relevant because, as I argued previously in the chapter, two key factors behind the creation of market bubbles are the lack of experience and depleted self-control. Depleted self-control is the result of higher cognitive load, and Covid-19 certainly presented plenty of that. In work with David Dickinson and Ryan Greenaway-McGrevy, we show that higher cognitive load and depleted self-control may also result from sleep deprivation. In our study, we bring together traders from the US and New Zealand, one group operating at a decent time of the day while the other is operating at a seriously suboptimal time given the time difference. For instance, the US participants may be playing at 12 noon while for their New Zealand counterparts it is 4 a.m. the next morning. We find that those traders operating at suboptimal times of the day make systematic errors, which are exploited by those operating at better times. The net result is that those traders who are more alert make higher profits at the expense of those who are sleepier. Cognitive loads and lack of experience played a critical role in fueling speculative bubbles during the Covid-19 pandemic.

Therefore, it was not surprising that the entry of new inexperienced investors into the share market set off a speculative frenzy. Eventually the bubble will burst and, even if it does not, some of the inexperienced investors will suffer catastrophic losses. However, the experienced investors will not lose out, and the net effect of this bubble-and-crash pattern will be an increase in the wealth of those already well-off at the expense of those who are not; particularly those of lower socio-economic status who are nowhere near the threshold of owning either property or shares.[16] The value of engaging in printing money to lower interest rates seems grossly counter-productive and the support for this from progressive politicians, ostensibly deeply concerned about growing inequality, completely escapes me.

* * *

In this chapter, I have explained how it is that in the midst of a pandemic, asset prices continued to soar, with little association with the rest of the economy. I have argued that this was driven to a large extent by expansionary fiscal and monetary policies adopted by governments and central banks. These policies were adopted to a large extent to fight a recession that those same governments were exacerbating, if not creating in the first instance, via stringent lockdowns. I have also argued that the net effect of this will be growing income and wealth inequality, both across countries and within countries. I alluded to some of the reasons for this growing cross-country inequality in previous chapters, via increased demand for automation and reduced demand for specific types of low-skilled labor. However, even within countries, particularly developed countries, a large part of growing inequality, especially in the form of wealth inequality, will be brought about by government policies. This is yet another unintended consequence and uncounted cost of lockdowns.

NOTES

1. Krugman, P. (2020). Crashing economy, rising stocks: What's going on? *New York Times*, 30 April. https://www.nytimes.com/2020/04/30/opinion/economy-stock-market-coronavirus.html; Rogoff, K. (2020). Why are stock market prices rising despite the Covid pandemic? *Guardian*, 6 October. https://www.theguard ian.com/business/2020/oct/06/stock-market-prices-covid-pandemic-business.
2. For now, think of it this way. Suppose you own shares of a company with investments in a depletable natural resource, such as a copper, gold or coal mine. This natural resource will generate cash flow in the form of dividends while the company is in operation but, at some time in the future, the resource will get depleted, rendering those shares valueless. This is a simplification and the type of market that Smith and his colleagues looked at. Even if we allow for longer-lived or even infinitely lived assets, we still observe similar bubble phenomena.
3. These decision-making experiments are now an integral part of mainstream economics. Yes, they suffer from a degree of artificiality, but they also provide an enormous amount of control. Studying phenomena such as asset bubbles in the real world is made difficult as so many things can change and are changing simultaneously. Interest rates may be going up or down, the economy may go into or out of a recession, unemployment may be high or low. Laboratory experiments provide the unique advantage that within the laboratory, we can control for all these potential confounds by changing one thing at a time. A laboratory experiment thus serves as a microcosm of society, where the experimenter can

look at what happens when one thing changes while everything else is held constant. The argument is that if we observe asset bubbles in the relatively sterile confines of the laboratory, where most things are being controlled for and cannot influence decisions, then these bubbles are even more likely in the real world where there are many more potential aspects that can change and many more decision-making biases that come into play. This branch of economics goes by the name of behavioral economics and incorporates psychological insights into traditional economic theories. For those who are interested in learning more about this, a good place to start is my book *Behavioural Economics and Experiments* published by Routledge, a British publisher and hence the "u" in "behavioural".

4. This was the War of Spanish Succession (1701–1714). It was set off with the death of the childless Charles II of Spain in 1700. Philip of Anjou, grandson of Louis XIV of France, inherited an undivided Spanish Empire. Disputes over territorial and commercial rights led to war in 1701 between the Bourbons of France and Spain, and the Grand Alliance, including Britain, Holland and Austria, whose candidate was Charles, younger son of Leopold I, Holy Roman Emperor.

5. Government officials who had oversight responsibilities for the company were gifted shares and were given cash loans backed by those same shares to spend on purchasing more shares.

6. See, for instance, work undertaken by Roy Baumeister. Baumeister had two groups of participants placed in two separate rooms around a table. In one room, the table had a bowl of freshly cut cauliflowers. The table in the other room had a bowl of freshly baked cookies, whose aroma filled the room. Participants were admonished from consuming any of the contents of the bowls in either room. Afterwards, both sets of participants were given challenging mathematical problems to solve. It turned out that the group that had been in the room with the cookies gave up much more quickly on trying to solve the problems, as opposed to the people in the room with the cauliflowers. (Baumeister, R. F., Bratslavsky, E., Muraven, M., and Tice, D. M. (1998). Ego depletion: Is the active self a limited resource? *Journal of Personality and Social Psychology, 74*(5), 1252–1265.) In the interests of full disclosure, I note that later researchers have had difficulty replicating the results of this particular study, but that is a debate for another time.

7. There is one difference. When the government spends the money, whether in buying things itself or giving it out in welfare benefits, this money is injected into the economy and has an immediate impact. Tax cuts are more roundabout in that they will stimulate economic activity if and when the recipients spend that extra money. This comes with a caveat; those who are less well-off tend to spend most of this extra income, while those who are more well-off end up saving most of it. So, tax cuts received by the latter will typically not stimulate economic activity to the same extent. This is why, in general, many governments prefer to increase government spending via deficit financing to fight recessions, rather than cutting taxes.

8. Readers will understand that there are many different interest rates in the economy. The interest rates that depositors receive on their savings accounts is different from that on term deposits. Similarly, the mortgage interest rates that homeowners pay when they borrow to buy a house is also different. I am going to write about this as though there is only one interest rate with the implication that all these different interest rates are closely correlated and when one rises the others will too. If the savings interest rate is higher then so will the mortgage interest rate be. As we say in academic circles, we can make this assumption without any loss of generality.

9. The late 1990s saw large-scale business in subprime loans. These were loans made at interest rates greatly below the prime (that is, market) interest rates to start with, but the rates increased sharply later. In most instances, these loans were made to people who had little ability to repay them. In turn, investment banks, such as Lehman Brothers, created a set of bonds named collateralized debt obligations (CDOs) on the basis of these mortgage payments. These are essentially bonds (pieces of paper) that people hold, where the payment on the bonds depends on a steady stream of regular mortgage payments. When the US housing market collapsed and the homeowners, who often had little ability to service the loans, defaulted, so did these mortgage assets, resulting in heavy losses for all those holding them.

10. Krugman has written extensively on the need for expansionary fiscal policy via debt financing to combat recessions both in his books and his columns. For a recent example see Krugman, P. (2021). How Democrats learned to seize the day. *New York Times*, 8 February. https://www.nytimes.com/2021/02/08/opinion/democrats-covid-stimulus.html.

11. These views are opposed by all serious scholars in economics, including Paul Krugman on the left and Greg Mankiw, Chair of George W. Bush's Council of Economic Advisors, on the right. I am not aware of any serious mainstream economist who supports the view that governments can continually pay off debt by printing money.

12. This is not a course in macroeconomics and I do not want to bombard readers with too much information. In any event, the way to think about this is that if and when depositors put money into their accounts, banks hold back a fraction of this amount while loaning out the rest. In the US, for instance, banks are required to hold a fraction of their deposits in the form of required reserve ratios. Banks are free to hold more in addition to that as excess reserves, depending on how much demand there is for loans from private individuals or businesses. Both the required and excess reserves are held with the country's central bank and earn interest, albeit small, but if the reserves are large then even a small interest on it can work out to a large sum. The Reserve Bank of New Zealand does not impose a required reserve ratio on commercial banks. Instead, it tries to influence the market interest rate by directly manipulating the Official Cash Rate (OCR), which is the rate at which the Reserve Bank lends money to banks. The OCR acts as the lower bound of retail interest rates; a higher (lower) OCR means higher (lower) retail rates. The OCR in New Zealand acts as the overnight

lending rate. This is similar to the London Interbank Offered Rate (LIBOR). In these instances, the aim is the same; by raising and lowering the interest rates that banks need to pay to the central bank (effectively a cost for the commercial banks), the central bank tries to influence the price that banks charge their retail customers.

13. Edwards wrote this in 2019.

14. Tibshraeny, J. (2020). A look at how much Covid-19 support property owners are receiving through low interest rates versus what non-property owners are receiving from the Government. *interest.co.nz*, 22 September. https://www.interest.co.nz/news/107161/look-how-much-covid-19-support-property-owners-are-receiving-through-low-interest-rates.

15. See Fitzgerald, M. (2020). Penny stock-loving Robinhood traders raised bubble concerns, but most retail investors are selling. *CNBC*, 25 June. https://www.cnbc.com/2020/06/25/penny-stock-loving-robinhood-traders-raised-bubble-concerns-but-most-retail-investors-are-selling.html.

16. Popper, N. (2020). Robinhood has lured young traders, sometimes with devastating results. *New York Times*, 8 July. https://www.nytimes.com/2020/07/08/technology/robinhood-risky-trading.html. Robinhood has also been accused of relying on behavioral nudges to encourage new investors to invest more and take on more risky positions. In February 2020, Robinhood was hit with a wrongful death lawsuit for such practices. See Fitzgerald, M. (2021). Robinhood sued by family of 20-year-old trader who killed himself after believing he racked up huge losses. *CNBC*, 8 February. https://www.cnbc.com/2021/02/08/robinhood-sued-by-family-of-alex-kearns-20-year-old-trader-who-killed-himself-.html. In their complaint, the parents and sister of Alex Kearns, the victim, write: "This case centers on Robinhood's aggressive tactics and strategy to lure inexperienced and unsophisticated investors, including Alex, to take big risks with the lure of tantalizing profits."

7. Epilogue

In this chapter, I wrap up my discussion with some concluding thoughts. Here, I:

- discuss the uncomfortable racial and/or socio-economic divide inherent in Covid-19 policy making within and across countries;
- answer frequently asked questions from those who support lockdowns, and refute some typical arguments;
- explore lessons learned from the current pandemic and implications for decision making in future pandemics.

* * *

In April 2020, India enacted one of the most stringent lockdowns to fight Covid-19. Among other effects, this was catastrophic for India's migrant worker community who travel long distances from one state to another to find work. Bapan Bhattacharya was one of these migrant workers employed as a mason in Chennai, a southern city of India. When he came to learn that his 4-year-old son was to undergo surgery for meningitis at the NRS Medical College and Hospital in Calcutta, with no other recourse, he cycled over 1600 kilometers in less than ten days to see his son. This included days without guarantee of food or shelter. According to Bhattacharya, his toughest trial was near the Odisha–Bengal border, where he walked 5 kilometers along railway tracks at night to bypass a rigorous police checkpoint enforcing Covid-19 restrictions.[1] I sincerely hope that his child is doing well. As the father of two young daughters, I cannot imagine the anguish this man went through as he tried to reach his son. Was this anguish for him and for numerous others around the world necessary?

RACE AND COVID-19

The world has faced pandemics before but at no time in the recent past have we responded with such hysteria effectively shutting down most social and economic activities. Given what we know now, it is difficult to avoid the conclusion that this was in large part because Covid-19 threatened rich white lives rather than poor black and brown lives. This is not hyperbole. In Figure 7.1, I present data on median age across countries and deaths per million. The vertical bars in the background show the median age. I have arranged this in ascending order of median age and this is measured on the left-hand axis. On the extreme left, we have Niger with a median age of around 16 (50 percent of Niger's population are under 16 years old while the remaining are over 16 years old). Countries such as the Democratic Republic of Congo, Gambia, Senegal, Burundi, Tanzania, Zimbabwe or Liberia have young populations as well. Space constraints prevent me from showing the names of all the countries represented. At the other extreme, we have countries such as Portugal or San Marino with a median age of around 45 years. Other countries with relatively older populations include Japan, Italy and Spain. Rich, western and industrialized nations have considerably higher proportions of older people among their population. There are more than 100 countries in the world where the median age is less than 30. That is, 50 percent of the population of these countries are less than 30 years old.[2] However, most of the countries in the West have older populations with a median age of 40 or more.[3] The solid jagged line in Figure 7.1 shows the death rates per million across different countries. (The dashed line is the linear approximation of the solid jagged line.) There are lots of ups and downs here but the pattern is clear. Deaths per million increased with an increase in the median age. Countries where 50 percent of the population are under the age of 30 had very low mortality. The mortality rate climbs sharply as the population got older.

There are outliers. Some countries, such as Iran, Mexico, Bolivia, Ecuador, Peru or Panama, which have a relatively young population have reported high death rates. South Africa is also a huge outlier with a relatively young population but a relatively high death count of 774 per million. More on South Africa shortly. At the right-hand end of Figure 7.1 we also have outlier countries with considerably higher mortality rates compared with other countries with a similar median

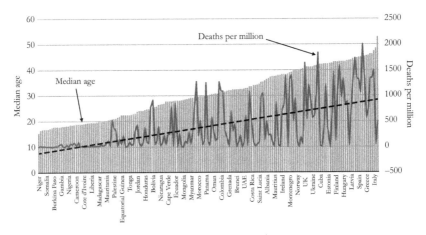

Figure 7.1   Median age and Covid-19 deaths per million across the world

age. This list will be less surprising and includes countries like Italy, San Marino, France, the UK, Belgium and the Czech Republic. But equally, Japan, with one of the older populations in the world, has exhibited a decidedly lower death rate. However, the basic pattern remains undeniable. As the median age increases and a country's population gets older on average, the death rate soared. On average, a one-year increase in median age will lead to 71 more deaths per million. This is striking given that the public health systems in most of the developing countries on the left-hand side of this chart are rudimentary to say the least.[4]

In Figure 7.2, I have blown up the left-hand side of Figure 7.1 in order to focus on 59 low Covid-19 incidence countries, mostly countries in Africa with a smattering in Asia and Latin America. As before, the vertical bars show the median age across the different countries. This is arranged in ascending order and is measured on the left-hand vertical scale. The deaths per million are shown by the solid jagged line and are measured on the right-hand vertical axis. Again, there are outliers, such as Swaziland, Palestine, Iraq, Guatemala, Jordan and Honduras, but for most of the rest (more than 50 countries), the death rate is around 100 per million or less, that is, about 1 in 10 000.

This, in turn, implies that many of the countries located on the left-hand side of Figure 7.2 with relatively younger populations could have done very little (and quite possibly did little), and the outcome would not have been dramatically different. According to John

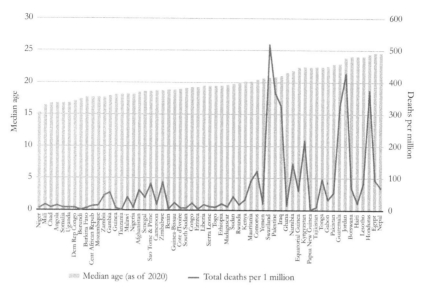

Figure 7.2   Median age and Covid-19 deaths per million in low incidence countries

Ioannidis of Stanford, for some of these countries the infection fatality ratio from Covid-19 is to the order of 0.09 percent, which is less than 1 in 1000 (about 9 in 10 000).[5] Compare this with Belgium, which has a median age of 42 and 1837 deaths per million or more than 18 deaths per 10 000.[6]

For many developing countries, there are other, far more imminent, threats to life, including HIV/AIDS, malaria, cholera and tuberculosis. Covid-19 did not pose that much more of a health threat to these countries. South Africa has reported approximately 49 000 deaths from Covid-19 over the course of 2020. In 2019, about 72 000 people died from HIV/AIDS in South Africa. Some of these will be assigned to Covid-19 in 2020 but immune-compromised people with HIV/ AIDS die from a multitude of other causes, such as tuberculosis. According to the World Bank, 1 in every 5 South Africans between the ages of 15 and 49 suffers from HIV/AIDS.[7] The HIV prevalence rate for adults aged 15 to 49 was 37 percent in Swaziland, 25 percent in Lesotho and 25 percent in Botswana. Since 1985, more than 2 million people have died of AIDS in South Africa. There has been no mad scramble to come up with a vaccine for AIDS as compared to Covid-19. In 2001, more than 40 pharmaceutical companies, many of them the world's largest and most powerful, including Merck, GlaxoSmithKline and Roche, sued the South African government to try to stop it from enacting legislation aimed at reducing the price of medicines for South Africans by adopting generic substitutes.[8] I noted in a previous chapter that the high-income countries of the world banded together under the World Trade Organization's TRIPS protocol (for governing intellectual property rights) to ensure that there will be no generic production of Covid-19 vaccines.

In a recent article, Mary Jane Rotheram-Borus of UCLA and Mark Tomlinson of Stellenbosch University of South Africa argue that the global policy response to Covid-19 has been driven by high-income countries. Yet, low- and middle-income countries face different challenges. There is greater emphasis on community solutions; families live in far more dense communities, making shelter-in-place mandates questionable; and strengthening existing health systems is more important than novel services. They go on to argue that, based on decades of lessons from the HIV epidemic, the low- and middle-income countries need to design and implement their own Covid-19 policies, to build on their strengths and to have the courage to resist policy and financial directives from the high-income countries.[9]

In Chapter 1, I wrote that the single-minded focus on Covid-19 was going to prove detrimental to the world's poor, especially children in low-income countries via channels such as deferred or canceled vaccinations and reduced focus on all the other diseases that are bigger killers than Covid-19. In December 2020, David Bell and Muhammad Usman Khan of pandata.org wrote the following in their article "COVID-19, the vaccine, and the betrayal of sub-Saharan Africa":[10]

> The "Global Health Community" that previously prioritized these diseases and the other big child killer, malaria, implicitly considers these avoidable deaths an acceptable cost in the attempt to reduce transmission of SARS-COV-2 ... As wealthy countries and private philanthropy plan to divert large donations to this cause and a global alliance under the COVAX umbrella is gearing up to lead it, there is an urgent need to examine whether this is an undeniable global health good, of benefit to the people for whom it is intended, and whether it really has anything to do with equity.

They go on to argue that we have arrived at a

> new paradigm for global health – vaccinating children not for their own health, but in order to protect a small cohort of elderly citizens – who, through acquired immunity, are expected to become less vulnerable to the disease as time passes. … If we believe the SARS-COV-2 virus can and should be eradicated globally, but we recognize that diverting resources for this programme will cost lives, then we need to acknowledge that the children who are no longer benefiting from other health interventions, are dying for the benefit of mostly elderly and chronically-sick people in far wealthier nations who wish to reduce their own Covid-19 risk.

The author C. S. Lewis said:

> Of all tyrannies, a tyranny sincerely exercised for the good of its victims may be the most oppressive. It would be better to live under robber barons than under omnipotent moral busybodies. The robber baron's cruelty may sometimes sleep, his cupidity may at some point be satiated; but those who torment us for our own good will torment us without end for they do so with the approval of their own conscience.

I end this section with a personal anecdote, which would be funny if it were not so tragic. In May 2020, Cyclone Amphan hit parts of Eastern India causing 128 deaths, mostly in India but with a few in Bangladesh and Sri Lanka during the course of a weekend. It also rendered many homeless. These natural calamities regularly affect the lives of the poor in developing countries. Some of these occurred in Calcutta, the city where I was born. Calcutta, or Kolkata, as it is known these days, is a modern megalopolis with more than 10 million people. According to a news report in *The Times of India*, the day after the cyclone hit Kolkata, citizens woke up to find at least 11 bodies floating in the water-logged streets at various parts of the city. Most of these deaths had been caused by electrocution when live electricity wires fell into water-logged streets. Yet, in spite of this calamity, the friends and relatives we talked to at the time all remained firmly fixated on Covid-19.[11] This was not even a trade-off between identified lives and statistical lives. It was a trade-off between some identified lives and other identified lives. However, people were so wrapped up with Covid-19 hysteria that they found it hard to focus on this other calamity unfolding right in front of their eyes.

In my decision-making courses I often show students a short video on the impact of cognitive load on mental acuity. Students see a clip where a group of eight athletes, four in white jerseys and the other four in black, are playing basketball. The clip starts by asking the viewers how many passes the players in white jerseys make during the course of the clip. Part way through the clip, a person dressed as a grizzly bear moon-dances through the court, between the basketball players. Surprisingly, a large majority of people are so engrossed trying to count the passes made by the white team that they completely fail to notice the bear. My point is that Covid-19 and the surrounding hysteria placed so much cognitive load on us that we found it virtually impossible to focus on anything else.[12]

WHY CAN WE JUST NOT TRUST THE SCIENCE?

During the pandemic, we were often told that we should just "trust the science". By this, what interlocutors meant was listening to the advice of epidemiological experts. The problem is that this was a narrowly defined view of what the relevant science was. The science that we needed to listen to extended into many other fields beyond epidemiology. Indeed, one of the lessons of the pandemic was for scientists to realize the limits of their expertise and not go beyond that. For instance, it is absolutely fine for an epidemiologist to indicate the IFR of a disease or its prospective path of transmission, but what we do with that data, what level of risk we are willing to tolerate, what costs we are willing to bear and what freedoms we are willing to sacrifice is no longer a question for epidemiologists. In fact, this is not a question that should be left to them. This requires expertise from others in social sciences and humanities.

I have highlighted previously the problems inherent in the SIR models that the epidemiologists were relying on. I have also shown that work carried out by economists, who incorporated more realistic assumptions about human behavior in those SIR models, demonstrated that lockdowns were not the proper course of action. There were other intermediate actions available which would have maximized the common good. This science also needs to be understood and acknowledged. I suggest that those who insist on listening to no one other than epidemiologists are guilty of adopting an anti-science posture. The epidemiological view is highly blinkered and incomplete; enough to make it incorrect by ignoring a swathe of related and pressing scientific issues. In the prologue, I briefly referred to a column by Ross Douthat in the *New York Times*. This is what Douthat wrote in that column:

> But for many crucial decisions of the last year, that unobjectionable version of trust the science didn't get you very far. (It represented) ... an abdication by elected officials of responsibility for decisions that are fundamentally political in nature ... When we look back over the pandemic era, one of the signal failures will be the inability to acknowledge that many key decisions – from our vaccine policy to our lockdown strategy to our approach to businesses and schools – are fundamentally questions of statesmanship, involving not just the right principles or the right technical understanding of the problem but the prudential balancing of many competing goods ... On the libertarian and populist right, that failure usually involved a recourse to "freedom" as a conversation-stopper, a way to deny that even a deadly disease required any compromises with normal life at all. But for liberals, especially blue-state politicians and officials, the failure has more often involved invoking capital-S Science to evade their own responsibilities: pretending that a certain kind of scientific knowledge, ideally backed by impeccable credentials, can substitute for prudential and moral judgments that we are all qualified to argue over, and that our elected leaders, not our scientists, have the final responsibility to make.

WHERE WOULD YOU RATHER BE IF NOT IN NEW ZEALAND?

New Zealand's relative success in reducing community transmission, to a large extent by shutting its borders and implementing a costly and cumbersome managed isolation system, meant that, inside the country, New Zealanders (Kiwis) could go about their lives with a much greater degree of freedom than people in many other countries. Kiwis could go out to eat, shop at malls, watch plays, performances and movies, attend sports events and pursue numerous other activities that make day-to-day living joyful.

Consequently, when I express my dissenting opinion about how we handled Covid-19, some, particularly colleagues at my own university, often say things along the following lines. Look how well New Zealand has done! What are you complaining about? Where else would you rather be? Look at the United States; what a mess they are in. Would you rather be in the US than in New Zealand? To me, these questions evince an alarming degree of naiveté and nationalism, the latter bordering on xenophobia. First, the interlocutors seemed to not understand that the identity of the person being asked this question matters. What was true of a middle-aged tenured professor at a research university with a high degree of job security may not necessarily be true of an unemployed young man with a mortgage and young children. While a large number of people were looking to buy investment properties, owing to the prevailing low interest rates, there were plenty of others who were struggling to make their mortgage payments.[13]

According to data provided by Statistics New Zealand, the country's unemployment rate at the end of 2020 was 22 percent higher than at the end of 2019. According to the Ministry of Social Development, over the course of the year, the number of Kiwis receiving jobseeker work-ready support increased by around 50 000 from 85 000 to 135 000. At the same time, data provided by Statistics New Zealand suggests that the "underutilization" rate, which includes people who are both unemployed and underemployed (those who are working fewer hours but are able and willing to work longer) went up by 58 000 during the course of 2020.[14] Again, Covid-19 would have most likely accounted for some of these job losses but it is my contention that by shutting down significant sections of the economy, including the largest export industry of tourism, the government exacerbated the economic maladies.

What the interlocutors also failed to understand was that the perspectives of native-born citizens were fundamentally different from that of the very large number of immigrants who call New Zealand home. Many of the latter had close family members including spouses stuck outside the country's borders.[15] Since they would need to self-isolate upon returning to New Zealand and pay a substantial sum for this (provided they could even get leave for that long as well as the isolation vouchers that they needed in order to even get on a flight), numerous immigrants were unable to visit ailing relatives at the time of the latter's need. In some instances, New Zealand citizens with foreign spouses chose to travel overseas to bring their spouses back with them at great inconvenience and expense. These efforts were not always successful.[16] I am not certain if asked "Where would you rather be?" the answer from all of these people would unambiguously be New Zealand.

Further, many of the people extolling the freedoms enjoyed by Kiwis took as their frame of reference what was happening in the industrialized nations of the West, which were suffering more restrictions. This is where they had friends and relatives. Consequently, they failed to understand that they were wrong about vast swaths of the world, including countries with younger populations, where Covid-19 was not so deadly after all. The latter set of countries, with their relatively younger populations, went on with their lives. (It was also the case that the Kiwis were celebrating prematurely. Covid did reach the country and spread within; albeit later than most others. Once it did, New Zealand also experienced stringent and long drawn lockdowns, the same as others, with the difference that New Zealand's lockdowns were often far more stringent and, therefore, far more debilitating, than those imposed by other countries.)

Finally, this argument that we are so much better off in New Zealand reflects an extremely narrow-minded view based on preservation of one's own self and that of one's near and dear ones. This view refuses to acknowledge the glaring racial divide that I alluded to previously: the disparities in outcomes for the richer, older nations that are disproportionately white and the poorer nations that are disproportionately non-white. New Zealand and other developed countries of the West are all equally guilty of propagating the myth that lockdowns were the panacea to tackle this pandemic and that this was true for everyone around the world. The policies promoted by the richer countries of the world certainly benefited them but to the tremendous detriment of the poorer nations of the world. The idea that somehow New Zealand (or another country) could keep borders closed, isolate itself until a vaccine came along, and that this could be regarded as an acceptable way of living regardless of the misery it caused elsewhere, was abhorrent to me. Any solution to the pandemic had to be a global solution. There was no other outcome to this disregard for global reality than to further exacerbate the already yawning gap between the rich and the poor; both within and across countries. I take the view espoused by John Donne in 1623:

No man is an island, entire of itself; every man is a piece of the continent, a part of the main; if a clod be washed away by the sea, Europe is the less, as well as if a promontory were, as well as if a manor of thy friend's or of thine own were; any man's death diminishes me, because I am involved in mankind, and therefore never send to know for whom the bell tolls; it tolls for thee.

BUT, WHAT ABOUT THE UNITED STATES?

I have noted previously that the US looms large in the psyche of other countries, particularly the English-speaking world. We empathize with the US because so much of our contemporary social mores and culture are driven by events in the US. Our movies, music and social attitudes are all guided by the US. We pay obsessive attention to their politics and their culture wars; my 16-year-old daughter gets much of her news and her entertainment from the likes of Stephen Colbert, Trevor Noah, Jimmy Kimmel and John Oliver, and knows the names of all the Supreme Court Justices. For many years prior to that, we turned to Jon Stewart for speaking truth to power on Comedy Central. My morning coffee is accompanied by looking through the *New York Times* even 18 years after I left the US to move to New Zealand. However, no matter how much US politicians or US media propagate the myth of American exceptionalism, it remains a country afflicted with deep-seated problems. The US is not a microcosm of the world, even though it often appears that way.

It is tempting to blame Trump for the fiasco that constituted the US response to Covid-19, but this would be incorrect. The real problem lies with a fractious healthcare system that varies dramatically from state to state and has been starved of funds for many years in the name of fiscal discipline. The system was never going to be able to handle a pandemic, just as it fails to deal effectively with many other crises. The difference this time was that this failure was being lit up on front pages of newspapers and television screens not only in the US but also around the world. If Trump bears blame, it is for minimizing the threat and for not making sure that there was a unified message being broadcast around the country whether about social distancing, hand-washing or mask-wearing. However, even then, the US probably would have struggled. They would have struggled because the US is alone among the developed nations in not having a nationalized healthcare system of some type. Also, many rich, developed countries, particularly the US and the UK, embarked on a policy of austerity in the aftermath of the GFC and these measures had a severe adverse impact on public services including healthcare.[17] The problem with enacting severe cuts in healthcare as opposed to, say, in education is that in the former, faced with a crisis, people die. In the latter, the destructive impact is much more gradual and less obvious to the general public.

Health insurance in the US is still dependent on your employment and provided by the employer. No wonder then that as millions lost their jobs, they also lost their healthcare. Most had little financial ability to sign up for alternative health coverage such as COBRA.[18] This meant that many, probably most, of those who lost their job could not seek medical help when needed. The US also has some of the most restrictive leave policies, including sick leave benefits, with a large proportion of workers working for hourly wages. This, in turn, meant that people could ill afford to take time off or engage in social distancing even when unwell, since that would mean going without a paycheck.

Hopefully, in the aftermath of the Trump Presidency and everything that transpired in recent times, we will have a better understanding of how truly schizophrenic a country the US is. A country that has acted as peacekeeper for the world struggled to protect its own lawmakers from a rampaging mob. A country that provided the template for written constitutions to much of the world witnessed a President egging on rioters against his own Vice-President to stop the peaceful transition of power. Equally, while the newspapers blared in 48-point font about the 500 000 deaths from Covid-19 in the US, they failed to note that more than 600 000 die in any given year from heart disease. Covid-19 being a notifiable disease guaranteed that anyone who dies and tests positive for (or even is suspected of having contracted) Covid-19 is considered to be a Covid-19 death, even if there were one or more underlying co-morbidities.[19] This is not excess mortality, or not overly so; it is merely displaced mortality. Most of the people who died of Covid-19 this year would have died, but from a multitude of other causes. Since those are not notifiable diseases, they would have not made the headlines. The real tragedy is not that the US could not prevent deaths from Covid-19; the real tragedy is that one of the richest nations of the world routinely fails to save lives from eminently preventable causes, including a variety of social ills such as homelessness, addiction or racial injustice.

A final thought about New Zealand and the US. In Chapter 5, I wrote about the work of Hunt Allcott and his colleagues showing that with Covid-19 it was possible to err on either side. Some erred by not doing enough social distancing and engaging in too many economic and social activities. Equally, others erred by engaging in too much social distancing and not enough social and economic activities. Both of these impose costs and benefits. So, one way to think of this is as follows. Given its location in the middle of the South Pacific, New Zealand would have likely escaped the worst ravages of Covid-19 in any case. Given that, it is my contention that New Zealand did too much. Its strategies, including social distancing and shutting down borders, represented an excessive degree of risk aversion. In effect, New Zealand could have achieved similar fatality rates at much lower economic cost. The US did the opposite. It engaged in too little social distancing. The net result is that the US economy would not suffer as much of a decline as many other developed countries. However, the US could have achieved the same economic goals while sacrificing fewer people to Covid-19 by maintaining a consistent message. Whatever this message was in relation to protective measures adopted, it had to create a sense of common comprehension. It did not help when the President was routinely contradicting the Head of the Centers for Disease Control and Prevention (CDC) on policy prescriptions.

WHY DID THE WORLD SHUT DOWN FOR COVID-19?

In Chapter 1, I raised the question as to why the world shut down owing to Covid-19 but not for diseases such as SARS or MERS. According to lockdown proponents, this is because, while those other diseases may be more deadly, they are not as contagious as Covid-19, particularly given its potential for asymptomatic transmission. Let me now address aspects of this. Table 7.1 shows the fatality rates from some past influenza epidemics. To a large extent, a great deal of early public policy was based on the 3.4 percent estimate of the case fatality

Table 7.1   Deaths from some prior influenza pandemics

Name	Date	R_0	Total deaths	Fatality rate (%)
1889–90 flu	1889–90	2.10	1 million	0.10–0.28
1918 Spanish flu	1918–20	1.80	17–100 million	2–3/~4/~10
Asian flu	1957–58	1.65	1–4 million	0.2–0.67
Hong Kong flu	1968–69	1.80	1–4 million	<0.2
2009 flu pandemic	2009–10	1.46	0.15–0.575 million	0.01
Typical seasonal flu	Every year	1.28	0.29–0.65 million	<0.1

Source: Data taken from Potter (2001).

ratio provided by the WHO; the idea that Covid-19 is ten times more deadly than seasonal influenza. Eventually this was dialed down to around 0.65 percent, with a range from 0.2 percent to 0.8 percent. This means that in terms of lethality, Covid-19 is certainly far more deadly than the yearly seasonal flu or other historical flu pandemics, but it is less deadly than the 1918 Spanish Flu. Covid-19 is generally comparable to the 1957–58 Asian flu pandemic. Covid-19 comes in at the upper end of the fatality rate of prior influenza pandemics and, so, is more deadly than most types of influenza. However, the difference is not ten-fold as originally proposed. Furthermore, unlike influenza, Covid-19 is not deadly for children and adults without co-morbidities. It is far more deadly for people older than 70. It is probably not worth laboring this point any further, but the implications are clear. Since Covid-19 rarely kills children or even most adults, the underlying age profile of Covid-19 deaths is not dramatically different from the typical mortality profile for most populations.

In Figure 7.3, I show the distribution of deaths from Covid-19 in New Zealand and New Zealand's general mortality profile (the usual pattern of deaths) in 2019.[20] The dashed line shows the general pattern of deaths in New Zealand in 2019 while the solid line shows the deaths from Covid-19. Total deaths are measured on the left-hand vertical axis while the right-hand axis counts the deaths from Covid-19. It is clear that these two shapes effectively lie one on top of the other. This implies that the general pattern of deaths in

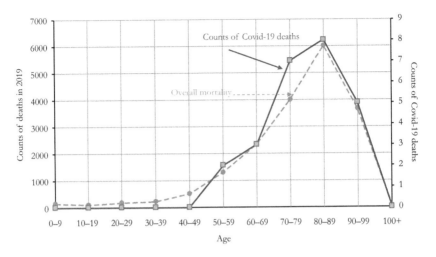

Source: Figure created by author on the basis of data from Thornley (2020).

Figure 7.3 Counts of deaths in 2019 and counts of Covid-19 deaths in New Zealand

New Zealand is no different from what would have happened in any other year. Those who died from Covid-19 in 2020 would have died in any event, except possibly from another disease. There is nothing particularly callous in stating this. In any given year, somewhere between 50 and 60 million people die around the world from age-related reasons. While I have not shown this for other countries, the pattern on total age-related mortality and deaths from Covid-19 would be similar for other rich, industrialized, Western nations. Generally, Covid-19 did not radically alter the mortality profile in these countries, with the possible exception of the US.

There are other ways of asking this question regarding the impact of Covid-19 on the mortality profile. For instance, a group of researchers led by Steven Woolf of Virginia Commonwealth University looked at life expectancy between 2010 and 2018, and projected life expectancy for the period between 2018 and 2020, that is, pre- and post-Covid in the US and 16 other high-income "peer" countries.[21] The US data come from National Center for Health Statistics, while the data for the peer countries come from the Human Mortality Database. The results are shown in Figure 7.4. These are projected results based on simulations and need to be interpreted with caution. Two facts stand out. First, across the 16 peer countries, the average decrease in life expectancy in 2020 was modest (0.22 years). This suggests that Covid-19 did not radically change life expectancy for that year on average. Decreases in life expectancy ranged from 0.12 years for Sweden to 1.09 years in Spain. However, it is equally obvious that there was a much larger impact in the US, where life expectancy was estimated to have declined by 1.87 years. I have not shown this in Figure 7.4, but this decline was significantly more pronounced among African Americans (projected decline of 3.25 years) and Hispanic Americans (projected decline of 3.88 years; pre-pandemic, the life expectancy of Hispanic Americans was above the US average). However, it should be noted that the gap in life expectancy between the US and the peer nations was widening long before the pandemic, beginning as long ago as the 1990s. By 2010, the average life expectancy in the peer nations was 80.5 years but was 78.7 years in the US, a gap of around 1.8 years. By 2018, this gap had increased to slightly more than three years (an average of 81.8 years for the peer nations and 78.7 for the US). Although the gap was expected to continue widening after 2018, it does appear that Covid-19 accelerated this process, widening the gap to 4.69 years in 2020.

A key argument behind lockdowns was the supposedly high probability of asymptomatic transmission. Under this view, Covid-19 is more deadly than many others because there may be little or no outward manifestation of the disease. Carriers of the disease could be walking around spreading the disease and creating havoc, all the while being unaware that they were infectious. In addition to the otherwise mistaken and inflated view of a more than 3 percent fatality rate, a big factor behind the arguments for stringent social distancing was the high prevalence of asymptomatic transmission and the assumption that asymptomatic carriers were as likely to spread infection as the symptomatic carriers.

A group of researchers from Australia's Bond University, led by Oyungerel Byambasuren, undertook a meta-analysis to understand the extent of asymptomatic transmission. They searched a large number of public repositories and screened more than 2000 published articles. Diagnosis in all studies was confirmed using a real-time reverse transcription–polymerase chain reaction (RT-PCR) test. They found that across many studies, the proportion of asymptomatic cases averaged 17 percent, with the average ranging

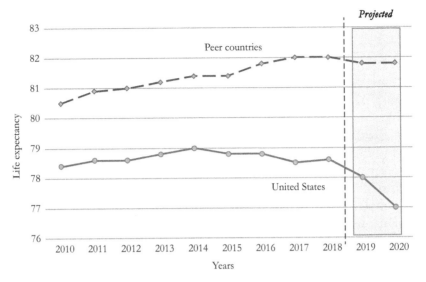

Source: Figure recreated by author on the basis of data from Woolf et al. (2021).

Figure 7.4 Life expectancy and projected life expectancy in the US and other high-income peer countries, 2010–18 and 2018–20

from 14 percent to 20 percent. This stands in stark contrast to some early studies that suggested rates of asymptomatic transmission as high as 81 percent.[22] Byambasuren and colleagues also found that asymptomatic carriers are about half as likely to pass the disease on compared with those displaying symptoms; the exact relative risk of asymptomatic transmission was 42 percent lower than that for symptomatic transmission. Byambasuren et al. go on to conclude that their "one-in-six estimate of the prevalence of asymptomatic COVID-19 cases and asymptomatic transmission rates is lower than those of many highly publicized studies". Unfortunately, it were those early highly publicized studies that were instrumental in creating a great deal of the fear and hysteria that came to characterize policy making during Covid-19.

What is also surprising to me is the lack of proportionality in the response. Many people believe that Covid-19 is especially virulent and the possibility of asymptomatic transmission makes this a particularly deadly disease. This makes the overwrought response to it justified. However, in reality there are diseases around that are far more deadly than Covid-19; that are and remain a cause for real fear.

In a review article, Berhanu Mekibib of the Institute of Tropical Medicine in Belgium and Kevin Ariën of Hawassa University of Ethiopia discuss the lethality of the *Filoviridae* family of viruses that consists of the genera *Marburgvirus*, *Cuevavirus* and *Ebolavirus*. According to these authors:

> Filoviruses are categorized among the deadliest zoonotic viruses known to affect human beings with mortality rates reaching up to 90% depending on the viral species and host. … The appearance of filoviruses and other emerging diseases is often attributed to urbanization with the concomitant invasion of animal habitats, climate change and deforestation, changing socio-economic conditions, increased global connectivity, and changes in biological characteristics of the viral species. The emergence and re-emergence in Africa, the potential for introductions into countries previously free from the disease through human mobility and the international transport of infected animals or animal products make filoviruses a worldwide public health concern.

Mekibib and Ariën note that the infrequent outbreaks of Ebola suggest the presence of *Ebolavirus* in a rare or ecologically isolated animal reservoir having few contacts with humans and non-human primates. While this reservoir remains unclear, accumulating evidence is identifying fruit bats as the natural reservoir of the virus. Mekibib and Ariën add that contact with bodily fluids from Ebola patients remains the most likely route of transmission. However, cases have been reported from the Democratic Republic of Congo that had no direct physical contact with an infected person. These observations indicate other routes, such as human to human aerosol transmission, or may suggest that other, unidentified, animal sources are involved in transmission to humans. While the aerosol mode remains "highly controversial", still there are some epidemiological and experimental studies supporting this mode.[23]

There are, thus, far more deadly diseases out there that pose a greater threat to human existence than Covid-19 does. Some of these may be highly transmissible via zoonotic, aerosol or airborne methods. This may occur naturally as is most probable with Covid-19 or, even, potentially as an act of bio-terrorism. It seems to me that the lockdowns we implemented were in the nature of nuclear options and that we have used up the most potent tool in our kit of non-pharmaceutical interventions. What is left if indeed we were confronted with something as deadly as Ebola? Also, given the experience of Covid-19 and the recognition that we may have over-reacted, what happens if people ignore social distancing recommendations if there is an Ebola outbreak?

WHY DID INTENSIVE CARE UNITS GET INUNDATED? WHAT ABOUT LONG COVID?

I venture into this section with trepidation since the evidence here, particularly as regards the impact of invasive mechanical ventilation in acute Covid-19 cases, is in its nascent stage and requires further corroboration. This requires time. Nevertheless, it may make sense to keep records in a contemporaneous manner so that we can compare the eventual reality with the original perception. This is what journalists do; capture in real time events whose true significance becomes clear only with the passage of time. This is different from the approach of the historian or the researcher who has the luxury of evaluating events with the benefit of hindsight. Unfortunately, while the second approach affords greater scientific validity and certainty, it fails to have any impact on current policy.

Since the early fatality estimate of Covid-19 was much higher than the reality, initial medical guidelines to clinicians advised in favor of mechanical ventilation and against the use of non-invasive positive pressure ventilation (NIPPV) or high-flow nasal cannula (HFNC), since these are aerosol-generating procedures and therefore created the fear of nosocomial or hospital associated infections. Neither the risk nor the fear should be minimized but, as a consequence, early in the pandemic the emphasis was on invasive mechanical ventilation (IMV) in intensive care units (ICUs). Current evidence suggests that in addition to the excessive pressure put on ICUs as a result, these IMV efforts may have led to higher mortality.

The OutcomeRea study group is a part of the Société de Réanimation de Langue Française (SRLF) or French Language Resuscitation Society, a learned society founded in 1971.[24] The SRLF is engaged in continuing education, postgraduate education as well as the promotion of clinical research and the evaluation of resuscitation activity in hospitals. This group of researchers analyzed longitudinal data for 245 patients admitted to ICUs of the OutcomeRea network in

Paris.[25] Of these patients, 187 were male and the median age was 61 years (range 52–69 years), and 157 patients, or 64 percent, had one or more co-morbidities, with obesity and cardiovascular disease being the most common in 89 (36 percent) and 61 (25 percent) patients, respectively. The median duration from onset of symptoms to ICU admission was 10 days (range 7–12 days) and between hospital and ICU admission was 2 days (range 1–4 days). Their results are sobering. Controlling for a wide range of co-variates such as age, gender, body mass index, PaO2/FiO2 ratio,[26] and so on, the 60-day mortality rate in the whole study population was about 32 percent. It was higher in the early than in the non-early IMV group: 43 percent versus 22 percent, respectively. The 83 patients (or 34 percent) who did not receive IMV had the best survival rate with a 60-day mortality rate of 11 percent.

The OutcomeRea researchers know that their results will require further confirmation. They argue in favor of non-invasive ventilation measures, such as HFNC, for acute respiratory failure. According to this group of researchers, HFNC reduces the risks from endotracheal intubation and improves oxygenation while reducing "excessive respiratory efforts, pleural pressure swings and exacerbation of lung injury".

* * *

I end this section with a brief discussion of long Covid, or as it is known medically, PASC (Post-Acute Sequelae of SARS-CoV-2). Given my limited knowledge in this area, I discuss what has been written on this topic by David Katz. Katz has an MD from the Albert Einstein College of Medicine and a Masters of Public Health from Yale. He is the founding director of Yale University's Yale-Griffin Prevention Research Center, Past-President of the American College of Lifestyle Medicine, and Founder/President of the True Health Initiative, a non-profit organization established "to defend and disseminate the science, sense, and global expert consensus about healthy, sustainable diet and lifestyle". I discussed Katz previously in the Prologue where I referred to his *New York Times* op-ed asking whether our fight against Covid-19 was making things worse than the disease.

As someone who had to be hospitalized for pneumonia a few years ago, I have long been aware that many respiratory diseases can have long-lasting effects. In that regard, I expected Covid-19 to be no different. Equally, while Covid-19 can have long-term health effects, many of my interlocutors seem to ignore that this is true of other respiratory diseases too. So, it was something of a relief to receive corroboration from a medical professional such as Katz. As he notes, while PASC is garnering a unique level of attention, this syndrome is not unique to Covid-19. According to Katz:[27]

> Many illnesses, and most injuries engender their own suite of post-acute sequelae. ... Community acquired pneumonia, for instance, is deemed mild when it does not require hospitalization – but that doesn't mean it disappears when the course of antibiotics ends. Patients routinely take months to feel back to baseline. So, too, for any of the other infections that assault a vital organ, from pyelonephritis, to septic arthritis, to prostatitis, and perhaps even to cellulitis; infection of the skin.
>
> As for viruses, many are notoriously "long". Varicella, the virus that gives us chickenpox, resides within for decades, emerging to cause shingles. Herpes simplex never goes away, and can cause recurrent cold sores for a lifetime. These and other common viral exposures may even cause a long-form illness much like PASC, which we call by other names: chronic fatigue syndrome, or fibromyalgia. ... There is another relevant consideration. We routinely say "illness and injury" as if the two are mutually exclusive. They are not. Many illnesses, SARS-CoV-2 clearly among them, cause tissue injury. Injured tissue takes time to heal.

CONCLUDING THOUGHTS

Before concluding, let us take a minute to look ahead and discuss how governments around the world should tackle pandemics in the future. Pandemics affect conservatives and liberals alike; therefore pandemic response should be a bipartisan affair. This will allow for significantly greater buy-in from larger segments of society. As far as practicable, the design of policy should be handed over to an independent group of people, who may well report to a Minister of Health or similar, since someone needs to make executive decisions. It is important to insulate a group of this type from the surrounding political pressures so that their findings are treated as being objective and unbiased. This also guarantees that a group like this would be able and willing to listen to a diverse cross-section of experts, both those supporting the popular view and those espousing minority (and therefore, unpopular) views in order to sieve out good ideas from bad.

However, at the core of these activities there needs to be a willingness to have an explicit Devil's advocate, often known as "red-teaming" in military or intelligence parlance. Defense forces do this routinely because, for them, the cost of messing up is high in numbers of lives lost. The cost of messing up and losing lives is also very high, though not often sufficiently acknowledged, when faulty policies are promulgated. The *advocatus diaboli* (Devil's advocate) is a former official position within the Catholic Church. The role of the Devil's advocate is to argue against the canonization of candidates in order to uncover any character flaws or other evidence that would argue against the canonization. Wikipedia suggests that the office was established in 1587 during the reign of Pope Sixtus V. Pope John Paul II reduced the power and changed the role of the office in 1983. It has been argued that this change led to numerous more canonizations than there would have been in a previous era,[28] including the canonization of Pope John Paul II himself.[29]

Very often, leaders, whether in business or in government, take a blinkered view of reality and there is no one around the boardroom or cabinet table who dares contradict the boss or the majority view. As I have argued previously, going against the group and/or conventional wisdom is psychologically discomfiting. However, contradiction is often essential, which is why the Church assigned this contradictory role formally to an official. This guaranteed that if and when this official expressed his or her contrarian view, he or she was not seen as a gadfly creating needless dissension but as someone who was performing a key role in questioning the validity or robustness of the choices. In my experience, this type of active solicitation of contrary views is unusual, whether in private corporations or public service. Engaging in it may lead to a more drawn-out process, but it is worth it since it leads to better engagement, wider dissemination of dissenting views and, eventually, better policy.[30]

* * *

Covid-19 is not the last pandemic that we will face but it is the first pandemic we have faced in the age of social media. This enabled particular beliefs and opinions to be magnified massively and spread rapidly around the world. However, our future as a society depends on basing policy making on evidence and a careful weighing of costs and benefits; of engaging not only with those who support our policies but also those who question it. This is both the scientific as well as the democratic approach. Not doing so is tantamount to discarding science in favor of gut feelings and instinctive decision making, which does not bode well for our ability to fight future epidemics.

In designing policy, it is important to bear in mind the idea of trade-offs and opportunity costs. Resources are not infinite; devoting them to one use invariably implies taking them away from another use. A good rule in undertaking this allocation is to either maximize the total benefit or minimize the total harm. The concept of opportunity cost is deceptively simple, yet is often overlooked. These trade-offs apply even to the nature of incentives. Both extrinsic incentives and intrinsic incentives matter. If we put too much emphasis on formal compliance, on explicit carrots and sticks, then this may reduce people's intrinsic incentive to do the right thing. Excessive demands for compliance may end up being counter-productive.

I am sure detractors will find a multitude of criticisms against arguments put forward in this book, and I welcome these criticisms. My aim in writing this book is not necessarily to criticize people for the decisions they made, since I do not for a moment doubt that many, if not most, of them were acting out of good will. I did not set out to write an Emile Zola-esque *J'accuse*. My aim is to ask questions that should have been asked but were not; or when asked were dismissed out of hand. My claim is that the science of human decision making can shed important light on why policy makers and members of the public reacted the way we did; why we were so willing to accept such restrictive policies and curbs on our liberties. These behavioral insights should have been incorporated in our policy responses but were not, and not doing so meant that the models we put so much faith in were incomplete and, therefore, often incorrect. This is why the initial predictions about Covid-19 deaths were so far off the mark. In attempting to highlight the cognitive biases that often led to mistaken policy, my goal is to make sure that when the next crisis comes along, and it will sooner or later, we are better prepared to deal with it and, more importantly, are better aware of the typical decision-making pitfalls that beset our approaches in these crises.

This book does not pretend to be a comprehensive analysis of the Covid-19 pandemic. Indeed, it is doubtful that any single book can do so and, if tried, would run to hundreds of pages. The Covid-19 pandemic and the global response to it can be studied from many angles. There are certainly stories of heroism on the part of front-line workers and the scientists who came up with a vaccine in short order. These vaccines, especially the mRNA vaccines, in spite of their limited efficacy, represent a major scientific breakthrough, which will be important in the development of future treatments. There is also a story to be told about the role of big pharmaceutical companies and how and why we came to spend billions of dollars on a relatively innocuous disease at the expense of other more deadly diseases.

My aim in writing this book was more modest. I have tried to answer a question that was posed by many, albeit a minority, about the justification of the extensive lockdowns. The evidence, I have suggested, shows that the costs of lockdowns exceed the benefits. This is most likely true for high-income nations with older populations and certainly is for low-income nations with younger populations. Given this, why was there such unquestioning acceptance of such stringent restrictions and curbs on normal life, civil liberties and fundamental rights? As I wrote at the outset, this is a question that needs to be asked. Here, in my limited way, I have tried to provide an answer to why what happened did happen. I am sure others will have further insights to present.

With apologies to Dennis Miller from when he used to read the "fake" news on *Saturday Night Live* a lifetime ago: This is my story and I am sticking to it.

POSTSCRIPT

I finished work on this book in early 2021. The book then went through an extended review process, following which the book went to the publisher in July 2021. At this time there was scope for updating material, correcting mistakes and setting the record straight. However, I have changed little in the text other than correcting typos. The only addition to the previous material is the discussion in this chapter around Figure 7.4, regarding whether Covid-19 has radically altered the mortality picture in industrialized nations. I decided to leave things alone so that the book could stand as a historical record of the contemporaneous arguments made by opponents of lockdowns, mistakes and all. This way, I could not be accused of *ex post facto* rationalizations or hindsight bias (saying I got something right when I knew it to be correct only in hindsight). The other reason is that, in carefully reading the book over, it did not seem to me that large-scale changes were called for. My arguments about the cognitive errors and biases that led policy makers to impose costly lockdowns and the public to accept these massive onslaughts on our civil liberties and the loss of statistical lives (and livelihoods) remain valid. If anything, there is now greater recognition of these biases and other failings.

As this book goes to print, the world remains in a state of disruption and uncertainty. The vaccines made by the Western pharmaceutical companies have been rolled out with varying degrees of success. Not surprisingly, new mutant strains of Covid-19 appeared in early 2021 and the existing vaccines did not prove particularly successful. In many instances, people who had been vaccinated still contracted Covid-19. One of these incidents that made the headlines was when a number of players for the New York Yankees who had already been vaccinated were found to have Covid-19.[31] This was not particularly surprising given that the compressed timeframe for the vaccine trials precluded testing for long-term efficacy. Lockdown proponents and vaccine supporters argued that such infections among vaccinated people was not a cause for concern and that, in the absence of the vaccines, they would have been much more seriously ill. While this may well be true, we will need a lot more data to draw definitive conclusions. This takes time and, therefore, such claims await rigorous validation. The vast majority of people who contract Covid-19 get mild symptoms in any event. Establishing the counter-factual, that they would have had more severe symptoms in the absence of vaccination, is not easy. It also seems surprising that people are contracting the disease literally weeks after being vaccinated. Evidently the vaccines are not that effective; they were not designed to be, but to not provide immunity beyond a few weeks still seems bizarre.

In the meantime, the argument about vaccine haves and vaccine have-nots have generally come true. Some countries have done well, others less so. This is problematic in different ways. Globally, pressure has been building to create vaccine passports that would allow people to travel (or not) across borders. I doubt I need to point out that this will yet again discriminate against people from developing countries who are reliant on the COVAX facility to get their vaccine supplies. According to *Our World in Data*, by mid-June 2021, there were around 120 countries around the world that had not managed to fully vaccinate even 10 percent of their citizens.[32] This list consists disproportionately of developing nations. It is not clear what the herd immunity threshold is, but a large part of the developing world is nowhere near it. This implies that people from those countries may not be allowed to travel to developed nations and people from developed nations may not be able to travel to these "high-risk" countries. This has obvious adverse implications for these countries' future economic and social well-being.[33]

For countries such as Palestine, the future is particularly fraught, given that they are not in charge of their own destiny. While Israel has been at the forefront of getting its citizens vaccinated, with nearly 60 percent fully vaccinated by mid-2021, Palestine has fared much worse. Israel has faced strong criticism for its unwillingness to help Palestinians.[34] However, even for the other countries that are ostensibly in control of their own fate, the future remains uncertain since these countries are critically dependent on Gavi and COVAX for their vaccine doses.

In the meantime, countries such as New Zealand, which aimed for an elimination strategy, have struggled to open their borders. Early attempts at opening up have faltered in the face of excessive risk aversion. In one instance, a travel bubble with New South Wales was hastily shut down because of one case in that state; a situation that the Premier of New South Wales referred to as "an overreaction".[35]

The availability of new data made it possible to answer more definitively two questions that lie at the heart of the debate. First, was a strong health response also the best possible economic response? The proponents of this view argue that the stringent lockdowns made sense because they helped economic growth by preventing community transmission of the disease. According to this view, not implementing these strong measures would cause greater economic devastation. John Gibson of Waikato University synthesizes data on the Covid-19 Stringency Index, available from Oxford University, with data from 32 OECD (Organisation for Economic Co-operation and Development) countries where there is data for both GDP growth rates as well as mortality (from the Human Mortality database). For these 32 OECD countries with weekly mortality data available, GDP growth rates in 2020 were lower the more restrictive the early response to Covid-19. I show this in Figure 7.5.[36]

Gibson goes on to argue that for these 32 countries:

> GDP growth rates in 2020 were lower the more restrictive the early response to Covid. ... The Level 4 lockdown in NZ was the most stringent early response in the world. If stringency had been at the median ... an OxCGRT index of 79.6 rather than 96.3, New Zealand's 2020 GDP growth rate is predicted to have been three percentage points higher.

Once again, detractors will reiterate that I am fixating on dollars and cents. After all, can we really put a dollar value on human life? Yes we can, but let us leave that debate aside. Proponents of lockdowns continue to insist that lockdowns save lives. So, what if the benefits do not necessarily stack up to the costs? In any event, we are comparing statistical lives with identified lives. Statistical lives are exactly that, *statistical, based on expectations and probabilities,* intangible things that we cannot readily see, but lockdowns are saving tangible lives that we can see right in front of our eyes. If this view is correct, then we should expect to see more stringent lockdowns resulting in fewer deaths. Unfortunately, new data makes it clear that proponents of

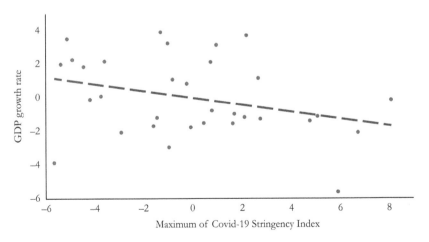

Source: Figure recreated by author on the basis of data from Gibson (2021).

Figure 7.5   Stringency Index and growth rates across 32 OECD countries

lockdowns have little cause for comfort. There is no evidence that harder lockdowns result in lower numbers of deaths compared with less harsh lockdowns.

Christian Bjørnskov of Aarhus University of Denmark looks at the association between severity of lockdown policies and mortality rates during the first half (the first 26 weeks) of 2020 in 24 European countries.[37] Deaths here include all deaths, from Covid-19 as well as from other causes. Figure 7.6 shows the results. The horizontal axis shows the first 26 weeks of 2020, while the vertical axis depicts deaths per million. Bjørnskov defines two types of lockdowns, "hard" or "easy", that is, those above or below the median, respectively, using the same Oxford University Stringency Index that Gibson uses. It is evident from Figure 7.6 that, compared with easier lockdowns, harder lockdowns did not succeed in reducing total death rates during the first half of 2020.

When Bjørnskov looks at mortality figures in these countries for the first half of 2020 and compares them with average mortality between

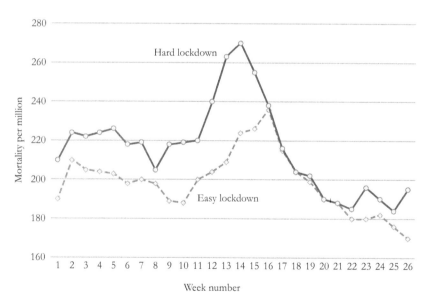

Source: Figure recreated by author on the basis of data provided by Bjørnskov (2021).

Figure 7.6 Severity of lockdowns and mortality rates for 24 European countries

2017 and 2019, he finds that for 15 out of 24 countries, mortality in 2020 was lower than the 2017–19 average. That is, there were fewer deaths in the first half of 2020 for those 15 countries compared to the average number of deaths in those countries between 2017 and 2019. For Switzerland, the number of deaths in 2020 was the same as its 2017–19 average. Surprisingly, the two countries that lead the table in higher numbers of deaths compared with their average for the past three years are the UK and Belgium. This implies that for these two countries, there were many more deaths in 2020 than during the same timeframe averaged over the previous three years. It is worth noting that Belgium is widely recognized for having implemented hard lockdowns. Yet, it reported much higher mortality numbers than the historical average. It may be further worth noting that Sweden, the media's favorite scapegoat, is not the table topper in higher death counts, even though Sweden did report more deaths in 2020 compared to its 2017–19 average.

An argument made repeatedly by lockdown proponents is that the timing of lockdowns mattered crucially; countries such as New Zealand that went "hard and early" (to use the phrase popularized by New Zealand's Prime Minister) fared much better than countries that were soft and/or went late. Remember, a critical argument was that earlier implementation of lockdowns may have saved lives by preventing healthcare systems from becoming overwhelmed. Early implementation of lockdowns also may have made it more feasible to not have to implement further and/or harder lockdowns in the future. Unfortunately, according to Bjørnskov: "the results do not support the claim that lockdowns are more effective when implemented early. In addition, exploring the data suggests that early lockdowns did not help governments avoid hard lockdowns, as there is no clear pattern between early timing and subsequent severity."

* * *

Based on the evidence, the extensive lockdowns will go down as serious mistakes and public health calamities. It is likely that history will not look kindly on those who proposed such stringent social distancing measures or those who continue to support the same in spite of the voluminous evidence against this view. This, again, may not be surprising. Manias, once they find a foothold in human minds, are not easy to get rid of. António Egas Moniz was awarded the Nobel Prize in 1949 for frontal lobotomy, a supposed cure for mental illness. Ultimately, however, Moniz and the Nobel committee were wrong. The operation did irreparable harm to over 50 000 patients and the results were far from the claimed cure. I end with some words written by Jay Bhattacharya of Stanford University, who, together with Sunetra Gupta of Oxford and Martin Kulldorff of Harvard (those of Great Barrington Declaration fame/notoriety), has fought a lonely but courageous battle against the conventional wisdom regarding Covid-19. This is what Bhattacharya wrote in the first issue of the newly launched *Collateral Global* newsletter:[38]

> In 1915, chemistry lost its innocence when mustard gas poisoned British troops in Ypres, Belgium. Physics lost its innocence in 1945 amongst the radioactive rubble of Hiroshima, Japan. Public health lost its innocence in March 2020 when the world adopted lockdowns as a primary tool to control the COVID-19 pandemic. The idea of lockdown was simple and beguiling – if we reduced all human contact to an absolute minimum, the virus would not spread, and our hospitals would not be overwhelmed. However, the reality proved to be much more complicated and, indeed, much more harmful as governments sought to show how much they care about the mortality risks from COVID-19 at the expense of so many others … In other words, it takes the wholehearted embrace of panic as a public health strategy. The scope of these effects is even more wide-ranging than those of poison gas or the nuclear bomb in war.

NOTES

1. Phadikar, A. (2020). 1600km ride to meet ailing son. *The Telegraph of Calcutta*, 5 May. https://www.telegraphindia.com/west-bengal/coronavirus-lockdown-mason-quarantined-after-cycling-from-chennai/cid/1771996.
2. These include, in ascending order: Niger, Mali, Chad, Angola, Somalia, Uganda, Congo, Burundi, Burkina Faso, Central African Republic, Mozambique, Zambia, Gambia, Guinea, Tanzania, Malawi, Nigeria, Afghanistan, Senegal, São Tomé and Príncipe, Cameroon, Zimbabwe, Benin, Guinea-Bissau, Côte d'Ivoire, South Sudan, Congo Republic, Eritrea, Liberia, Sierra Leone, Togo, Ethiopia, Madagascar, Sudan, Solomon Islands, Rwanda, Kenya, Mauritania, East Timor (Timor-Leste), Comoros, Yemen, Swaziland (Eswatini), Palestine, Iraq, Vanuatu, Ghana, Namibia, Samoa, Equatorial Guinea, Kyrgyzstan, Papua

New Guinea, Tajikistan, Tonga, Gabon, Pakistan, Guatemala, Kiribati, Jordan, Marshall Islands, Botswana, Haiti, Lesotho, Honduras, Laos, Micronesia, Egypt, Nepal, Belize, Bolivia, Cambodia, Syria, the Philippines, Paraguay, Nicaragua, Djibouti, Tuvalu, Guyana, Turkmenistan, Nauru, Bangladesh, Cape Verde, El Salvador, South Africa, Uzbekistan, Ecuador, Fiji, Dominican Republic, Bhutan, Mongolia, India, Algeria, Libya, Myanmar, Suriname, Kosovo, Mexico, Morocco, Lebanon, Venezuela, Indonesia, Panama and the Maldives.

3. The United Kingdom, Canada, Sweden, Slovakia, Ukraine, Serbia, Poland, Belgium, Cuba, Singapore, Denmark, France, Estonia, Malta, Bosnia and Herzegovina, Finland, Switzerland, Czech Republic, Romania, Hungary, the Netherlands, Austria, Latvia, Croatia, Slovenia, Bulgaria, Spain, Lithuania, San Marino, Liechtenstein, Greece, Germany, Andorra, Portugal, Italy, Japan and Monaco. The United States of America has a median age of 38.

4. This chart has been constructed on the basis of data available from the following sources: https://population.un.org/wpp/Download/Standard/Population/; https://ourworldindata.org/age-structure; https://ourworldindata.org/corona virus; https://ourworldindata.org/covid-deaths.

5. Ioannidis, J. (2021). Infection fatality rate of COVID-19 inferred from seroprevalence data. *Bulletin of the World Health Organization*, 99(1), 19.

6. This chart has been constructed on the basis of data available from the following sources: https://population.un.org/wpp/Download/Standard/Population/; https://ourworldindata.org/age-structure; https://ourworldindata.org/corona virus; https://ourworldindata.org/covid-deaths.

7. UNAIDS. (n.d.). Incidence of HIV, ages 15–49 (per 1,000 uninfected population ages 15–49). Data set. World Bank. https://data.worldbank.org/indicator/SH.HIV.INCD.ZS.

8. See, for instance, Sidley, P. (2001). Drug companies sue South African government over generics. *British Medical Journal*, 322(7284), 447. doi:10.1136/bmj.322.7284.447.

9. Rotheram-Borus, M. J., and Tomlinson, M. (2020). Not remembering history, dooms us to repeat it: Using the lessons of the global HIV response to address COVID-19. *AIDS and Behavior*, 24(12), 3288–3290. doi:10.1007/s10461-020-03066-y.

10. Bell, D., and Khan, M. U. (2020). COVID-19, the vaccine, and the betrayal of sub-Saharan Africa. *PANDA*. https://www.pandata.org/wp-content/uploa ds/PANDAArticles-COVID-19-the-vaccine-and-the-betrayal-of-sub-Saharan-Africa.pdf.

11. Banerjee, R. (2020). Kolkata: Electrocuted bodies float up in waterlogged streets. *Times of India*, 22 May. https://timesofindia.indiatimes.com/city/kolk ata/electrocuted-bodies-float-up-in-waterlogged-streets/articleshow/75878701. cms.

12. You can watch Drozdovskis's (2012) basketball test video at https://www.you tube.com/watch?v=KB_lTKZm1Ts&ab_channel=AleksasDrozdovskis. Now that I have told you about this, you will be mentally alert to the appearance of the bear. So, do not take my word for it. Ask a few others to watch the video and see

whether they pick up on the bear dancing through. I dare say you will be surprised by the responses.

13. Corlett, E. (2020). Thousands default on mortgage payments, others rush to get home finance. *New Zealand Herald*, 21 August. https://www.nzherald.co.nz/ business/thousands-default-on-mortgage-payments-others-rush-to-get-home-fi nance/QP3YH7HRKPCLC7GUPEBQRTK6SU/.

14. I have not provided a specific reference since this is all publicly available data taken from the websites of various government agencies. There is no dispute about these figures. They can be viewed at https://stats.govt.nz and https://msd. govt.nz. While these numbers look small, bear in mind that the entire labor force of the country in 2020 amounted to 2 874 000. The reported unemployment rate for the last quarter of 2020 was 4.9 percent, implying a total of 141 000 unemployed. However, one problem with the way the unemployment rate is calculated (and this is international practice rather than being unique to New Zealand) is that it reports the fraction of adults between 15 and 64 who are unemployed out of the total number actively looking for a job during the previous four-week period. Therefore, anyone who is not actively looking for a job is not considered to be part of the labor force and will also not be counted as unemployed. This is why the underutilization rate is a better measure of the degree of slack in the economy. For instance, if we assume that the 50 000 people who were receiving jobseeker support but were not looking for a job or have stopped looking for jobs, then the total number of unemployed increases to 191 000 or 6.5 percent, which is significantly different from 4.9 percent and with very different macroeconomic policy implications. For a more detailed analysis, see Chaudhuri, A. (2021b). Latest NZ unemployment figures may not give true picture of the number of people out of work. *The Conversation*, 18 February. https://theconversation.com/latest-nz-unemployment-figure-may-not-give-a-tr ue-picture-of-the-number-of-people-out-of-work-155362.

15. Robson, S. (2020). Coronavirus: Families split by Covid-19 border restrictions. *Radio New Zealand*, 20 April. https://www.stuff.co.nz/life-style/well-good/ 121128131/coronavirus-families-split-by-covid19-border-restrictions.

16. Franks, J., and Tokalau, T. (2020). "A Covid-laced Band-Aid": Kiwi couples split by borders plan "risky" trips to reunite. *Stuff*, 6 September. https://www. stuff.co.nz/national/health/coronavirus/122637916/a-covidlaced-bandaid-kiwi- couples-split-by-borders-plan-risky-trips-to-reunite.

17. See for instance: Krugman, P. (2019). The legacy of destructive austerity. *New York Times*, 30 December. https://www.nytimes.com/2019/12/30/opinion/ deficits-economy.html. Krugman wrote this just prior to the Covid-19 outbreak and the article appears prescient in retrospect. The impact of austerity on healthcare is hardly disputed. But for further evidence, see: (1) Stuckler, D., Reeves, A., Loopstra, R., Karanikolos, M., and McKee, M. (2017). Austerity and health: the impact in the UK and Europe. *European Journal of Public Health*, 27(suppl. 4), 18–21. doi:10.1093/eurpub/ckx167; and (2) McCartney, G., Fenton, L., Minton, J., Fischbacher, C., Taulbut, M., Little, K., et al. (2020). Is austerity responsible for the recent change in mortality trends across

high-income nations? A protocol for an observational study. *BMJ Open*, *10*(1), e034832. doi:10.1136/bmjopen-2019-034832.

18. From the Department of Labor website (https://www.dol.gov/general/topic/health-plans/cobra):

> The Consolidated Omnibus Budget Reconciliation Act (COBRA) gives workers and their families who lose their health benefits the right to choose to continue group health benefits provided by their group health plan for limited periods of time under certain circumstances such as voluntary or involuntary job loss, reduction in the hours worked, transition between jobs, death, divorce, and other life events. Qualified individuals may be required to pay the entire premium for coverage up to 102% of the cost to the plan.

19. It is also generally conceded that in most countries the count of Covid-19 deaths include those who died *from* Covid-19 as well as those who died *with* Covid-19 but from other causes. For Italy, see: Newey, S. (2020). Why have so many coronavirus patients died in Italy? *Telegraph*, 23 March. https://www.telegraph.co.uk/global-health/science-and-disease/have-many-coronavirus-patients-died-italy/. The Director General of Health for New Zealand, Dr Ashley Bloomfield, recently said: "Most countries are doing this, for example in the UK they categorize everyone who dies within 28 days of being hospitalized with COVID-19 as being categorized as a COVID-19-related death." See Kronast, H. (2021). Dr Ashley Bloomfield clarifies difference between COVID-19 and COVID-related deaths. *Newshub*, 18 February. https://www.newshub.co.nz/home/new-zealand/2021/02/dr-ashley-bloomfield-clarifies-difference-between-covid-19-and-covid-related-deaths.html.

20. I thank Simon Thornley for providing me with this data.

21. Woolf, S. H., Masters, R. K., and Aron, L. Y. (2021). Effect of Covid-19 pandemic in 2020 on life expectancy across populations in the US and other high income countries: simulations of provisional mortality data. *BMJ*, *373*(1343). doi:10.1136/bmj.n1343. The 16 high-income peer countries include Austria, Belgium, Denmark, Finland, France, Israel, the Netherlands, New Zealand, Norway, South Korea, Portugal, Spain, Sweden, Switzerland, Taiwan and the United Kingdom.

22. Ing, A. J., Cocks, C., and Green, J. P. (2020). COVID-19: in the footsteps of Ernest Shackleton. *Thorax*, *75*(8), 693–694.

23. Aerosol transmission implies direct contact transmission where respiratory droplets carrying infectious pathogens transmit infection when they travel directly from the respiratory tract of the infectious individual to susceptible recipients, generally over short distances. Airborne transmission is potentially far more dangerous. Here, infection transmission results from the inhalation of small respirable particles that remain infectious over time and distance and can be dispersed over long distances by air currents. For further discussion of aerosol transmission of filoviruses, see: (1) Osterholm, M. T., Moore, K. A., Kelley, N. S., Brosseau, L. M., Wong, G., Murphy, F. A., et al. (2015). Transmission of Ebola viruses: What we know and what we do not know. *MBio*, *6*(2), e00137-15; (2) Prescott, J., Bushmaker, T., Fischer, R., Miazgowicz, K., Judson, S., and Munster, V. J. (2015). Postmortem stability of Ebola virus.

Emerging Infectious Diseases, *21*(5), 856–859; (3) Jones, R. M., and Brosseau, L. M. (2014). Ebola virus transmission via contact and aerosol – a new paradigm. Center for Infectious Disease Research and Policy, University of Minnesota, Minneapolis, MN; and (4) Francesconi, P., Yoti, Z., Declich, S., Onek, P. A., Fabiani, M., Olango, J., et al. (2003). Ebola hemorrhagic fever transmission and risk factors of contacts, Uganda. *Emerging Infectious Diseases*, *9*(11), 1430–1437.

24. https://www.srlf.org/auteur/outcomerea-study-group.
25. Dupuis, C., Bouadma, L., de Montmollin, E., Goldgran-Toledano, D., Schwebel, C., Reignier, J., et al. (2021). Association between early invasive mechanical ventilation and 60-day mortality in acute hypoxemic respiratory failure related to coronavirus disease-2019 pneumonia. *Critical Care Explorations*, *3*(1), e0329. doi:10.1097/CCE.0000000000000329. These findings are supported, to an extent, by a report from the Intensive Care National Audit and Research Centre (ICNARC). However, the findings of the latter study in relation to the detrimental effects of invasive mechanical ventilation is far less definitive than the results reported by the OutcomeRea group. See Ferrando-Vivas, P., Doidge, J., Thomas, K., Gould, D. W., Mouncey, P., Shankar-Hari, M., et al. (2020). Prognostic factors for 30-day mortality in critically ill patients with coronavirus disease 2019: An observational study. *Critical Care Medicine*, *49*(1), 102–111. doi:10.1097/CCM.0000000000004740.
26. Also known as P/F ratio, this is a measure of how much oxygen the patient is receiving. A P/F ratio less than 300 millimeters of mercury (mmHg) indicates mild respiratory failure, less than 200 is moderate and less than 100 is considered acute respiratory failure.
27. Katz has written extensively on Covid-19. See Katz, D. L. (n.d.). Coronavirus: Information and resources. https://davidkatzmd.com/coronavirus-information-and-resources/. This quote is taken from Katz, D. L. (2021, 20 March). Gaps in the tale of COVID's long tail. *LinkedIn*. https://www.linkedin.com/pulse/gaps-tale-covids-long-tail-david-l-katz-md-mph-facpm-facp-faclm/.
28. Catanoso, J. (2008). A saint in the family. *Los Angeles Times*, 19 July. https://www.latimes.com/archives/la-xpm-2008-jul-19-oe-catanoso19-story.html. Catanoso writes: "Pope Benedict XVI has made no secret of his disdain for the high volume of saints named by his predecessor, Pope John Paul II, who died in 2005. John Paul II conducted 482 canonizations, naming more saints in 26 years than his predecessors had canonized in the previous four centuries."
29. Horowitz, J. (2020). Sainted too soon? Vatican report cast John Paul II in harsh new light. *New York Times*, 14 November. https://www.nytimes.com/2020/11/14/world/europe/john-paul-vatican.html.
30. I served an extended period as Chair of a department that had a history of dysfunction. When I carried out annual performance reviews for my staff, at the very end, I asked every person to tell me one thing that happened during the year where they thought I was wrong, mistaken or unfair. In response, I tried to explain as far as practicable why I did or acted in the way I did. At times, this brought up issues or grievances that I was unaware of. Thankfully there were not a lot of these, which is probably why I ended up serving for an extended

period. More importantly, my query made people feel comfortable about stating dissenting views since I was explicitly soliciting them. In my view, this works much better than other popular options such as 360-degree reviews. See, for instance, the following article: Buckingham, M. (2011). The fatal flaw with 360 surveys. *Harvard Business Review*, 17 October. https://hbr.org/2011/10/the-fatal-flaw-with-360-survey. I was talking to a journalist once about the potential costs and benefits of New Zealand's managed isolation and quarantine facility. During the conversation, this journalist said to me: "Presumably, someone has done this analysis." In reality no one had, and no one sought to question this because everyone thought that someone must have done the analysis and/or inquired about the existence of this analysis.

31. Wagner, J. (2021). Eight people from the New York Yankees organization tested positive, despite having been vaccinated. Here's what to know. *New York Times*, 14 May. https://www.nytimes.com/2021/05/14/sports/baseball/eight-people-from-the-new-york-yankees-organization-tested-positive-despite-having-been-vaccinated-heres-what-to-know.html.

32. The list includes: Afghanistan, Algeria, Angola, Argentina, Armenia, Australia, Azerbaijan, Bangladesh, Belarus, Belize, Benin, Bhutan, Bolivia, Bosnia and Herzegovina, Botswana, Brunei, Burkina Faso, Cameroon, Cape Verde, Caribbean Netherlands, Central African Republic, Chad, China, Colombia, Comoros, Côte d'Ivoire, Cuba, Democratic Republic of the Congo, Djibouti, Ecuador, Egypt, Equatorial Guinea, Eswatini, Ethiopia, Fiji, Gabon, Georgia, Ghana, Grenada, Guatemala, Guernsey, Guinea, Guinea-Bissau, Honduras, India, Indonesia, Iran, Iraq, Jamaica, Japan, Jordan, Kazakhstan, Kenya, Kosovo, Kuwait, Kyrgyzstan, Laos, Lebanon, Lesotho, Liberia, Libya, Madagascar, Malawi, Malaysia, Mali, Mauritania, Moldova, Mozambique, Myanmar (Burma), Namibia, Nauru, Nepal, New Zealand, Nicaragua, Niger, Nigeria, North Macedonia, Oman, Pakistan, Palau, Palestine, Papua New Guinea, Paraguay, Peru, the Philippines, Republic of the Congo, Russia, Rwanda, Saint Vincent and the Grenadines, Samoa, São Tomé and Príncipe, Saudi Arabia, Senegal, Sierra Leone, Solomon Islands, Somalia, South Africa, South Korea, South Sudan, Sri Lanka, Sudan, Suriname, Syria, Taiwan, Tajikistan, Thailand, The Bahamas, The Gambia, Timor-Leste, Togo, Tonga, Trinidad and Tobago, Tunisia, Turkmenistan, Tuvalu, Uganda, Ukraine, Uzbekistan, Vanuatu, Venezuela, Vietnam, Yemen, Zambia and Zimbabwe.

33. It is also important not to underestimate the racial bias inherent in many of these decisions. For instance, in early 2021, when India reported a second wave, both Australia and New Zealand responded by stopping all flights from that country. This included citizens of Indian ethnicity or others who happened to be in India. Australia even threatened jail if any citizens tried to return from India. This was surprising, since at its peak, India reported around 280 Covid-19 cases per million, where cases really meant positive RT-PCR tests. Judges in Portugal rejected this standard by stating: "In view of current scientific evidence, this test shows itself to be unable to determine beyond reasonable doubt that such positivity corresponds, in fact, to the infection of a person by the SARS-CoV-2

virus." (See Covid PCR test reliability doubtful – Portugal judges. (2020). *The Portugal News*, 27 November. https://www.theportugalnews.com/news/2020-11-27/covid-pcr-test-reliability-doubtful-portugal-judges/56962.) Yet, in 2020, countries such as the UK or France were reporting more than 800 cases per million but there was never any consideration of stopping flights from those countries. The refrain was that cases from India were being under-reported. The façade quickly broke down when New Zealand players playing for large sums of money in the lucrative Indian Premier League cricket tournament in India were all allowed to return to New Zealand (including players who had tested positive for Covid-19) but New Zealand or Australian citizens of Indian origin remained barred from returning.

34. Rasgon, A. (2021). Israel's vaccine success unleashes a debate on Palestinian inequities. *New York Times*, 4 February. https://www.nytimes.com/2021/02/04/world/middleeast/israel-palestinians-vaccine.html.

35. Brown, V. (2021). Covid 19 coronavirus: NSW Premier calls transtasman bubble pause "an overreaction". *New Zealand Herald*, 7 May. https://www.nzherald.co.nz/nz/covid-19-coronavirus-nsw-premier-calls-transtasman-bubble-pause-an-overreaction/LLRA4C3DTMGA5CBYYJOPRPW4TE/.

36. Figure 7.5 is based on results from an instrumental variable regression where the treatment variable is the maximum of the Oxford University Stringency Index (by 31 March 2020) and the instrument is the maximum stringency of neighboring OECD countries. The latter is a suitable instrument based on results reported in Sebhatu et al. (2020) about the extent of mimicry in most countries' approach to lockdowns. The regression controls for pre-pandemic economic growth rates and economic structure (from the World Bank's World Development Indicators for 2019). This is needed because a pandemic especially affects economic activity in services, given that these have more face-to-face interaction of buyers and sellers than is typical for agriculture or industry. The outcome variable is the 2020 calendar year real GDP growth rate, from the May 2021 OECD Economic Outlook. In order to get the instrumental variable estimation results into the bivariate one shown in Figure 7.5, Gibson partials out the effect of industry structure and 2019 growth rates, using the added variable approach to instrumental variable estimation. This puts the first stage residuals into the main model, which turns it into a control function approach. This gives a slope of negative 0.206, which is the same as the instrumental variable estimator, as well as that of the control function.

37. Bjørnskov, C. (2021). Did lockdown work? An economist's cross-country comparison. *CESifo Economic Studies*, 1–14. doi:10.1093/cesifo/ifab003. The countries included in the study are Austria, Belgium, Bulgaria, Czech Republic, Denmark, Estonia, Finland, France, Germany, Hungary, Iceland, Italy, Latvia, Lithuania, Luxembourg, the Netherlands, Norway, Poland, Portugal, Slovakia, Spain, Sweden, Switzerland and the United Kingdom.

38. Bhattacharya, J. (2021). Editor's note – week one. *Collateral Global*. https://collateralglobal.org/article/editors-note-1/.

Bibliography

Abadie, A., and Gay, S. (2006). The impact of presumed consent legislation on cadaveric organ donation: A cross-country study. *Journal of Health Economics*, *25*(4), 599–620.

Accident Compensation Corporation. (n.d.). *Injury Claim Statistics*. https://www.acc.co.nz/newsroom/media-resources/injury-claim-statistics/.

Adorno, T. W., Frenkel-Brunswik, E., Levinson, D. J., and Sanford, R. N. (1950). *The Authoritarian Personality*. New York: Harper & Row.

Akerlof, G. A. (1982). Labor contracts as partial gift exchange. *Quarterly Journal of Economics*, *97*(4), 543–569.

Akoorie, N. (2020). Covid 19 coronavirus: Tangiwai Wilson's whānau desperate to take her body through Auckland to Northland for tangi. *New Zealand Herald*, 19 August. https://www.nzherald.co.nz/nz/covid-19-coronavirus-tangiwai-wilsons-whanau-desperate-to-take-her-body-through-auckland-to-northland-for-tangi/OK PMXTLUFGC5ILYYCB5YUD5E6E/.

Allcott, H., Boxell, L., Conway, J., Gentzkow, M., Thaler, M., and Yang, D. (2020). Polarization and public health: Partisan differences in social distancing during the coronavirus pandemic. *Journal of Public Economics*, *191*, 104254.

Altemeyer, B. (1981). *Right-wing Authoritarianism*. University of Manitoba Press.

Aluja, A., Garcia, O., and Garcia, L. F. (2003). Relationship among extraversion, openness to experience and sensation seeking. *Personality and Individual Difference*, *35*(3), 671–680.

Alwan, N. A., Burgess, R. A., Ashworth, S., Beale, R., Bhadelia, N., Bogaert, D., et al. (2020). Scientific consensus on the COVID-19 pandemic: we need to act now. *The Lancet*, *396*(10260), e71–e72.

Anderson, T. (2019). *Brain Games How Many Gumballs?* [Video recording]. YouTube, 5 April. https://www.youtube.com/watch?v=Qfh-k9P8ZPI&ab_channel=TylerAnderson.

Ariely, D. (2008). *Predictably Irrational*. HarperCollins.

Asch, S. E. (1951). Effects of group pressure upon the modification and distortion of judgments. In H. Guetzkow (ed.), *Groups, Leadership and Men: Research in Human Relations* (pp. 177–190). Carnegie Press.

Asch, S. E. (1955). Opinions and social pressure. *Scientific American*, *193*(5), 31–35.

Asch, S. E. (1956). Studies of independence and conformity: I. A minority of one against a unanimous majority. *Psychological Monographs: General and Applied*, *70*(9), 1–70.

Associated Press. (2004). 43rd president is "gut player" who eschews personal change. *NBC News*, 29 August. https://www.nbcnews.com/id/wbna5762240.

Bakker, B. N., Schumacher, G., Gothreau, C., and Arceneaux, K. (2020). Conservatives and liberals have similar physiological responses to threats. *Nature Human Behaviour*, *4*, 613–621.

Banerjee, R. (2020). Kolkata: Electrocuted bodies float up in waterlogged streets. *Times of India*, 22 May. https://timesofindia.indiatimes.com/city/kolkata/electro cuted-bodies-float-up-in-waterlogged-streets/articleshow/75878701.cms.

Baron, J. N., Hannan, M. T., and Burton, M. D. (2001). Labor pains: Change in organizational models and employee turnover in young, high-tech firms. *American Journal of Sociology*, 106(4), 960–1012.

Baumeister, R. F., Bratslavsky, E., Muraven, M., and Tice, D. M. (1998). Ego depletion: Is the active self a limited resource? *Journal of Personality and Social Psychology*, 74(5), 1252–1265.

Bayes, T. (1763). An essay towards solving a problem in the doctrine of chances. By the late Rev. Mr. Bayes, F. R. S. communicated by Mr. Price, in a letter to John Canton, A. M. F. R. S. *Philosophical Transactions of the Royal Society of London*, 53, 370–418.

BBC. (2020). Covid-19: PM announces four-week England lockdown. *BBC News*, 31 October. https://www.bbc.com/news/uk-54763956.

Bell, D., and Khan, M. U. (2020). COVID-19, the vaccine, and the betrayal of sub-Saharan Africa. *PANDA*. https://www.pandata.org/wp-content/uploads/PANDAArticles-COVID-19-the-vaccine-and-the-betrayal-of-sub-Saharan-Africa.pdf.

Bentham, J. (2009). *An Introduction to the Principles of Morals and Legislation*. Dover. (Original work published 1789.)

Berg, J., Dickhaut, J., and McCabe, K. (1995). Trust, reciprocity, and social history. *Games and Economic Behavior*, 10(1), 122–142.

Berka, M. (2020). Protecting lives and livelihoods: The data on why New Zealand should relax its coronavirus lockdown from Thursday. *The Conversation*, 17 April. https://theconversation.com/protecting-lives-and-livelihoods-the-data-on-why-new-zealand-should-relax-its-coronavirus-lockdown-from-thursday-136242.

Bernoulli, D. (1954). Exposition of a new theory on the measurement of risk. (L. Sommer, trans.), *Econometrica*, 22(1), 23–36. (Original work published 1738.)

Bhattacharya, J. (2021). Editor's note – week one. *Collateral Global*. https://col lateralglobal.org/article/editors-note-1/.

Biddle, D.-L. (2020a). South Auckland Mad Butcher owner dies suddenly after business goes into liquidation. *Stuff*, 12 May. https://www.stuff.co.nz/busi ness/121491315/south-auckland-mad-butcher-owner-dies-suddenly-after-business-goes-into-liquidation.

Biddle, D.-L. (2020b). Family of Auckland butcher who died suddenly say Covid-19 restrictions "added to burden". *Stuff*, 13 May. https://www.stuff.co.nz/national/121497895/family-of-auckland-butcher-who-died-suddenly-say-covid19-restrictions-added-to-burden.

Bjørnskov, C. (2021). Did lockdown work? An economist's cross-country compari-son. *CESifo Economic Studies*, 1–14. doi:10.1093/cesifo/ifab003.

Blinder, A. (1988). *Hard Heads, Soft Hearts: Tough Minded Economics for a Just Society*. Basic Books.

Bostian, A. J., and Holt, C. A. (2009). Price bubbles with discounting: A web-based classroom experiment. *Journal of Economic Education*, 40(1), 27–37.

Bostian, A. J., Goeree, J., and Holt, C. A. (2005). Price bubbles in asset market experiments with a flat fundamental value. In draft for the Experimental Finance Conference, Federal Reserve Bank of Atlanta, 23 September.

Brandt, M. J., Turner-Zwinkels, F. M., Karapirinler, B., van Leeuwen, F., Bender, M., van Osch, Y., et al. (2021). The association between threat and politics depends on the type of threat, the political domain, and the country. *Personality and Social Psychology Bulletin, 47*(2), 324–343. https://doi.org/10.1177/0146167220946187.

Brown, V. (2021). Covid 19 coronavirus: NSW Premier calls transtasman bubble pause "an overreaction". *New Zealand Herald*, 7 May. https://www.nzherald. co.nz/nz/covid-19-coronavirus-nsw-premier-calls-transtasman-bubble-pause-an-overreaction/LLRA4C3DTMGA5CBYYJOPRPW4TE/.

Buckingham, M. (2011). The fatal flaw with 360 surveys. *Harvard Business Review*, 17 October. https://hbr.org/2011/10/the-fatal-flaw-with-360-survey.

Bursztyn, L., Rao, A., Roth, C. P., and Yanagizawa-Drott, D. H. (2020). Misinformation during a pandemic. NBER Working Paper. National Bureau of Economic Research.

Byambasuren, O., Cardona, M., Bell, K., Clark, J., McLaws, M-L., and Glasziou, P. (2020). Estimating the extent of asymptomatic COVID-19 and its potential for community transmission: Systematic review and meta-analysis. *Official Journal of the Association of Medical Microbiology and Infectious Disease Canada, 5*(4), 223–234.

Calvillo, D. P., Ross, B. J., Garcia, R. J. B., Smelter, T. J., and Rutchick, A. M. (2020). Political ideology predicts perceptions of the threat of COVID-19 (and susceptibility to fake news about it). *Social Psychological and Personality Science, 11*(8), 1119–1128.

Cameron, L. A. (1999). Raising the stakes in the ultimatum game: Experimental evidence from Indonesia. *Economic Inquiry, 37*(1), 47–59.

Camus, A. (1960). *The Plague*. (S. Gilbert, trans.). Penguin. (Original work published 1947.)

Cardenas, J. C., Stranlund, J., and Willis, C. (2002). Economic inequality and burden-sharing in the provision of local environmental quality. *Ecological Economics, 40*(3), 379–395.

Carpenter, J. P. (2007). Punishing free-riders: How group size affects mutual monitoring and the provision of public goods. *Games and Economic Behavior, 60*(1), 31–51.

Carroll, A. (2020). When it comes to Covid-19, most of us have risk exactly backward. *New York Times*, 28 August. https://www.nytimes.com/2020/08/28/opinion/coronavirus-schools-tradeoffs.html.

Catanoso, J. (2008). A saint in the family. *Los Angeles Times*, 19 July. https://www.latimes.com/archives/la-xpm-2008-jul-19-oe-catanoso19-story.html.

Chari, V. V., Kirpalani, R., and Phelan, C. (2021). The hammer and the scalpel: On the economics of indiscriminate versus targeted isolation policies during pandemics. *Review of Economic Dynamics, 42*, 1–14. https://doi.org/10.1016/j.red.2020.11.004.

Chaudhry, R., Dranitsaris, G., Mubashir, T., Bartoszko, J., and Riazia, S. (2020). A country level analysis measuring the impact of government actions, country preparedness and socioeconomic factors on COVID-19 mortality and related health outcomes. *EClinicalMedicine, 25*, 100464. https://doi.org/10.1016/j.eclinm.2020.100464.

Chaudhuri, A. (2009). *Experiments in Economics: Playing Fair with Money*. Routledge.

Chaudhuri, A. (2020a). A different perspective on Covid-19. *Newsroom*, 8 April. https://www.newsroom.co.nz/ideasroom/2020/04/08/1119994/a-different-perspective-on-covid-19.

Chaudhuri, A. (2020b). Don't make Kiwis pay for Covid-19 quarantine. *Newsroom*, 29 June. https://www.newsroom.co.nz/ideasroom/1256268/dont-make-kiwis-pay-for-quarantine.

Chaudhuri, A. (2020c). Time to walk the talk, Minister. *New Zealand Herald*, 22 September.

Chaudhuri, A. (2020d). Election 2020: Why the Nats fared so poorly. *Stuff*, 20 October. https://www.stuff.co.nz/opinion/123135666/election-2020-why-the-nats-fared-so-poorly.

Chaudhuri, A. (2021a). *Behavioural Economics and Experiments*. Routledge.

Chaudhuri, A. (2021b). Latest NZ unemployment figures may not give true picture of the number of people out of work. *The Conversation*, 18 February. https://theconversation.com/latest-nz-unemployment-figure-may-not-give-a-true-picture-of-the-number-of-people-out-of-work-155362.

Chaudhuri, A., Graziano, S., and Maitra, P. (2006). Social learning and norms in a public goods experiment with inter-generational advice. *Review of Economic Studies*, 73(2), 357–380.

Chaudhuri, A., Li, Y., and Paichayontvijit, T. (2016). What's in a frame? Goal framing, trust and reciprocity. *Journal of Economic Psychology*, 57, 117–135.

Chaudhuri, A., Schotter, A., and Sopher, B. (2009). Talking ourselves to efficiency: Coordination in inter-generational minimum effort games with private, almost common and common knowledge of advice. *Economic Journal*, 119(534), 91–122.

Claessens, S., Fischer, K., Chaudhuri, A., Sibley, C. G., and Atkinson, Q. D. (2020a). The dual evolutionary foundations of political ideology. *Nature Human Behaviour*, 4, 336–345. https://doi.org/10.1038/s41562-020-0850-9.

Claessens, S., Sibley, C., Chaudhuri, A., and Atkinson, Q. (2020b). Cooperative phenotype predicts economic conservatism, policy views, and political party support. *PsyArXive preprints*. https://psyarxiv.com/t7rqb/.

Colbert, S. (2006). Stephen Colbert: "We're not brainiacs on the nerd patrol. We're not members of the factinista. We go straight from the gut, right sir?" Correspondents Dinner – 2006. *Speakola*, 29 April. https://speakola.com/political/colbert-correspondents-dinner-2006.

Corlett, E. (2020). Thousands default on mortgage payments, others rush to get home finance. *New Zealand Herald*, 21 August. https://www.nzherald.co.nz/business/thousands-default-on-mortgage-payments-others-rush-to-get-home-finance/QP3YH7HRKPCLC7GUPEBQRTK6SU/.

Coughlan, T. (2020). Coalition MPs say no to grilling Bloomfield over outbreak. *Stuff*, 20 August. https://www.stuff.co.nz/national/politics/300087522/coronavirus-coalition-mps-say-no-to-grilling-bloomfield-over-outbreak.

Covid Plan B. (2020). *Watch the COVID-19 Science and Policy Symposium – 17/08/2020*. https://www.covidplanb.co.nz/videos/.

Covid PCR test reliability doubtful – Portugal judges. (2020). *The Portugal News*, 27 November. https://www.theportugalnews.com/news/2020-11-27/covid-pcr-test-reliability-doubtful-portugal-judges/56962.

Cowen, T. (2020). Bill Gates is really worried about the coronavirus: Here's why. *Bloomberg*, 4 March. https://www.bloomberg.com/opinion/articles/2020-03-03/how-fast-will-the-new-coronavirus-spread-two-sides-of-the-debate.

Cronk, L. (2007). The influence of cultural framing on play in the trust game: A Maasai example. *Evolution and Human Behavior*, 28(5), 352–358.

Daaldar, M. (2020). "Contrarian" academics oppose lockdown. *Newsroom*, 14 April. https://www.newsroom.co.nz/contrarian-academics-oppose-nz-lockdown.

Davison, I. (2020). Stateless: New Zealanders working overseas struggle to return home. *New Zealand Herald*, 23 November. https://www.nzherald.co.nz/nz/

stateless-new-zealanders-working-overseas-struggle-to-return-home/AYPH3OTM
DMMH7MJJNZYMHTZCPI/.

Dawes, R. M., and Thaler, R. H. (1988). Anomalies: Cooperation. *Journal of Economic Perspectives, 2*(3), 187–197.

De Waal, F. (1997). *Good Natured: The Origins of Right and Wrong in Humans and Other Animals.* Harvard University Press.

De Waal, F. (2007). *Chimpanzee Politics: Power and Sex Among Apes.* Johns Hopkins University Press.

De Waal, F. (2014). *The Bonobo and the Atheist: In Search of Humanism Among the Primates.* W. W. Norton & Company.

Deci, E. L. (1971). Effects of externally mediated rewards on intrinsic motivation. *Journal of Personality and Social Psychology, 18*(1), 105–115.

Deci, E. L., Koestner, R., and Ryan, R. M. (1999). A meta-analytic review of experiments examining the effects of extrinsic rewards on intrinsic motivation. *Psychological Bulletin, 125*(6), 627–668.

Dickinson, D. L., Chaudhuri, A., and Greenaway-McGrevy, R. (2020). Trading while sleepy? Circadian mismatch and mispricing in a global experimental asset market. *Experimental Economics, 23*(2), 526–553.

Dillane, T. (2020). Booze run vs father's funeral: questions of systemic racism over quarantine escapees' contrasting sentences. *New Zealand Herald,* 29 August. https://www.nzherald.co.nz/nz/booze-run-vs-fathers-funeral-questions-of-systemic-racism-over-quarantine-escapees-contrasting-sentences/FLG5GV3EX GPNU4HY35KWTBU23A/.

Doctors Without Borders. (2020). COVID-19 Vaccine Global Access (COVAX) Facility: Key considerations for Gavi's new global financing mechanism. MSF Media Briefing, June. https://msfaccess.org/sites/default/files/2020-06/MSF-AC_ COVID-19_Gavi-COVAXFacility_briefing-document.pdf.

Donaldson, L. J., Rutter, P. D., Ellis, B. M., Greaves, F. E., Mytton, O. T., Pebody R. G., et al. (2009). Mortality from pandemic A/H1N1 2009 influenza in England: public health surveillance study. *BMJ, 339,* b5213. doi:10.1136/bmj.b5213. PMC 2791802. PMID 20007665.

Donne, J., and Savage, E. (1975). *John Donne's Devotions upon Emergent Occasions: A Critical Edition with Introduction & Commentary.* Institut für Englische Sprache und Literatur, Universität Salzburg.

Donnell, H. (2020). A backlash over tough questions for Dr Ashley Bloomfield. *Radio New Zealand,* 23 August. https://www.rnz.co.nz/national/programmes/mediawa tch/audio/2018760556/a-backlash-over-tough-questions-for-dr-ashleybloomfield.

Donnelly, L., and Gilbert, D. (2020). Non-virus deaths at home behind surge in excess fatalities, figures show. *Telegraph,* 2 September. https://www.telegraph.co.uk/ news/2020/09/02/patients-dying-home-causes-covid-19-fuelling-excess-uk-deaths/.

Doshi, P. (2020). Will covid-19 vaccines save lives? Current trials aren't designed to tell us. *BMJ, 371,* m4037. https://www.bmj.com/content/371/bmj.m4037.

Douthat, R. (2020). When you can't just "trust the science". *New York Times,* 19 December. https://www.nytimes.com/2020/12/19/opinion/sunday/coronavirus-science.html.

Drozdovskis, A. (2012). *Basketball Awareness Test* [Video recording]. YouTube. 20 April. https://www.youtube.com/watch?v=KB_lTKZm1Ts&ab_channel= AleksasDrozdovskis.

Duckitt, J., and Sibley, C. G. (2009). A dual-process motivational model of ideology, politics, and prejudice. *Psychological Inquiry, 20*(2), 98–109.

Dupuis, C., Bouadma, L., de Montmollin, E., Goldgran-Toledano, D., Schwebel, C., Reignier, J., et al. (2021). Association between early invasive mechanical ventilation and 60-day mortality in acute hypoxemic respiratory failure related to coronavirus disease-2019 pneumonia. *Critical Care Explorations*, *3*(1), e0329. doi:10.1097/CCE.0000000000000329.

Eastwood, C. (Director). (2016). *Sully* [Film]. Village Roadshow Pictures; Flashlight Films; The Kennedy/Marshall Company; Malpaso Productions; Orange Corp.

Eckel, C. C., and Wilson, R. K. (2004). Is trust a risky decision? *Journal of Economic Behavior and Organization*, *55*(4), 447–465.

Edwards, S. (2019). Modern monetary disasters. Copyright: Project Syndicate, 2019. Reprinted with permission in *Interest.co.nz*, 19 May.

Eichenbaum, M. S., Rebelo, S., and Trabandt, M. (2020a). The macroeconomics of epidemics. Working Paper No. 26882. National Bureau of Economic Research.

Eichenbaum, M. S., Rebelo, S., and Trabandt, M. (2020b). The macroeconomics of testing and quarantining. Working Paper No. 27104. National Bureau of Economic Research.

Eichenbaum, M. S., Rebelo, S., and Trabandt, M. (2020c). Epidemics in the neoclassical and new Keynesian models. NBER Working Paper No. 27430. National Bureau of Economic Research.

Emerson, R. W. (1911). *Essays* (first, second and third series). Ward Lock.

Fama, E. F. (1970). Efficient capital markets: A review of theory and empirical work. *Journal of Finance*, *25*(2), 383–417.

Fathi, M., Bateson, M., and Nettle, D. (2014). Effects of watching eyes and norm cues on charitable giving in a surreptitious behavioral experiment. *Evolutionary Psychology*, *12*(5), 878–887.

Fehr, E., and Rockenbach, B. (2003). Detrimental effects of sanctions on human altruism. *Nature*, *422*(6928), 137–140.

Fehr, E., Gächter, S., and Kirchsteiger, G. (1997). Reciprocity as a contract enforcement device: Experimental evidence. *Econometrica*, *65*(4), 833–860.

Fehr, E., Kirchsteiger, G., and Riedl, A. (1993). Does fairness prevent market clearing? An experimental investigation. *Quarterly Journal of Economics*, *108*(2), 437–459.

Fehr, E., Kirchsteiger, G., and Riedl, A. (1998). Gift exchange and reciprocity in competitive experimental markets. *European Economic Review*, *42*(1), 1–34.

Fehr, E., Kirchler, E., Weichbold, A., and Gächter, S. (1998). When social norms overpower competition: Gift exchange in experimental labor markets. *Journal of Labor Economics*, *16*(2), 324–351.

Ferguson, N., Laydon, D., Nedjati Gilani, G., Imai, N., Ainslie, K., Baguelin, M., et al. (2020). Report 9: Impact of non-pharmaceutical interventions (NPIs) to reduce COVID-19 mortality and healthcare demand. *Imperial College Covid-19 Response Team Research Report*. Imperial College, London.

Ferrando-Vivas, P., Doidge, J., Thomas, K., Gould, D. W., Mouncey, P., Shankar-Hari, M., et al. (2020). Prognostic factors for 30-day mortality in critically ill patients with coronavirus disease 2019: An observational study. *Critical Care Medicine*, *49*(1), 102–111. doi:10.1097/CCM.0000000000004740.

Fischer, K., Chaudhuri, A., and Atkinson, Q. D. (2020). The dual evolutionary foundations of political ideology predict responses to the COVID-19 pandemic. Unpublished manuscript. University of Auckland.

Fitzgerald, M. (2020). Penny stock-loving Robinhood traders raised bubble concerns, but most retail investors are selling. *CNBC*, 25 June. https://www.cnbc.

com/2020/06/25/penny-stock-loving-robinhood-traders-raised-bubble-concerns-but-most-retail-investors-are-selling.html.

Fitzgerald, M. (2021). Robinhood sued by family of 20-year-old trader who killed himself after believing he racked up huge losses. *CNBC*, 8 February. https://www.cnbc.com/2021/02/08/robinhood-sued-by-family-of-alex-kearns-20-year-old-trader-who-killed-himself-.html.

Forster, N. (2018). Unemployment, income affect life expectancy. *Associated Press*, 15 December. https://apnews.com/article/ea3be7fb82bf4bec90a00d75957f833b.

Francesconi, P., Yoti, Z., Declich, S., Onek, P. A., Fabiani, M., Olango, J., et al. (2003). Ebola hemorrhagic fever transmission and risk factors of contacts, Uganda. *Emerging Infectious Diseases*, 9(11), 1430–1437.

Franks, J., and Tokalau, T. (2020). "A Covid-laced Band-Aid": Kiwi couples split by borders plan "risky" trips to reunite. *Stuff*, 6 September. https://www.stuff.co.nz/national/health/coronavirus/122637916/a-covidlaced-bandaid-kiwi-couples-split-by-borders-plan-risky-trips-to-reunite.

Frederick, S. (2005). Cognitive reflection and decision making. *Journal of Economic Perspectives*, 19(4), 25–42.

Frey, B. S. (1997). *Not Just for the Money: An Economic Theory of Personal Motivation.* Edward Elgar.

Frey, B. S., and Oberholzer-Gee, F. (1997). The cost of price incentives: An empirical analysis of motivation crowding-out. *American Economic Review*, 87(4), 746–755.

Gardiner, J. M., Willem, L., Van Der Wijngaart, W., Kamerlin, S. C. L., Brusselaers, N., and Kasson, P. (2020). Intervention strategies against COVID-19 and their estimated impact on Swedish healthcare capacity. *MedRxiv*, 15 April. https://doi.org/10.1101/2020.04.11.20062133.

Geddis, A., and Geiringer, C. (2020). The legal basis for the lockdown may not be as solid as we've been led to believe. *The Spinoff*, 28 April. https://thespinoff.co.nz/covid-19/28-04-2020/the-legal-basis-for-the-lockdown-may-not-be-as-solid-as-weve-been-led-to-believe/.

Geisel, T. (Dr Seuss). (1990). *Oh, the Places You'll Go!* Random House.

Gibson, J. (2020a). Government mandated lockdowns do not reduce Covid-19 deaths: Implications for evaluating the stringent New Zealand response. *New Zealand Economic Papers*. doi:10.1080/00779954.2020.1844786.

Gibson, J. (2020b). Hard, not early: Putting the New Zealand Covid-19 response in context. *New Zealand Economic Papers*. doi:10.1080/00779954.2020.1842796.

Gibson, J. (2021). *Life expectancy reductions from New Zealand's unbalanced Covid response* [Poster]. New Zealand Association of Economists Annual Conference, Wellington. 23 June.

Gigerenzer, G. (2007). *Gut Feelings: The Intelligence of the Unconscious.* Viking Books.

Gigerenzer, G. (2013). *Risk Savvy: How to Make Good Decisions.* Penguin Books.

Gladwell, M. (2005). *Blink: The Power of Thinking Without Thinking.* Little, Brown.

Gneezy, A., Gneezy, U., Riener, G., and Nelson, L. D. (2012). Pay-what-you-want, identity, and self-signaling in markets. *Proceedings of the National Academy of Sciences*, 109(19), 7236–7240.

Gneezy, U., and List, J. (2006). Putting behavioral economics to work: Testing for gift exchange in labor markets using field experiments. *Econometrica*, 74(5), 1365–1384.

Graham, J., Haidt, J., and Nosek, B. (2009). Liberals and conservatives rely on differ-ent sets of moral foundations. *Journal of Personality and Social Psychology*, 96(5), 1029–1046.

Gupta, S. (2020). Talk at Covid-19 Science and Policy Symposium organized by Covid Plan B, 17 August. https://www.covidplanb.co.nz/videos/.

Haidt, J. (2012). *The Righteous Mind: Why Good People Are Divided by Politics and Religion*. Pantheon Books.

Harris, J. R. (1998). *The Nurture Assumption: Why Children Turn Out the Way They Do*. Macmillan.

Haruvy, E., Lahav, Y., and Noussair, C. N. (2007). Traders' expectations in asset markets: Experimental evidence. *American Economic Review*, 97(5), 1901–1920.

Heatley, D. (2020). *A Cost Benefit Analysis of 5 Extra Days at COVID-19 Alert Level 4* (Research Note 2020/02). New Zealand Productivity Commission. https://www.productivity.govt.nz/research/cost-benefit-analysis-covid-alert-4/.

Heller, J. (1961). *Catch-22*. Simon & Schuster.

Henley, J. (2020). Latest coronavirus lockdowns spark protest around Europe. *Guardian*, 2 November. https://www.theguardian.com/world/2020/nov/02/latest-coronavirus-lockdowns-spark-protests-across-europe.

Henrich, J., and Gil-White, F. J. (2001). The evolution of prestige: Freely conferred deference as a mechanism for enhancing the benefits of cultural transmission. *Evolution and Human Behavior*, 22(3), 165–196.

Hibbing, J. R., Smith, K. B., and Alford, J. R. (2013). *Predisposed: Liberals, conserva-tives, and the biology of political differences*. Routledge.

Hickey, S. (2020). Maajid Nawaz corners epidemiologist over cost of second lock-down. *LBC*, 31 October. https://www.lbc.co.uk/radio/presenters/maajid-nawaz/epidemiologist-on-cost-of-second-lockdown-coronavirus/.

Hoffman, J. (2020). Polio and measles could surge after disruption of vaccine pro-grams. *New York Times*, 22 May. https://www.nytimes.com/2020/05/22/health/coronavirus-polio-measles-immunizations.html.

Homans, G. C. (1954). The cash posters: A study of a group of working girls. *American Sociological Review*, 19(6), 724–733.

Horowitz, J. (2020). Sainted too soon? Vatican report cast John Paul II in harsh new light. *New York Times*, 14 November. https://www.nytimes.com/2020/11/14/world/europe/john-paul-vatican.html.

Illmer, A. (2017). What's behind New Zealand's shocking youth suicide rate? *BBC*, 15 June. https://www.bbc.com/news/world-asia-40284130.

Ing, A. J., Cocks, C., and Green, J. P. (2020). COVID-19: in the footsteps of Ernest Shackleton. *Thorax*, 75(8), 693–694.

Inglesby, T. V., Nuzzo, J. B., O'Toole, T., and Henderson, D. A. (2006). Disease mitigation measures in the control of pandemic influenza. *Biosecurity and Bioterrorism: Biodefense Strategy, Practice, and Science*, 4(4), 366–375. doi:10.1089/bsp.2006.4.366.

Ioannidis, J. (2021). Infection fatality rate of COVID-19 inferred from seroprevalence data. *Bulletin of the World Health Organization*, 99(1), 19.

Ioannidis, J., Axfors, C., and Contopoulos-Ioannidis, D. G. (2020). Population-level COVID-19 mortality risk for non-elderly individuals overall and for non-elderly individuals without underlying diseases in pandemic epicenters. *Environmental Research*, 188, 109890. https://doi.org/10.1101/2020.04.05.20054361.

Jones, R. M., and Brosseau, L. M. (2014). Ebola virus transmission via contact and aerosol – a new paradigm. Center for Infectious Disease Research and Policy, University of Minnesota, Minneapolis, MN.

Jost, J. T. (2017). Ideological asymmetries and the essence of political psychology. *Political Psychology*, 38(2), 167–208.

Jost, J. T., Glaser, J., Kruglanski, A. W., and Sulloway, F. J. (2003). Political conservatism as motivated social cognition. *Psychological Bulletin*, 129(3), 339–375.

Kahan, D. M. (2013). Ideology, motivated reasoning, and cognitive reflection. *Judgment and Decision Making*, 8(4), 407–424.

Kahan, D. M., Jenkins-Smith, H., and Braman, D. (2011). Cultural cognition of scientific consensus. *Journal of Risk Research*, 14(2), 147–174.

Kahneman, D. (2011). *Thinking, Fast and Slow*. Farrar, Straus and Giroux.

Kahneman, D., and Tversky, A. (1979). Prospect theory: An analysis of decision under risk. *Econometrica*, 47(2), 263–292.

Kanai, R., Feilden, T., Firth, C., and Rees, G. (2011). Political orientations are correlated with brain structure in young adults. *Current Biology*, 21(8), 677–680.

Katz, D. L. (2020). Is our fight against coronavirus worse than the disease? *New York Times*, 20 March. https://www.nytimes.com/2020/03/20/opinion/coronavirus-pandemic-social-distancing.html.

Katz, D. L. (2021). Gaps in the tale of COVID's long tail. *LinkedIn*. 20 March. https://www.linkedin.com/pulse/gaps-tale-covids-long-tail-david-l-katz-md-mph-facpm-facp-faclm/.

Katz, D. L. (n.d.). Coronavirus: Information and resources. https://davidkatzmd.com/coronavirus-information-and-resources/.

Kermack, W. O., and McKendrick, A. G. (1927). A contribution to the mathematical theory of epidemics. *Proceedings of the Royal Society A*, 115(772), 700–721.

Keynes, J. M. (1936). *The General Theory of Employment, Interest and Money*. Palgrave Macmillan.

Kocher, M. G., Lucks, K. E., and Schindler, D. (2019). Unleashing animal spirits: Self-control and overpricing in experimental asset markets. *Review of Financial Studies*, 32(6), 2149–2178.

Kosfeld, M., Heinrichs, M., Zak, P. J., Fischbacher, U., and Fehr, E. (2005). Oxytocin increases trust in humans. *Nature*, 435(7042), 673–676.

Kronast, H. (2021). Dr Ashley Bloomfield clarifies difference between COVID-19 and COVID-related deaths. *Newshub*, 18 February. https://www.newshub.co.nz/home/new-zealand/2021/02/dr-ashley-bloomfield-clarifies-difference-between-covid-19-and-covid-related-deaths.html.

Krugman, P. (2019). The legacy of destructive austerity. *New York Times*, 30 December. https://www.nytimes.com/2019/12/30/opinion/deficits-economy.html.

Krugman, P. (2020). Crashing economy, rising stocks: What's going on? *New York Times*, 30 April. https://www.nytimes.com/2020/04/30/opinion/economy-stock-market-coronavirus.html.

Krugman, P. (2021). How Democrats learned to seize the day. *New York Times*, 8 February. https://www.nytimes.com/2021/02/08/opinion/democrats-covid-stimulus.html.

Kulldorff, M., Gupta, S., and Bhattacharya, J. (2020). *Great Barrington Declaration*. Great Barrington Declaration. 4 October. https://gbdeclaration.org/.

Kunreuther, H., and Easterling, D. (1990). Are risk-benefit tradeoffs possible in siting hazardous facilities? *American Economic Review*, 80(2), 252–256.

Kunreuther, H., and Easterling, D. (1996). The role of compensation in siting hazardous facilities. *Journal of Policy Analysis and Management*, 15(4), 601–622.

Landler, M., and Castle, S. (2020). Behind the virus report that jarred the U.S. and the
U.K. to action. *New York Times*, 2 April. https://www.nytimes.com/2020/03/17/
world/europe/coronavirus-imperial-college-johnson.html.

Lee, E. (2021). "Known unknowns": Donald Rumsfeld's most famous – and
infamous – quotes. *Yahoo News*, 1 July.

Lei, V., Noussair, C. N., and Plott, C. R. (2001). Nonspeculative bubbles in
experimental asset markets: Lack of common knowledge of rationality vs. actual
irrationality. *Econometrica*, 69(4), 831–859.

Lepper, M. R., Greene, D., and Nisbett, R. E. (1973). Undermining children's
intrinsic interest with extrinsic reward: A test of the "overjustification" hypothesis.
Journal of Personality and Social Psychology, 28(1), 129–137.

Lewis, C. S., in Hooper, W. (ed.). (1970). *God in the Dock: Essays on Theology and
Ethics*. William B. Eerdmans.

Lewis, M. (2010a). Betting on the blind side. *Vanity Fair*, 1 March.

Lewis, M. (2010b). *The Big Short: Inside the Doomsday Machine*. W. W. Norton.

Lippman, D. (2019). The Purell presidency: Trump aides learn the president's
real red line. *Politico*, 7 July. https://www.politico.com/story/2019/07/07/
donald-trump-germaphobe-1399258.

Lo, A. W., Repin, D. V., and Steenbarger, B. N. (2005). Fear and greed in financial
markets: A clinical study of day-traders. *American Economic Review*, 95(2), 352–359.

Lord, C. G., Ross, L., and Lepper, M. R. (1979). Biased assimilation and attitude
polarization: The effects of prior theories on subsequently considered evidence.
Journal of Personality and Social Psychology, 37(11), 2098–2109.

Lumet, S. (Director). (1957). *12 Angry Men* [Film]. Orion-Nova Productions.

Mackay, C. (1841). *Extraordinary Popular Delusions and the Madness of Crowds*.
Richard Bentley.

MacNamara, K. (2020a). Why productivity at the Productivity Commission seems
to be a low ebb. *New Zealand Herald*, 11 September. https://www.nzherald.co.nz/
business/kate-macnamara-why-productivity-at-the-productivity-commission-see
ms-to-be-at-a-low-ebb/XR7PNKKLTZ5N4FV7YMUOHKO3R4/.

MacNamara, K. (2020b). Can we put a cost on a human life? *New Zealand Herald*,
14 September. https://www.nzherald.co.nz/business/kate-macnamara-can-we-put-
a-cost-on-a-human-life/AP7GDUZRSHVNXFG723OTA2ECQ4/.

Malik, S. (2021). COVID-19: Supreme Court advises Centre, states to impose
lockdown. *Yahoo News*, 3 May.

McCartney, G., Fenton, L., Minton, J., Fischbacher, C., Taulbut, M., Little, K., et al.
(2020). Is austerity responsible for the recent change in mortality trends across
high-income nations? A protocol for an observational study. *BMJ Open*, 10(1),
e034832. doi:10.1136/bmjopen-2019-034832.

McKay, A. (Director). (2015). *The Big Short* [Film]. Regency Enterprises; Plan B
Entertainment.

Mekibib, B., and Ariën, K. (2016). Aerosol transmission of filoviruses. *Viruses*, 8(5),
148. doi:10.3390/v8050148.

Merlo, A., and Schotter, A. (1999). A surprise-quiz view of learning in economic
experiments. *Games and Economic Behavior*, 28(1), 25–54.

Meszaros, L. (2020). Top 10 causes of death in the US in 2020. *MDLinx*. 28 February.
https://www.mdlinx.com/article/top-10-causes-of-death-in-the-us-in-2020/MNp
EowpA8DXKBUNcbmkpY.

Meunier, T.A. (2020). Full lockdown policies in Western Europe countries have no evident impacts on the COVID-19 epidemic. *MedRxiv*. https://doi.org/10.1101/2 020.04.24.20078717. (Not peer reviewed at the time of writing.)

Miles, D. (2020). The UK lockdown: Balancing costs against benefits. *VoxEU*, 13 July.

Miles, D., Stedman, M., and Heald, A. (2020). Living with Covid-19: Balancing costs against benefits in the face of the virus. *National Institute Economic Review, 253*, R60–R76. https://doi.org/10.1017/nie.2020.30. Published online by Cambridge University Press, 28 July.

Mills, C. E., Robins, J. M., and Lipsitch, M. (2004). Transmissibility of 1918 pandemic influenza. *Nature, 432*(7019), 904–906. doi:10.1038/nature03063.

Mockus, A. (2015). The art of changing a city. *New York Times*, 16 July. http://www.nytimes.com/2015/07/17/opinion/the-art-of-changing-a-city.html.

Neale, M. A., and Bazerman, M. H. (1985). The effects of framing and negotiator overconfidence on bargaining behaviors and outcomes. *Academy of Management Journal, 28*(1), 34–49.

Nettle, D. (2006). The evolution of personality variation in humans and other animals. *American Psychologist, 61*(6), 622–631.

Newey, S. (2020). Why have so many coronavirus patients died in Italy? *Telegraph*, 23 March. https://www.telegraph.co.uk/global-health/science-and-disease/have-many-coronavirus-patients-died-italy/.

Nickol, M. E., and Kindrachuk, J. (2019). A year of terror and a century of reflection: perspectives on the great influenza pandemic of 1918–1919. *BMC Infectious Diseases, 19*(1), 1–10. doi:10.1186/s12879-019-3750-8.

Nightingale, M. (2020). Coronavirus lockdown unlawful for first nine days high court finds but says action was justified. *New Zealand Herald*, 19 August. https://www.nzherald.co.nz/nz/covid-19-coronavirus-lockdown-unlawful-for-first-nine-days-high-court-finds-but-says-action-was-justified/AI2WQ3PZ5QYEWUYGST S3MNKE6Q/.

Northcraft, G. B., and Neale, M. A. (1987). Experts, amateurs, and real estate: An anchoring-and-adjustment perspective on property pricing decisions. *Organizational Behavior and Human Decision Processes, 39*(1), 84–97.

Nyman, R., and Ormerod, P. (2020). How many lives has lockdown saved in the UK? *MedRxiv*, 21 August. https://doi.org/10.1101/2020.06.24.20139196.

NZ Herald. (2020). In awe of NZ: How world media reacted to New Zealand eliminating Covid-19. *New Zealand Herald*, 9 June. (No byline.) https://www.nzherald.co.nz/nz/in-awe-of-nz-how-world-media-reacted-to-new-zealand-eliminating-covid-19/MMOWHK3HHQCYU3TWV7G3TSJJK4/.

Oppenheim, M. (2018). Bizarre video of Rudy Giuliani dressed in drag while being seduced by Donald Trump resurfaces. *Independent*, 10 May. https://www.independent.co.uk/news/world/americas/rudy-guiliani-donald-trump-drag-video-seduce-new-york-mayor-us-president-a8344921.html.

Ortmann, A., Fitzgerald, J., and Boeing, C. (2000). Trust, reciprocity, and social history: A re-examination. *Experimental Economics, 3*(1), 81–100.

Osterholm, M. T., Moore, K. A., Kelley, N. S., Brosseau, L. M., Wong, G., Murphy, F. A., et al. (2015). Transmission of Ebola viruses: What we know and what we do not know. *MBio, 6*(2), e00137-15.

Ostrom, E. (1990). *Governing the Commons: The Evolution of Institutions for Collective Action*. Cambridge University Press.

Ostrom, E., Gardner, R., and Walker, J. (1994). *Rules, Games, and Common-Pool Resources*. University of Michigan Press.

Ostrom, E., Walker, J., and Gardner, R. (1992). Covenants with and without a sword: Self-governance is possible. *American Political Science Review*, 86(2), 404–417.

Palan, S. (2013). A review of bubbles and crashes in experimental asset markets. *Journal of Economic Surveys*, 27(3), 570–588.

Pennycook, G., and Rand, D. G. (2019a). Lazy, not biased: Susceptibility to partisan fake news is better explained by lack of reasoning than by motivated reasoning. *Cognition*, 188, 39–50.

Pennycook, G., and Rand, D. G. (2019b). Who falls for fake news? The roles of bullshit receptivity, overclaiming, familiarity, and analytic thinking. *Journal of Personality*, 88(2), 185–200.

Pennycook, G., McPhetres, J., Bago, B., and Rand, D. G. (2020). Attitudes about COVID-19 in Canada, the U.K., and the U.S.A.: A novel test of political polarization and motivated reasoning. Unpublished manuscript. University of Regina, Saskatchewan.

Phadikar, A. (2020). 1600km ride to meet ailing son. *The Telegraph of Calcutta*, 5 May. https://www.telegraphindia.com/west-bengal/coronavirus-lockdown-ma son-quarantined-after-cycling-from-chennai/cid/1771996.

Piketty, T. (2014). *Capital in the Twenty-First Century* (A. Goldhammer, trans.). Harvard University Press. (Original work published 2013.)

Pinker, S. (2012). *The Better Angels of Our Nature: Why Violence Has Declined*. Random House.

Pinker, S. (2018). *Enlightenment Now: The Case for Reason, Science, Humanism, and Progress*. Viking.

Popper, N. (2020). Robinhood has lured young traders, sometimes with devastating results. *New York Times*, 8 July. https://www.nytimes.com/2020/07/08/technol ogy/robinhood-risky-trading.html.

Pospichal, J. (2020). Questions for lockdown apologists. *The Medium*, 24 May. https://medium.com/@JohnPospichal/questions-for-lockdown-apologists-32a9bb f2e247.

Potter, C. W. (2001). A history of influenza. *Journal of Applied Microbiology*, 91(4), 572–579. doi:10.1046/j.1365-2672.2001.01492.x.

Prescott, J., Bushmaker, T., Fischer, R., Miazgowicz, K., Judson, S., and Munster, V. J. (2015). Postmortem stability of Ebola virus. *Emerging Infectious Diseases*, 21(5), 856–859.

Pullar-Strecker, T. (2020). Sam Morgan gives up on CovidCard in frustration with Ministry of Health. *Stuff*, 1 September. https://www.stuff.co.nz/business/122626 522/sam-morgan-gives-up-on-covidcard-in-frustration-with-ministry-of-health.

Rasgon, A. (2021). Israel's vaccine success unleashes a debate on Palestinian inequities. *New York Times*, 4 February. https://www.nytimes.com/2021/02/04/world/ middleeast/israel-palestinians-vaccine.html.

Rawls, J. (1999). *A Theory of Justice*. Belknap Press.

Reiner, R. (Director). (1992). *A Few Good Men* [Film]. Castle Rock Entertainment.

Resnick, B. (2019). Oxytocin, the so-called "hug hormone," is way more sophisticated than we thought. *Vox*, 13 February. https://www.vox.com/science-and-health/2019/2/13/18221876/oxytocin-morality-valentines.

Richerson, P. J. and Boyd, R. (2005). *Not by Genes Alone: How Culture Transformed Human Evolution*. University of Chicago Press.

Ritchie, H., and Roser, M. (2019). Age structure. *Our World in Data*. https:// ourworldindata.org/age-structure.

Ritchie, H., Ortiz-Ospina, E., Beltekian, D., Mathieu, E., Hasell, J., Macdonald, B., et al. (2020a). Coronavirus pandemic (COVID-19). *Our World in Data*. https://ourworldindata.org/coronavirus.

Ritchie, H., Ortiz-Ospina, E., Beltekian, D., Mathieu, E., Hasell, J., Macdonald, B., et al. (2020b). Coronavirus (COVID-19) deaths. *Our World in Data*. https://ourworldindata.org/covid-deaths.

Robson, S. (2020). Coronavirus: Families split by Covid-19 border restrictions. *Radio New Zealand*, 20 April. https://www.stuff.co.nz/life-style/well-good/121128131/coronavirus-families-split-by-covid19-border-restrictions.

Rogers, K. (2020). Why did the world shut down for COVID-19 but not Ebola, SARS or swine flu? *FiveThirtyEight*, 14 April. https://fivethirtyeight.com/features/why-did-the-world-shut-down-for-covid-19-but-not-ebola-sars-or-swine-flu/.

Rogoff, K. (2020). Why are stock market prices rising despite the Covid pandemic? *Guardian*, 6 October. https://www.theguardian.com/business/2020/oct/06/stock-market-prices-covid-pandemic-business.

Romer, P., and Garber, A. (2020). Will our economy die from coronavirus? *New York Times*, 23 March. https://www.nytimes.com/2020/03/23/opinion/coronavirus-depression.html.

Rosling, H., Rosling, O., and Rönnlund, A. R. (2018). *Factfulness: Ten Reasons We're Wrong about the World – and Why Things Are Better than You Think*. Flatiron Books.

Rotheram-Borus, M. J., and Tomlinson, M. (2020). Not remembering history, dooms us to repeat it: Using the lessons of the global HIV response to address COVID-19. *AIDS and Behavior*, 24(12), 3288–3290. doi:10.1007/s10461-020-03066-y.

Rubin, J. (2020). Fox News has succeeded – in misinforming millions of Americans. *Washington Post*, 1 April. https://www.washingtonpost.com/opinions/2020/04/01/fox-news-has-succeeded-misinforming-millions-americans.

Sachdeva, S. (2020a). Coronavirus: Officials pitched OIA suspension during Covid-19 lockdown. *Newsroom*, 24 April. https://www.stuff.co.nz/national/politics/121237698/coronavirus-officials-pitched-oia-suspension-during-covid19-lockdown.

Sachdeva, S. (2020b). Covid-19 powers approved under urgency. *Newsroom*, 13 May. https://www.newsroom.co.nz/2020/05/13/1171049/covid-19-powers-approved-under-urgency.

Samore, R., Fessler, D., Sparks, A. M., and Holbrook, C. (2020). Of pathogens and party lines: Social conservatism positively associates with COVID-19 precautions among Democrats but not Republicans. Unpublished manuscript. University of California, Los Angeles.

Sample, S. (2020). Why herd immunity strategy is regarded as fringe viewpoint. *Guardian*, 7 October. https://www.theguardian.com/world/2020/oct/07/why-herd-immunity-strategy-is-regarded-as-fringe-viewpoint.

Sanyal, A. (2020). 2,000 fine for not wearing mask in Delhi, up from 500, to tackle Covid. *NDTV*, 19 November. https://www.ndtv.com/india-news/coronavirus-rs-2-000-fine-for-those-not-wearing-masks-in-delhi-up-from-rs-500-says-arvind-kejriwal-2327352.

Schwarzmann, S. W., Adler, J. L., Sullivan, R. J., and Marine, W. M. (1971). Bacterial pneumonia during the Hong Kong influenza epidemic of 1968–1969. *Archives of Internal Medicine*, 127(6), 1037–1041. doi:10.1001/archinte.1971.00310180053006.

Sebhatu, A., Wennberg, K., Arora-Jonsson, S., and Lindberg, S. (2020). Explaining the homogeneous diffusion of Covid-19 nonpharmaceutical interventions across heterogenous countries. *Proceedings of the National Academy of Sciences*, 117(35), 21201–21208.

Sharma, R. (2020). Some countries face an awful question: Death by Coronavirus or by hunger? *New York Times*, 12 April.

Shiller, R. J. (2000). *Irrational Exuberance*. Princeton University Press.

Shils, E. (1954). *Authoritarianism "Right" and "Left"*. Free Press.

Shimmack, U., Heene, M., and Kesavan, K. (2017). Reconstruction of a train wreck: How priming research went off the rails. 2 February. https://replicationindex.com/2017/02/02/reconstruction-of-a-train-wreck-how-priming-research-went-of-the-rails/.

Sidanius, J., and Pratto, F. (1999). *Social Dominance: An Intergroup Theory of Social Hierarchy and Oppression*. Cambridge University Press.

Sidley, P. (2001). Drug companies sue South African government over generics. *British Medical Journal*, 322(7284), 447. doi:10.1136/bmj.322.7284.447.

Silva, J. (2011–). *Brain Games*. National Geographic Channel.

Smith, A. (2020). Woman given 14-day jail sentence for escaping isolation facility. *New Zealand Herald*, 28 August. https://www.nzherald.co.nz/nz/covid-19-coronavirus-woman-given-14-day-jail-sentence-for-escaping-isolation-facility/MVVSAPJWOYTG5MOHQMDPD4H334/.

Smith, V. L., Suchanek, G. L., and Williams, A. W. (1988). Bubbles, crashes, and endogenous expectations in experimental spot asset markets. *Econometrica*, 56(5), 1119–1151.

Smyth, J. (2020). New Zealand backs lockdown despite record contraction. *Financial Times*, 17 September.

So, T., Brown, P., Chaudhuri, A., Ryvkin, D., and Cameron, L. (2017). Piece-rates and tournaments: Implications for productivity and learning in a cognitively challenging task. *Journal of Economic Behavior and Organization*, 142, 11–23.

Société de Réanimation de Langue Française. (n.d.). *OUTCOMEREA Study Group*. https://www.srlf.org/auteur/outcomerea-study-group.

Stiglitz, J. (2020). The pandemic has laid bare deep divisions, but it's not too late to change course. *Conquering the Great Divide, International Monetary Fund Finance and Development*, (Fall). https://www.imf.org/external/pubs/ft/fandd/2020/09/COVID19-and-global-inequality-joseph-stiglitz.htm.

Stuckler, D., Reeves, A., Loopstra, R., Karanikolos, M., and McKee, M. (2017). Austerity and health: the impact in the UK and Europe. *European Journal of Public Health*, 27(suppl. 4), 18–21. doi:10.1093/eurpub/ckx167.

Surowiecki, J. (2005). *The Wisdom of Crowds*. (Reprint edition.) Anchor.

Swisher, K. (2020). Fox's fake news contagion. *New York Times*, 31 March. https://www.nytimes.com/2020/03/31/opinion/coronavirus-fox-news.html.

Taleb, N. N. (2010). *The Black Swan: The Impact of the Highly Improbable*. Random House.

Thaler, R. H., and Sunstein, C. R. (2008). *Nudge: Improving Decisions about Health, Wealth, and Happiness*. Yale University Press.

Thomson, S. A. (2020). How long will a vaccine really take? *New York Times*, 30 April. https://www.nytimes.com/interactive/2020/04/30/opinion/coronavirus-covid-vaccine.html.

Thornley, S. (2020). Do lockdowns work? Presentation at Covid Plan B Science and Policy Symposium, 17 August.

Thornley, S. (2021). Was SARS-Cov-2 around before Wuhan? What does this mean for Covid-19 policy? Presentation at Covid Plan B Science and Policy Symposium, 13 February.

Tibshraeny, J. (2020). A look at how much Covid-19 support property owners are receiving through low interest rates versus what non-property owners are receiving from the Government. *interest.co.nz*, 22 September. https://www.interest.co.nz/news/107161/look-how-much-covid-19-support-property-owners-are-receiving-through-low-interest-rates.

Titmuss, R. M. (1970). *The Gift Relationship*. Allen & Unwin.

Tversky, A., and Kahneman, D. (1983). Extensional versus intuitive reasoning: The conjunction fallacy in probability judgment. *Psychological Review*, *90*(4), 293–315.

UNAIDS. (n.d.). Incidence of HIV, ages 15–49 (per 1,000 uninfected population ages 15–49). Data set. World Bank. https://data.worldbank.org/indicator/SH.HIV.INCD.ZS.

University of Auckland. (n.d.). The New Zealand Attitudes and Values Study. https://www.psych.auckland.ac.nz/en/about/new-zealand-attitudes-and-values-study.html.

University of Oxford. (n.d.). *COVID-19 Government Response Tracker*. Blavatnik School of Government. https://www.bsg.ox.ac.uk/research/research-projects/covid-19-government-response-tracker.

Valleron, A. J., Cori, A., Valtat, S., Meurisse, S., Carrat, F., and Boëlle, P. Y. (2010). Transmissibility and geographic spread of the 1889 influenza pandemic. *Proceedings of the National Academy of Sciences of the United States of America*, *107*(19), 8778–8781. doi:10.1073/pnas.1000886107.

Van Elsland, S. L. (2020). COVID-19 deaths: Infection fatality ratio is about 1% says new report. Imperial College London, 29 October. https://www.imperial.ac.uk/news/207273/covid-19-deaths-infection-fatality-ratio-about/.

Wade, A. (2020). Covid 19 coronavirus: Winston Peters tells struggling migrant workers "you should probably go home". *New Zealand Herald*, 13 May. https://www.nzherald.co.nz/nz/covid-19-coronavirus-winston-peters-tells-struggling-migrant-workers-you-should-probably-go-home/C47ZGBC3BELTLBIND47N6J5JXM/.

Wagner, J. (2021). Eight people from the New York Yankees organization tested positive, despite having been vaccinated. Here's what to know. *New York Times*, 14 May. https://www.nytimes.com/2021/05/14/sports/baseball/eight-people-from-the-new-york-yankees-organization-tested-positive-despite-having-been-vaccinated-heres-what-to-know.html.

WebMD. (n.d.). Coronavirus recovery. *WebMD*. https://www.webmd.com/lung/covid-recovery-overview#1.

Whitcombe, A. L., McGregor, R., Craigie, A., James, A., Charlewood, R., Lorenz, N., et al. (2020). Comprehensive analysis of SARS-CoV-2 antibody dynamics in New Zealand. *MedRxiv*, 11 December. https://doi.org/10.1101/2020.12.10.20246751.

Wikipedia. (n.d.a). List of leading rugby union test try scorers. https://en.wikipedia.org/wiki/List_of_leading_rugby_union_test_try_scorers.

Wikipedia. (n.d.b). Philip Sidney. https://en.wikipedia.org/wiki/Philip_Sidney.

Wilkinson, B. (2020). IMF's fiscal forecasts make for grim reading for New Zealand. *New Zealand Herald*, 21 October. https://www.nzherald.co.nz/business/bryce-wilkinson-imfs-fiscal-forecasts-make-grim-reading-for-nz/JVUUSP2JUIJBGBTJGVTJTSHTRQ/.

Woolf, S. H., Masters, R. K., and Aron, L. Y. (2021). Effect of Covid-19 pandemic in 2020 on life expectancy across populations in the USA and other high income countries: simulations of provisional mortality data. *BMJ, 373*(1343). doi:10.1136/bmj.n1343.

World Health Organization. (2013). Framework for verifying elimination of measles and rubella. *Weekly Epidemiological Record, 88*(9), 89. https://www.who.int/wer/2013/wer8809.pdf.

World Health Organization. (2018). Influenza: Fact sheet. 6 November. Archived from the original on 17 December 2019. Retrieved 25 January 2020. https://www.who.int/news-room/fact-sheets/detail/influenza-(seasonal).

World Health Organization. (2020). At least 80 million children under one at risk of diseases such as diphtheria, measles and polio as COVID-19 disrupts routine vaccination efforts, warn Gavi, WHO and UNICEF. World Health Organization, 22 May. https://www.who.int/news/item/22-05-2020-at-least-80-million-children-under-one-at-risk-of-diseases-such-as-diphtheria-measles-and-polio-as-covid-19-disrupts-routine-vaccination-efforts-warn-gavi-who-and-unicef.

Wu, K. (2020a). In coronavirus testing, false positives are more hazardous than they might seem. *New York Times*, 25 October. https://www.nytimes.com/2020/10/25/world/in-coronavirus-testing-false-positives-are-more-hazardous-than-they-might-seem.html.

Wu, K. (2020b). Why false positives merit concern, too. *New York Times*, 15 December. https://www.nytimes.com/2020/10/25/health/coronavirus-testing-false-positive.html.

Wu, K. J., and Robbins, R. (2021). As rollout falters, scientists debate new vaccination tactics. *New York Times*, 3 January. https://www.nytimes.com/2021/01/03/health/coronavirus-vaccine-doses.html.

Yunus, M., and Jolis, A. (1998). *Banker to the Poor: Micro-Lending and the Battle against World Poverty*. Public Affairs.

Zola, E., and Jensen, M. K. (1992). *Emile Zola's J'accuse!* Bay Side Press.

Zuckerman, M. (1979). *Sensation Seeking: Beyond the Optimal Level of Arousal*. Lawrence Erlbaum.

Index

'In responding to the novel coronavirus pandemic, most governments abandoned the existing scientific and policy consensus and mimicked one another to embrace lockdowns of varying stringency. Remarkably, hardly any seemed to produce cost–benefit analysis. Unremarkably, the cost–benefit balance varied between rich and poor countries. In this rigorous, multi-disciplinary examination, written in clearly accessible language, Ananish Chaudhuri explores the reasons for the herd-like behaviour by governments and for the public compliance with their edicts. A must-read for understanding what really happened with Covid-19 and why, and for being better prepared for the inevitable next pandemic.'*

Ramesh Thakur, Director of the Centre for Nuclear Non-Proliferation and Disarmament (CNND), Crawford School, The Australian National University, Vice Rector and Senior Vice Rector of the United Nations University and Assistant Secretary-General of the United Nations 1998–2007

'This book is at once scholarly and readily accessible to all. The case Chaudhuri makes is not for any specific policy response, but rather for rational and fully informed decisions – for epidemiology over ideology. If the careful logic and vivid illustrations here pry open enough minds, we will be far better prepared for the next great public health crisis than we were for Covid-19.'*

David L. Katz, MD, MPH, President, True Health Initiative and Founding Director, Yale-Griffin Prevention Research Center, Yale University, USA, 1998–2019

'Professor Chaudhuri lays out the many irrationalities involved in the support for lockdowns in New Zealand and elsewhere: an inability to judge small probabilities, the problems with gut feelings, and many ex-post justification biases. Ananish lays out the argument carefully and yet manages to retain great humanism and compassion. A delight to read.'*

Paul Frijters, Professor in Wellbeing Economics, London School of Economics and Political Science, UK, and co-author of *An Economic Theory of Greed, Love, Groups, and Networks* and *The Great Covid Panic*

'In response to the Covid pandemic, many countries adopted containment policies that did not condition on people's health status or demographic characteristics. This timely and insightful book addresses the questions of what considerations led to those policies and whether those policies were well-informed. The book begins from the premise that the design of effective policy cannot be based solely on the insights of classic epidemiology models. The reason is both simple and sensible: those models don't take into account behavioral responses of people to policies like containment. The author's analysis is multidisciplinary in nature, blending economics, psychology, political science and epidemiology. The result is a rich and informative analysis. I highly recommend this well-written and timely book.'*

Martin Eichenbaum, Charles Moskos Professor of Economics and Co-Director, Center for International Macroeconomics, Northwestern University, USA

'This book is a very timely one for those, like me, who believe the democratic world's lockdown response to the Covid virus will go down as the worst public policy response of the last few centuries. It is sceptical. It is interesting. It is Great Barrington over Chief Medical Officer. There is more to living and the good life than fear of dying of Covid. All the politicians who focused on that matrix, and ignored other causes of death as well as all the benefits of living in a free society, and more, should have to read this book.'*

James Allan, Garrick Professor in Law, TC Beirne School of Law, University of Queensland, Australia

'This timely book asks some fundamental questions about policies adopted during the Covid pandemic. It uses the tools of economic analysis – most notably insights from behavioural economics – to question the wisdom of measures adopted in many developed countries. It offers insights into how decision making could be improved when, as is inevitable, the next pandemic arrives.'*

David Miles, CBE, Professor of Financial Economics, Imperial College London, UK

'In this book Ananish Chaudhuri achieves the impossible – he offers an easy-to-read book that delivers profound insights about our behavior which applies not just to pandemics, but to many other recurrent situations in our daily lives! A must-read for anyone that wants to make better decisions.'

Sudipta Sarangi, Professor and Chair, Department of Economics, Virginia Tech, USA, Co-Editor, *Journal of Economic Behavior and Organization* and author of *The Economics of Small Things*

'Careful comparison of costs and benefits is usually considered a hallmark of wise decision-making. Yet in 2020 many governments abandoned this standard as they tried to minimize deaths from Covid-19 regardless of cost. Traditional cost–benefit arguments were rebuked, by politicians who by nature rarely admit error, but also by ordinary folk affronted that someone would want to "kill granny". This book draws insights from experimental economics, political science and psychology to show how various biases in decision-making processes contributed to this situation. Fifty years ago,* Essence of Decision *led a generation of scholars to examine models of government decision-making. Hopefully Ananish Chaudhuri's lively book has a similar impact, for scholars, students and members of the public concerned about the retreat from rationality that is revealed by policy choices and public attitudes in the Covid-19 era.'

John Gibson, Professor of Economics, University of Waikato, New Zealand, Fellow of the Royal Society of New Zealand and Distinguished Fellow of the New Zealand Association of Economists

'This is an excellent book that nicely discusses cutting-edge applications in behavioural economics pertaining to the Covid-19 pandemic. It is thought-provoking and contains pioneering approaches that broaden the scope of behavioural research. Excellent writing style, making the content of the book accessible to a broad audience. Highly recommended!'

Michalis Drouvelis, Professor of Economics, University of Birmingham, UK and Co-ordinating Editor, *Theory and Decision*

'In New Zealand now it is hard to remember the shock of lockdown as a pandemic response. So much has happened. The virus has been kept at bay, so far. The predicted economic disaster has not happened – yet. Massive financial relief for businesses forcibly suspended and jobs at risk was followed by a rapid recovery when shops reopened. But Ananish Chaudhuri is by no means alone in thinking the country could pay a high and lingering price for its unprecedented lockdown, and that these costs, especially the human costs, should have been weighed against the risks the virus posed. His book uses fascinating behavioral studies of economic decision making and the psychology of popular risk assessment to question the merits of measures that New Zealand's Government took and New Zealanders overwhelmingly accepted. They should read this book and wonder if these were questions they should have asked.'

John Roughan, Political Columnist, *New Zealand Herald*